JEWISH ETHICS FOR THE TWENTY-FIRST CENTURY

Library of Jewish Philosophy

JEWISH ETHICS
for the
TWENTY-FIRST
CENTURY

Living in the Image of God

BYRON L. SHERWIN

WITH A FOREWORD BY LOUIS JACOBS

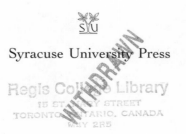

Syracuse University Press

First Edition 2000
00 01 02 03 04 05   6 5 4 3 2 1

The paper used in this publication meets the minimum requirements of
American National Standard for Information Sciences — Permanence of
Paper for Printed Library Materials, ANSI Z39.48-1984.

Library of Congress Cataloging-in-Publication Data
Sherwin, Byron L.
Jewish ethics for the twenty-first century : living in the image
of God / Byron L. Sherwin.
p. cm. — (Library of Jewish philosophy)
Includes bibliographical references and index.
ISBN 0-8156-2856-0 (cloth : alk. paper). — ISBN 0-8156-0624-9
(pbk. : alk. paper)
1. Ethics, Jewish.   2. Bioethics — Religious aspects — Judaism.
I. Title.   II. Series.
BJ1287.A155S54 1999
296.3′6 — dc21   99-41320

Manufactured in the United States of America

For Jan Lessem
For thirty years of devoted friendship . . . and more

Byron L. Sherwin is an ethicist, theologian, historian of Jewish ideas and an academic administrator. Ordained a rabbi by the Jewish Theological Seminary of America, he earned his Ph.D. from the Committee on the History of Culture at the University of Chicago. Listed in more than a dozen *Who's Who*s, he is the recipient of many awards, including a presidential medal, the Officer's Order of Merit from the Republic of Poland, and a Doctor of Hebrew Letters *honoris causa* from the Jewish Theological Seminary. He is the author or editor of twenty-one books and more than one hundred articles and monographs, most recently *Why Be Good?*, *Crafting the Soul*, and *Sparks Amidst the Ashes: The Spiritual Legacy of Polish Jewry*. He currently serves as Vice-President of Academic Affairs and Distinguished Service Professor of Jewish Philosophy and Mysticism at Spertus Institute of Jewish Studies in Chicago, Illinois.

Contents

Foreword, Louis Jacobs / ix

Preface / xvii

Abbreviations / xxi

1. In God's Image / 1

2. Health and Healing / 13

3. Euthanasia / 35

4. In Adam's Image / 62

5. Parent-Child Relations / 88

6. Cloning and Reproductive Biotechnology / 110

7. *Zedakah* as Social Welfare / 127

8. Repentance as Moral Rehabilitation / 151

Glossary / 169

Works Cited / 173

Index / 191

Foreword

IN A TALMUDIC LEGEND, King Manasseh accuses the prophet Isaiah of contradicting the words of Moses: "Your teacher Moses said: 'For men shall not see me and live' (Exod. 33:20) and yet you [i.e., Isaiah] said: 'I saw the Lord sitting on a throne' (Isa. 6:1)." The Talmud proceeds to resolve the contradiction. Moses' prophetic vision was through a clear glass (*aspaklaria ha-meirah*) whereas Isaiah's vision was "through a glass darkly" (*aspaklaria she-einah meirah*). As Rashi penetratingly explains it, Moses — he of the clear vision — knew that no human being can really see God. It was only in Isaiah's dimmed vision that he imagined he could see God (Rashi to *Yeb.*, 49b).

Since in the Talmud a sage is compared to a prophet (*BB*, 12a), it is not too far-fetched to detect the insight derived from each among Jewish theologians throughout the ages; though these latter have never claimed to be prophets, with the possible exception of Maimonides, if Heschel is right (see Heschel 1996b, 69–126). The more the theologian knows, the greater his or her degree of clarity, the more he or she becomes aware of the mystery; the more intense the illumination, the more opaque "the cloud of unknowing."

A striking feature of Byron Sherwin's thought lies precisely in the ability of his powerful mind and gifted pen to explore with great clarity that which can be known while acknowledging the existence of those mysterious realms impenetrable to the human mind. Sherwin repeatedly calls to our attention the theological dilemma. To say too much is to invite ridicule. To say too little can all too easily result in a vague agnosticism of no avail to the questing religious soul. Sherwin knows full well the complexities of human existence, that easy solutions are bogus solutions. For the world, he tells us, is both a terrible and a wonderful place and the struggle between good and evil is all too real. As Sherwin, in his magnum opus on Judah Loew of Prague (Maharal) —*Mystical Theology and Social Dissent* (1982) —describes the Maharal's thought: "Everything, except God, exists in a condition of dialectical opposition. Only God is truly one. Everything else exists in a stage of fragmented disunity. While God transcends all disunity, He is both the source and the resolution of all disunity and all fragmentation" (1982, 70).

Sherwin's dialectic is pervasive in all his work. For him, Judaism is not to be perceived chiefly in terms of either/or but of both this and that. For Sherwin, the Jew can both be secure in his religion and have a questing spirit. He or she can be a universalist while remaining a proud and committed Jew. Responsibilities to society need not compromise individuality. One can be both a liberal and a traditionalist, who sees no contradiction in an attitude of "progressive conservatism," a term used in the early twentieth century by Dr. Joseph H. Hertz to describe the religious position of the United Synagogue in Great Britain. In what follows, I want to examine how this dialectic operates in some of Sherwin's many publications, including the present one. If, here and there, I am critical of some of the positions he takes, he is too honest a thinker not to welcome it.

In Partnership with God, the title of one of Sherwin's books (1990), is a recurring theme in his work. For example, in one of his essays, Sherwin draws on the midrashic parable of the world as a palace that is on fire; a world from which a retreat into utopianism is for pitiful dreamers lacking the courage to enter the flaming palace in order to help God restore it (see chap. 7 below). In a neat pun, Sherwin sees Judaism as teaching that our world is not a redeemed *messianic* but an unredeemed and *messy* world and he warns against the entertainment of any ideas of realized eschatology. Even our best social, religious, educational and political institutions represent the commingling of good and evil. Sherwin quotes Ecclesiastes (7:20) "for there is not a *righteous* man upon this earth that does good and sins not." Like his teacher Abraham Joshua Heschel, Sherwin is fond of quoting the Kotzker Rebbe who similarly interpreted the verse in Leviticus (7:1), "This is the law of the guilt offering; it is most holy," to mean: Where is guilt to be found? In the most holy. And, taking issue with Kierkegaard's "leap of faith," he remarks that it is more prudent to look before one leaps; rushing ahead toward utopia can only lead to ultimate despair and to eventual inaction (1995b, 150–51). But Kierkegaard, whether one agrees with him or not, is certainly not thinking of a leap into a utopian vision. On the contrary, this religious existentialist would agree with Sherwin's thesis that we are living in an unredeemed world, though Kierkegaard is primarily concerned with the individual and may be far less concerned with the improvement of society than Sherwin.

In a famous illustration of Kierkegaard, when the sea is calm, the sun is shining, and the captain sober, and you have faith that the ship will reach its destination, that is not faith. When the seas are raging, the ship floundering, and the captain drunk, however, and you still have faith that the ship will reach its destination, that is really faith. For Kierkegaard, it is the ship of the individual, not of society, that is floundering. The Kotzker, whose religious torments Heschel sees as resembling those of Kierkegaard, is speaking of the individual as an individual not as a member of society. Similarly, when the Kotzker is invoked in favor of social action, this appeal overlooks the fact that the Kotzker lived for a large portion of his life secluded in his room.

The above is offered, not to critique Sherwin's essential position, presented by him so convincingly, but only to note that eclecticism, even at its best, must be cautious in calling to the aid of a normative approach such mavericks as Kierkegaard and the Kotzker. I have often wondered whether, in fact, there is any such thing as "normative Judaism."

Discussing the vexed question of euthanasia in one of the essays in the present volume, Sherwin surveys the halakhic literature on the question. He admits that the dominant view in the Jewish sources prohibits active euthanasia of any kind. Yet, "in view of contemporary realities," he defends a position within the framework of classical Jewish sources that would justify active euthanasia in at least certain circumstances. Through this essay, Sherwin raises two acute questions: 1) How far should "contemporary realities" influence halakhic decisions? 2) How far can extrahalakhic sources be used to determine what the *halakhah* (Jewish religious law) should

be? When Heschel was critical of "pan-Halakhism" he was referring to the attitude according to which all that matters in Judaism
is the *halakhah* (1955, 328). Sherwin goes further by introducing
extrahalakhic categories into the *halakhah* itself.

Sherwin is similarly original in his application in the present
volume of the Golem legend to the question of reproductive biotechnology (chaps. 4, 6). The use of sources dealing with fantasies
is not new in the *halakhah*, for example, witness the discussions in
contemporary responsa about artificial insemination on the basis of
the curious story of Ben Sira and the daughter of the prophet Jeremiah. But it has taken a Byron Sherwin to use the Golem legend
for the consideration of the status of an "artificial person" in Jewish
law and ethics. These essays, important in themselves, offer, as
Sherwin says, "a window of opportunity" for applying old texts to
new problems.

Discussing the Maharal's attitude to the body, Sherwin sees this
thinker as occupying a midway position between those who believe
the body and its appetites to be good in themselves and those who
have nothing but hatred for the body, which they see as a hindrance
to spiritual progress (1982, 111–23). For the Maharal, the body is
not good in itself but it becomes good when used as the means for
spiritual advance. Elsewhere, Sherwin further explores the theme of
the body from the wider perspective of Judaism in general, demonstrating that three attitudes prevail among Jewish thinkers — the
positive attitude, which considers the body to be a blessing; the
negative attitude, which sets the body in opposition to the soul; and
the neutral attitude, according to which everything depends on how
the body is used. With massive erudition, Sherwin surveys the
whole range of Jewish thought on the question (1991a, 129–47).
In the process he rightly observes that there have been Jewish
thinkers with a negative attitude to the body so that, whatever mod-
ernists might hold, it is a distortion of the religion to state categorically that asceticism is totally alien to Judaism. After all, there
were pious Jews who fasted from Sabbath to Sabbath; who engaged in self-flagellation, wore sackcloth and ashes, and even, as in
the curious medieval tale about the talmudic Rabbi Joseph, blinded
themselves in order not to be able to gaze outwards. This is far
removed from "normative Judaism." As the Victorian lady said on
witnessing a performance of *Cleopatra:* "How different, how very
different, from the home life of our own dear Queen!" Yet the phe-

nomenon of asceticism does exist and here, too, a question is put again to the whole notion of a normative interpretation of the Jewish religion. On a personal note, I was honored that Sherwin's essay, "The Human Body and the Image of God," excerpted in the present volume, was originally published in a Festschrift in my honor (see Sherwin 1991b).

Sherwin believes that unless theology and ethics are based on sound historical foundations, they are no more than a matter of personal preference. By definition a Jewish theology must take into account the facts of history. As the old lady said: "It isn't only *emes* [truth], it's a fact." At the same time, the theologian must avoid a historicism in which all that matters is what happened in the Jewish past. Solomon Schechter once said of some scholars that they are so lost in the past they never come back to the present and they ignore the future. In his preface to *In Partnership with God*, Sherwin boldly declares that he offers a variety of Jewish scholarship that is a continuation of what came before, and that it is not an objective "scientific" dissection of the Jewish past. In the first essay in that book, Sherwin offers in this vein "A Program for Jewish Scholarship," drawing on the analogy of the dwarf on the giant's shoulders. The dwarf without the giant cannot see further than his own nose, but if he stands on the giant's shoulders without availing himself of the wider vision that is now afforded him, he might just as well have remained down on the ground. "Yet, much of contemporary Jewish scholarship," Sherwin avers, "seems to suffer from restricted peripheral vision. Scholars seem prone to overspecialization in minute sub-areas of Jewish studies without surveying the breadth of classical Jewish sources" (1990, 3). Here, Sherwin bravely takes a swipe at the *Jüdische Wissenschaft* movement, quoting Scholem's observation that this movement aims at the liquidation of Judaism as a living organism. But this is not one of Scholem's happiest observations. Scholem himself rarely concerns himself with the kind of program Sherwin envisages and his plea is really for greater not less "objectivity" in Jewish studies. It can be argued that the Jewish scholar, qua scholar, in order to be true to his vocation, must confine himself to unbiased examination of the sources as if he were studying, say, Chinese metaphysics, leaving theology to the theologian who, admittedly, fails in his task if he does not take into account the researches of the historian. In other words, the ideal is for the theologian, while not necessarily engaged in historical research himself, to be extremely well informed about the conclusion arrived at in historical, objective scholarship and then proceed to foster his own discipline. Sherwin is one of the few Jewish theologians and ethicists working today to approximate to this ideal. In the present volume, Sherwin amplifies the use of this methodology with enviable erudition and skill.

Sherwin's writings here and elsewhere reflect the influence of the thought of Abraham Joshua Heschel and Solomon Schechter, two of his heroes who follow the same variety of Jewish learning in which impeccable scholarship is wedded to strong personal piety and total commitment to traditional Judaism. Of Heschel, Sherwin writes, "Heschel was no armchair philosopher, no 'ivory tower' theologian, no clinically detached academician. For Heschel, life is too precarious, too precious, to become a game of trivial pursuit" (1992, 50). Of Schechter, Sherwin has written that though scholarship was critical for him, it was insufficient in itself. Schechter's ideal of the Jewish role model was not simply the scholar, but what he called "the saint-scholar," for whom spiritual, as well as intellectual conviction was necessary to sustain and to inspire the religious life (see Sherwin 1993). Sparing Byron Sherwin' blushes, I shall not refer to him as a "saint-scholar" but am surely justified in noting that in all his work and general Jewish activity, he certainly follows this model as his ideal.

In one of his essays, Sherwin cites the talmudic story of the son of Rabbi Joshua ben Levi who was vouchsafed a vision of the next world, where he observed that those who are of little account here are of high account there, and those of high account here are of little account there (Sherwin 1995b, 149). However, Sherwin omits the punch line of the tale. "What of we scholars?" the father asked his son on the latter's return from the "world of truth." "We scholars," he replied, "are the same there as we are here." I understand this to mean that students of the Torah obtain so clear and true a picture of both life as it really is and of their own character here on earth that no celestial reversal is required for them. It can best be summed up by adapting the title of Heschel's famous study of Rabbi Mendel of Kotzk (1973). Sherwin, like his heroes, has "a passion for truth."

In his essay on my work published some years ago, Byron Sherwin wrote a generous appreciation of my work in which he paid me, by implication, the compliment that I would take kindly to criticism as well as to praise (1979, 95–108). It is in this spirit that I return the compliment. If, here and there, I have offered criticisms of his positions, this is because I believe he would have had me do no less. I yield to none in my admiration for Byron Sherwin and feel it a privilege to have been asked to provide the foreword to this original and highly stimulating book.

Preface

THE TERM "JEWISH ETHICS" may denote the ethics of Jews or the ethics of Judaism. Sometimes these two meanings coalesce; often, they do not. More often, they tend to be confused with one another. For example, in twentieth-century America there has been a pervasive tendency to identify the ethics of Judaism with the ethics of secular modern liberalism. Indeed, survey after survey indicates that many American Jews consider liberal politics and morality to be the basis of their identity as Jews, with theological beliefs and ritual practices of Judaism considered as anachronistic remnants of a to-be-discarded Jewish religious heritage (see, e.g., S. Cohen 1983; Liebman 1973, 135–59; Fein 1988, 222–44; Abrams 1997, 126–37). As one sociologist of American Jewry has put it, "Many American Jews were raised with the understanding that liberalism or political radicalism constituted the very essence of Judaism, that all the rest — the rituals, liturgy, communal organizations — were outdated, vestigial trappings for a religion with a great moral and political message embodied in liberalism" (S. Cohen 1983, 35). Or, as another keen observer of the American Jewish scene has put it, "Politics is our religion; our preferred denomination is liberalism" (Fein 1988, 224). However, the secular morality that many contemporary Jews identify with Judaism has little to do with the faith of their ancestors. It may be the ethics of groups of Jews but it is not the ethics of Judaism.

Judaism rests upon theistic assumptions. Yet, in the "civil religion" of American Jewry that both characterizes and expresses the identity of much of American Jewry, belief in God plays little visible role. As one observer of American Jewry has put it, "What is most striking . . . is the thoroughly insignificant role which any God-concept plays in the civil religion [of American Jewry]" (Woocher 1986, 92).

The ethics of Judaism is a form of theological or religious ethics. As such, it presumes certain theological claims and assumptions regarding God, human nature, revelation, and the interpretive tradition of texts considered sacred and significant. The ethics of Judaism is defined by those claims, texts, and traditions. The ethics of contemporary Judaism entails the application of the wisdom of the past to the ethical problems of the present. The ethics of Jews, in contrast, may be discerned through a sociological investigation of the behavior of groups of Jews as it relates to ethical issues, and of what groups of Jews at a given time and in a given place might consider ethical values and ethical behavior to be. The ethics of contemporary Jews may be determined by a description of how Jews behave at the present historical juncture.

Precisely because Jews have little awareness of the ethics of Judaism, the disjuncture of the ethics of Jews and the ethics of Judaism should not be surprising. For instance, the vast majority of Jews is unaware of or unfamiliar with the constitutive texts that characterize the ethics of Judaism. Furthermore, as was already noted, they tend to equate certain forms of secular ethics with the ethics of Judaism. This pervasive confusion of the ethics of Judaism with the ethics of Jews tends to influence popular Jewish and non-Jewish understandings of the nature of Jewish ethics.

The present volume deals with the ethics of Judaism and has four primary goals. The first is to portray the ethics of Judaism as a form of theological ethics defined by the beliefs, practices, and significant literature of Judaism. The second goal is to provide the reader with an awareness of some of the theological claims upon which the ethics of Judaism rests, and with access to the resources of classical Jewish ethical literature. The third goal is to demonstrate that the sacred and significant texts of the Jewish past may be effectively applied to the ethical problems of the present. The final goal is to apply those texts to a number of particular ethical issues confronting individuals at the current juncture in human history, such as: health and healing, euthanasia, relationships between humans and machines, genetic engineering, reproductive biotechnology, cloning, parent-child relations, social welfare, and the intersection of spirituality and ethics. The methodology utilized in achieving these goals has features in common with that used by other contemporary Jewish ethicists. This methodology is explained in a number of my earlier works (Sherwin 1990, 1991a). However, I am grateful to Professor Louis Newman for his perceptive analysis of my methodology from which I greatly benefited (1997), and which has stimulated me to further refine it.

Earlier versions of a number of the chapters that follow appeared in my previous book, *In Partnership with God: Contemporary Jewish Law and Ethics,* also published by Syracuse University Press (Sherwin 1990). To Dr. Robert Mandel, director of Syracuse University Press, I am grateful for the opportunity to recast them, to supplement them with new material, and to publish them along with a number of chapters written specifically for this volume.

To my esteemed colleague Rabbi Dr. Louis Jacobs of London, I am profoundly indebted for his thoughtful and thought-provoking foreword to this volume. For over thirty years, I have continued to learn from him, mostly through reading his erudite and stimulating works. For this reason, I consider him one of my most formative and formidable teachers.

This volume is dedicated to my devoted friend Dr. Jan Lessem. Despite our usually having been separated by considerable geographical distance, the closeness and warmth of our friendship of more than thirty-years never has diminished.

Without the consummate skill and forbearance of my secretary, Pamela Spitzner, this book would have remained a package of ink scrawls on paper. To her, my gratitude. To the staff of the Asher Library of Spertus Institute of Jewish Studies for their research assistance, and especially to Dan Sharon, I am most grateful. To my wife Judith and son Jason my gratitude for their forbearance in giving me time to write when they would have preferred me to be engaged in less solitary activities. To the Cohn Scholars' Fund for financial assistance related to the preparation of this volume, my thanks. Unless otherwise noted, translations of primary source material are my own.

Abbreviations

ABBREVIATIONS OF NAMES of biblical and apocryphal books follow standard forms of abbreviation. In addition, the following abbreviations are used:

Rabbinic Literature

M.	Mishnah
PT.	Palestinian Talmud
T.	Tosefta
Tos.	Tosafot

Talmudic Tractates (in Talmud with commentaries)

AZ	Avodah Zara	Ned.	Nedarim
BB	Bava Batra	Nid.	Niddah
BK	Bava Kamma	PA	Pirke Avot
BM	Bava Metzia	Pes.	Pesahim
Ber.	Berakhot	RH	Rosh ha-Shanah
Erub.	Erubin	San.	Sanhedrin
Git.	Gittin	Shab.	Shabbat
Hag.	Hagiga	Shek.	Shekalim
Ket.	Ketubot	Suk.	Sukkot
Kid.	Kiddushin	Ter.	Terumot
Meg.	Megillah	Yeb.	Yebamot
MK	Mo'ed Katan		

Titles of the following talmudic tractates have not been abbreviated: *Arakhin, Beitzah, Ohalot, Pe'ah, Sota, Ta'anit, Yoma.*

The following abbreviations have been used for these "minor tractates" of the Talmud:

ARN   *Avot d'Rabbi Natan.* 1887. Edited by Solomon Schechter. Vienna: N.p. Translated by Judah Goldin under the title *The Fathers According to Rabbi Nathan.* 1955. (New Haven: Yale University Press, 1955).

Sem.   *Semahot*

Sof.   *Soferim*

For an English translation of the "minor tractates," see *The Minor Tractates of the Talmud.* 1965. 2 vols. Edited by A. Cohen. London: Soncino Press.

Midrashic Collections

The following midrashic collections are referenced in the text by these abbreviations; others are referenced in the standard manner.

Midrash Rabbah

DR	*Deuteronomy Rabbah*
ER	*Ecclesiastes Rabbah*
Exod. R.	*Exodus Rabbah*
GR	*Genesis Rabbah*
LR	*Leviticus Rabbah*
NR	*Numbers Rabbah*
SSR	*Song of Songs Rabbah*

Midrash Rabbah to the five books of the Torah and the five "scrolls" was first published in 1545. The edition used here is 1921 (Vilna: Romm) [with commentaries]. English translation by H. Freedman and Maurice Simon, eds., 10 vols. (London: Soncino, 1939). Other midrashic collections:

MP   *Midrash Tehillim* [1592] 1891. Edited by So-
      lomon Buber. Vilna: Romm. Translated by
      William G. Braude under the title *Midrash
      on Psalms*. 1959. New Haven: Yale Univer-
      sity Press.

MRY   *Mekhilta d'Rabbi Yishmael* [1515] 1960. Edited
      by Hayyim Horovitz and Israel Rabin. Je-
      rusalem: Wahrmann. Translated by Jacob
      Lauterbach. 1933. 3 vols. Philadelphia: Jew-
      ish Publication Society of America.

PR   *Pesikta Rabbati*. 1880. Edited by Meir Fried-
      man. Vienna: Herausgebers. Translated by
      William G. Braude. 1968. 2 vols. Yale Uni-
      versity Press.

PRE   *Pirke d'Rabbi Eliezer* [1852] 1946. New York:
      Ohm. Translated by Gerald Friedlander.
      1916. London: N.p.

PRK   *Pesikta d'Rav Kahana*. 1868. Edited by So-
      lomon Buber. Lyck: Mekitzei Nirdamim.
      Translated by William G. Braude and Israel
      Kapstein. 1975. Philadelphia: Jewish Pub-
      lication Society of America.

Tan. *Midrash Tanhuma*. [1520] 1885. Edited by So-
      lomon Buber. 2 vols. Vienna: N.p.

YS   *Yalkut Shimoni*. [1595] 1944. 2 vols. New
      York: Pardes Press.

Works of Moses Maimonides

The following works of Maimonides are referenced in the text
by the following abbreviations; others are referenced in the standard manner:

CM   *Commentary on the Mishnah*. 1963. 3 vols. Ed-
      ited by Joseph Kapah. Jerusalem: Mosad
      ha-Rav Kook.

GP   *Guide of the Perplexed (Moreh Nevhuhim)* [1480].
      1963. Translated by Shlomo Pines. Chicago:
      University of Chicago Press.

SM   *Sefer ha-Mitzvot.* [1510]. 1971b. Edited by Joseph Kapah. Jerusalem: Mosad ha-Rav Kook.

Maimonides Legal Code — *Mishneh Torah*

MT   *Mishneh Torah* [1509] 1963. 6 vols. [with commentaries]. New York: Friedman.

Abbreviations are used for the following sections of *Mishneh Torah:*

MT—HD   *Mishneh Torah — Hilkhot De-ot (Laws of Beliefs)*

MT—HK   *Mishneh Torah — Hilkhot Kidushin (Laws of Marriage)*

MT—HN   *Mishneh Torah — Hilkhot Nedarim (Laws of Vows)*

MT—HS   *Mishneh Torah — Hilkhot Shekheinim (Laws of Neighbors)*

MT—HT   *Mishneh Torah — Hilkhot Teshuvah (Laws of Repentance)*

MT—LM   *Mishneh Torah — Hilkhot Rozeah (Laws of Murderers)*

MT—LR   *Mishneh Torah — Hilkhot Mamrim (Laws of Rebels)*

MT—MA   *Mishneh Torah — Hilkhot Matnat Ani''im (Laws of Gifts to the Poor)*

MT—TT   *Mishneh Torah — Hilkhot Talmud Torah (Laws of Torah Study)*

Other Medieval Legal Codes

Besides Maimonides's *Mishneh Torah,* references to two other medieval legal codes are given in abbreviated form. These are:

Ben Asher, Jacob. [1550]. Reprint: N.d. *Arba'ah Turim* [with commentaries]. 7 vols. New York: Grossman; and, Joseph Karo. [1564] 1911. *Shulhan Arukh.* 4 vols. Vilna: Romm.

AT   *Arba'ah Turim*
SA   *Shulḥan Arukh*

The names of the four sections of each of these two works are identical:

EH   *Even ha-Ezer*
HM   *Hoshen Mishpat*
OH   *Oraḥ Hayyim*
YD   *Yoreh De'ah*

Hence, for example, *AT — YD* refers to *Arba'ah Turim — Yoreh De'ah*, *SA — EH* refers to *Shulḥan Arukh — Even ha-Ezer*.

Works of Judah Loew of Prague

BG   *Be'er ha-Golah*
DH   *Derekh Hayyim*
GA   *Gur Aryeh*
HA   *Hiddushei Agadot*
NO   *Netivot Olom*
NY   *Nezaḥ Yisrael*
TY   *Tiferet Yisrael*

The edition of *Gur Aryeh* used is 1972. 5 vols. Jerusalem: Yahadut. The other works of Judah Loew are found in his collected works: *Kol Sifrei ha-Maharal me-Prag.* 1969. 12 vols. New York: Judaica Press.

Abbreviations of Other Works

EJ   *Encyclopedia Judaica.* 1971. Edited by Cecil Roth. Jerusalem: Keter.
ET   *Encyclopedia Talmudit.* 1947–. Jerusalem: Makhon ha-Encyclopedia ha-Talmudit.
MM   Ben Yekutiel, Yehiel. 1968. *Sefer Ma'alot ha-Middot.* Jerusalem: Eshkol.
OZ   *Orḥot Zaddikim.* 1960. Translated by Seymour J. Cohen. New York: Feldheim.

SH   *Sefer Hasidim*. [1538] 1924. Edited by Jehuda Wistinetzki and J. Freimann. Frankfurt: Wahrmann Verlag. Edited by Reuven Margaliot. 1960. Jerusalem: Mosad ha-Rav Kook.

JEWISH ETHICS FOR THE TWENTY-FIRST CENTURY

1

In God's Image

THE TALMUDIC RABBIS taught that God not only reveals the Torah, but that God also observes its commandments: "A human king issues a decree. The king may then choose to obey it; or, the king may choose to have only others obey it. Not so the Holy One. When God issues a decree, God is the first to obey it. As it is stated, 'And they shall observe my observances . . . I am the Lord' (Lev. 22:9). I [God] am the first to obey the commandments of the Torah" (*PT. Yeb.*, chap. 4, sec. 12). Yet, when creating human beings, God did not obey the commandments of the Torah. Though Scripture forbids making an image of God, when God created human beings, God made an image of God. Of all of God's creatures, only the human creature is described by Scripture as having been created in "the image and likeness of God" (Gen. 1:26–27; see also Gen. 5:1, 9:6). As Rabbi Joshua ben Levi said, "A procession of angels pass before a human being wherever he or she goes, proclaiming — Make way for the image of God" (*DR*, chap. 4, sec. 4; see also *MP*, chap. 17, sec. 8, 66a).

Rabbi Akiva taught that not only have human beings been created in the divine image, but that divine grace allows them to become aware of it: "Beloved are human beings for they were created in the [divine] image. Even more beloved are they, because they can be aware of having been created in the [divine] image. As it is written, 'For in the image of God, God made human beings' (Gen. 9:6)" (*PA*, chap. 3, sec. 14). Jewish ethics focuses upon how human beings can live out their lives in the awareness of their having been created in the image and likeness of God. But, what does it mean to

1

say that human beings have been created in "the image and likeness of God"?

In postbiblical Jewish religious literature, two interpretive approaches usually have been applied to this biblical phrase. One posits ontological analogies between God and human beings while the other offers behavioral analogies. Ontological analogies presume a similitude between God and human beings. The task is then to identify the attribute or attributes of God that human beings share with God. Behavioral analogies assume that human beings and God have no essential similitude. Therefore, behavioral analogies concentrate not on the nature of God, but on the actions of God. From this perspective, God's actions do not disclose God's nature (see, e.g., *GP*, bk. 1, chaps. 52–53, 114–23). Living in the image and likeness of God means emulating God's actions, rather than the attributes of God's unknowable essence (see *GP*, bk. 1, chap. 54, 128).

Behavioral analogies ask us to act as God acts. This means, for example, that "just as God clothes the naked, attends the sick, comforts the mourners and buries the dead, so you do likewise" (*Sota*, 14a). Just as God performs acts of love, mercy, compassion, righteousness, holiness, and truth, so should we do likewise (see, e.g., *Shab.*, 133b; *MRY*, 127; *MT—HD*, chap. 1, sec. 6). Whereas the Bible describes God as acting angrily, vengefully, and jealously, the rabbis exclude these types of actions from those that we ought to emulate.

Behavioral analogies identify *imago Dei* with *imitatio Dei* (see glossary) and ask us "to walk in God's ways" (see, e.g., Isa. 2:3). This phrase may denote both the ways in which God acts as well as the ways in which God has commanded us to act (see Shapiro 1963, 57–77). As will be discussed further below, the task of the Jewish ethicist and the halakhist is to explicate the specifics of that which God has commanded us to do.

Ontological analogies go further than behavioral analogies by positing a similitude not only between divine and human actions, but between essential attributes shared by God and human beings. From this perspective, theology anticipates anthropology, which in turn shapes ethics. How we perceive the nature of God informs our understanding of human nature which then fashions our expectations about human behavior. For example, were we to apprehend the divine as being subject to fate as did the ancient Babylonians, then human beings created in the divine image would be similarly devoid of moral volition. Ethics would not then be possible, since ethics presumes making and acting upon moral choices. The expectation of moral action presupposes the availability of moral volition. For biblical religion, human action is not rooted in tragic necessity or predetermined fate, but in the free exercise of the God-given and God-like expression of the moral will (see, e.g., Kaufmann 1960, 32–33, 328–29).

Throughout classical Jewish literature, there is a variety of interpretations of the term "image of God" that employs ontological analogies. For example, Maimonides considers God to be an essentially intellectual being. For him, the attribute that human beings share with God is the intellect, the rational faculty. As Maimonides states in the opening chapter of his philosophical magnum opus, *The Guide of the Perplexed* (*GP*, bk. 1, chap. 2), "It is on account of this intellectual apprehension that it is said of man, 'In the image of God, God created human beings'" (Gen. 1:26). Maimonides' interpretation became commonplace in subsequent Jewish philosophical literature (see, e.g., Altmann 1968, 254). For Maimonides, ethical behavior requires the employment of the intellect. A function of the intellect is making distinctions, and ethical behavior presumes the ability to make distinctions between truth and falsehood, good and bad actions (*GP*, bk. 1, chap. 2, 24–25).

The Image of Creative Freedom

The sixteenth-century mystic Judah Loew of Prague found Maimonides' view too restrictive. Though for Loew, the intellect is part of both divine and human nature, it is quintessential to neither. Commenting on the talmudic statement that human beings are aware of their having been created in the divine image, Loew identifies moral volition as the primary divine attribute that human beings share with God and as that which distinguishes human beings from both the angels and the animals (see Sherwin 1982, 118–21). Though angels have higher intellects than human beings, according to Loew, angels lack the ability to make choices. In Loew's words,

> In this way, human beings resemble God, in that they were created in the divine image. But, this is not the case with angels who have no choice. They only do what God appoints them to do, and they are incapable of altering their mission. But humans who

were created in God's image enjoy the benefit of making determinations for themselves, like God who does what God desires. And thus, humans control their own selves to do what they will, and are masters of their ability to choose. (*DH*, chap. 3, 148)

Animals, whose actions are controlled by their instincts, also lack moral choice. For Loew, the erect human stance is indicative of the moral posture that distinguishes human beings from animals. To be bent-over indicates subservience, while to be erect denotes sovereignty, independence, and self-determination. As God is sovereign of all of creation, so are human beings sovereign in the terrestrial realm. As Loew writes, "The human being alone is erect. The upright posture bespeaks still more marvelous notions regarding the human image which is erect. The sages indicated this in their dictum: 'Beloved are human beings for they were created in the divine image' [*PA*, chap. 3, sec. 14]. . . . In sum, the human stature is unique, accounting for the human superiority over the animals" (*TY*, chap. 16, 53). "Therefore, it is said of the human being whose posture is upright that he is in the image of God" (*DH*, chap. 3, sec. 14, 142).

Although Loew and Maimonides disagreed on the interpretation of the biblical phrase "image of God," they nonetheless agreed that moral choice is a vital and unique characteristic of human nature. For Loew moral volition is a shared attribute of humans and God whereas for Maimonides it is a divine gift bestowed upon humankind. In Maimonides' words:

The human species is unique in the world — there being no other species like it in the following respect; namely, that a person by himself, and by the exercise of intelligence and reason knows what is good and what is evil, and there is none who can prevent the human person from doing what is good or that which is evil. . . . This doctrine [of moral free will] is an important principle, the pillar of the Torah and the commandments. . . . If a person's destiny had been decreed, and his innate constitution drew him to that which he could not set himself free, then what purpose would there be for the whole of the Torah? (*MT — HT*, chap. 5, secs. 3, 4)

To the point in the biblical text where God is described as creating human beings in the divine image, all we are told of God is that

God creates. Therefore, one may interpret the phrase "image of God" to mean that human beings are like God in that they have the capacity to create. But, without will, creativity cannot occur. "Choice forms the base of creation" (Soloveichik 1983, 116). Human beings share the divine capacity to create because they share the divine attribute of will. However, creativity entails not only volition but also imagination. The nineteenth-century Hasidic master, Nahman of Bratslav, interprets the claim that human beings are created in the image and likeness of God to mean that like God, human beings are endowed with an imagination (1966, pt. 2, 10b; see Green 1979, 341).

Through a pun on the Hebrew word for "rock" (*tzur*), God is described as a creative artist (*tzayyar*). A talmudic text reads: "'There is none holy as the Lord, for there is none besides You, neither is there any rock like our God' (1 Sam. 2:2). What means 'neither is there any rock (*tzur*) like our God'? There is no artist (*tzayyar*) like our God" (*Ber.*, 10a; see also *MRY*, sec. "*Be-shalah*," 144). Like God, human beings can be creative artists. However, though God can create something from nothing, human creativity begins by re-creating raw materials already created by God (see, e.g., *GR*, chap. 1, sec. 12; Ha-Levi 1924, bk. 3, sec. 23, 163).

God's most superlative artwork is the human being, and it is the human mission to act as a cocreator with God to complete God's unfinished artistic masterpiece — the human person. According to the Talmud, human beings are not only God's creatures, but God's cocreators, God's "partner in the work of creation" (*Shab.*, 10a). Consequently, the divine image implanted in human beings is not a gratuitous gift but a challenge to be met (see Soloveichik 1978, 64). That challenge can be met through certain types of human creativity. As Rabbi Joseph B. Soloveichik put it (1983, 101), "The peak of religious ethical perfection to which Judaism aspires is man as creator." Ethics is a way in which each individual can create his or her life as a work of art.

Re-Creating the Divine Word

According to Scripture, Bezalel, who built the Tabernacle, was the first Jewish artist. The Talmud observes that Bezalel "knew how to combine the letters by which the heavens and the earth were created" (*Ber.*, 55a). These are the letters of the Hebrew alphabet, the letters of the Torah. Being God's partner in the work of creation is not limited to the cocreation of the individual human person, but extends to the cocreation of God's word, the Torah (see *AT — HM,* chap. 1, sec. 1). Through engaging in the art of interpretation of the Torah, one becomes God's coauthor of the Torah (see, e.g., Faur 1986, 123; and Idel 1988a, 214–15 and sources noted there); one completes the Torah. As a Hasidic master put it:

> Everything depends upon the interpretations of the sages. . . . Until they interpreted it, the Torah was not considered complete, but only half finished; it was the sages, through their interpretations, who made the Torah whole. Such is the case for each generation and its leaders; they complete the Torah. The Torah is interpreted in each generation according to the soul-root of those who live at that time. God thus enlightens the sages of the generation in [the interpretation of] God's Holy Torah. One who denies this is as if he denies the Torah itself. (Moses Hayyim Ephraim of Sudlykow 1963, sec. "*Bereshit,*" 6; see also Sherwin 1991a, 19–23)

Or, in the words of Judah Loew, "When we contemplate the works of God, [we realize that] everything God created requires repair (*tikkun*) and action. For example, that which is not created full grown needs human tending. . . . Scholars are those who are the repair (*tikkun*) and [bring about] the completion (*hashlamah*) of the Torah" (*TY,* chap. 69, 216). The tasks of augmenting and interpreting the Torah, and of creating life as a work of art, coalesce in Jewish ethics. Like the artist who transforms the raw materials of nature into something more than they previously had been, the Jewish ethicist is one who takes the raw materials conveyed through revelation and inherited from tradition and re-creates them, providing them with a voice that speaks to the task of creating life as a work of art, and to the challenge of addressing the particular ethical issues that characterize his or her juncture in history.

A Torah scroll contains only consonants; it has no vowels. According to Jewish law, a vocalized Torah scroll is unfit for ritual use. It is the reader who provides the vowels, the vocalization of the text. Medieval texts compare the consonants to the body and the vowels to the soul (see, e.g., *Sefer ha-Bahir* 1951, sec. 115, 51). The sixteenth-century halakhist and cabalist, David ibn Zimra, noted that "vocalization is like a commentary to the written Torah" (1781, vol. 3, no. 643, 43b; see also Zioni 1882, 2b). By vocalizing the text, the reader animates and interprets it, giving it life, allowing it to be spoken, heard, understood. The unvocalized word of God invites human articulation and vocalization. Without such vocalization and interpretation, the text remains moot, God's word remains unheard.

To animate God's words, to "walk in God's ways," and to cultivate the moral virtues, one must know what they are. This requires immersion in the resources of Jewish ethical literature. The goal here is not to amass information, but to engender spiritual transformation based upon what is gleaned from the harvest of study. The purpose is not to know for the sake of knowing, but to know for the sake of doing. As a blunt rabbinic statement puts it, "If one studies [Torah] without the intention of observing it, it is better that he had not been born" (*PT. Ber.*, chap. 1, sec. 2; *LR*, chap. 35, sec. 7).

Erudition is a prerequisite: "The unlearned cannot be pious" (*PA*, chap. 2, sec. 5). But, erudition is an invitation, not a destination. The purpose of studying ethical literature is to become what one studies (see, e.g., Abrahams 1926, 98). From the resources gathered in the mineworks of tradition, the ethicist must sift, distill, refine, and reformulate his or her findings in a manner that can address the problem of how to create one's life as a work of art in the context of one's own time and place. By using materials bequeathed by the past, what the ethicist re-creates becomes an organic extension of the tradition, and is therefore authentic. By transporting the past to the present, by reformulating past texts, the ethicist provides old texts with a voice that can speak not only to their times, but to our time as well.

Creating life as a work of art in the image of God entails cultivation of the moral virtues (*middot*) like love, justice, humility, compassion, repentance, and acts of loving-kindness — actions that emulate the ways of God. Through performing God-like actions one can articulate one's God-like nature. Analogies of action and ontological analogies thereby merge. Through what a person does, he or she can graduate from "walking after God" to becoming Godlike, from *imitatio Dei* to *imago Dei*. As a midrash puts it, "God says: All those who do as I do become as I am" (*Tan.*, sec. "*Behukotai*," 2:56a).

Jewish ethics is concerned not only with the cultivation of the moral virtues but with the propriety and impropriety of specific actions in particular situations. A function of Jewish law or *hala-khah* is to determine the disposition of specific ethical questions, even when such specificity is not explicitly available in past precedent.

The fifteenth-century Jewish philosopher Joseph Albo wrote: "The Torah of God could not be so complete as to be adequate for all times because the ever new details of human relations, their customs and their acts are too numerous to be embraced in a [single] work. Therefore, Moses was given orally certain general principles, only briefly alluded to in the Torah, by means of which the sages in every generation may innovate the details" (1930, bk. 3, chap. 23, 203). Similarly, commenting on the biblical verse, "Do what is right and good in the sight of the Lord" (Deut. 6:18), Nahmanides pointed out that since it is impossible to specify all of the details for individual and social ethics, it was necessary for the Torah to provide general rules such as is indicated by this verse (1960, 2:376). Likewise commenting on this verse (i.e., Deut. 6:18), Joseph Karo states that the details were not provided because "human virtues and behavior change according to the times and the people" (see his commentary *Maggid Mishnah* to *MT—HS*, chap. 14, sec. 5). In other words, God does not reveal halakhic decisions but halakhic possibilities. Consequently, it is the task of the ethicist and halakhist to creatively amplify and to apply what is available from the resources of tradition to the particular moral situations confronting his or her contemporaries. Here, too, the challenge is to apply yesterday's dicta to today's situations. "Let the Torah never be for you an antiquated decree . . . but as one issued this very day" (*PRK,* 102a). By correctly applying the wisdom of the past to the ethical situations of the present, one serves as "God's partner in the work of creation" (*MRY,* sec. "*Yitro,*" chap. 2, 196).

Theological and Secular Ethics

Where Jewish ethics differs from secular ethics is in Jewish ethics' resistance to the claim that ethics can be based upon individual subjective human criteria *alone.* Jewish tradition apparently found the human condition too precarious, human thought and emotion too unreliable, to leave the task of moral guidance to the vicissitudes of the human mind and heart alone (see, e.g., Sherwin 1990, 47–65). The limited wisdom and experience of an individual who must make an ethical decision in a particular situation cannot vie with the cumulative wisdom and experience of a long-standing tradition in deciding what course of action is ethical.

For Jewish ethics, objective moral norms inhere in a divine Creator. They are not the fabrications of random individuals. Dostoyevsky's famous observation that if there is no God, then everything is permitted, that is, there can be no viable ethics, was anticipated by the thirteenth-century talmudic commentator Menahem Meiri. According to Meiri, atheists and idolaters cannot be presumed to act ethically because they do not affirm a belief system that imposes objective moral constraints upon its believers (1965, 39).

The ethics of Judaism presupposes an objective foundation for moral behavior by rooting morality in the revelation God's will and in tradition's interpretation of the textual products of that revelation. These texts provide the raw materials for ethical decision making. However, though they are necessary, they are not sufficient in dealing with the adjudication of specific ethical issues at a particular time and place. More is required. Subjective human elements such as reason, intuition, and emotion must also be harnessed. Though God has the first word, human beings have the last word in determining a correct course of moral action. In the process of ethical decision making, the challenge is to link God's initial word with our last word, despite human fallibility. As Aryeh Leib Heller wrote in his nineteenth-century commentary to the *Shulhan Arukh*, "The Torah was not given to angels but to human beings who have intelligence. God gave us the Torah in conformity to the ability of the human mind to decide, even though it may not be the truth [objectively speaking], only that it be true according to the conclusions of the human mind. . . . 'Let truth emerge from the earth' (Ps. 85:12), that is, the truth as the sages decide using human intelligence" (1888, "Introduction"; see also Jacobs 1981, 184–217).

The ethics of Judaism utilizes both objective and subjective components in the process of ethical decision making. In this, it differs from secular ethics, which rejects the objective resources of revelation and tradition and which exclusively relies on the resources of the human mind and heart. Consequently, Jewish ethics offers a more complete, comprehensive, and "rounded" approach than secular ethics in that Jewish ethics includes a system of checks and balances between the objective and subjective components that inform the process of ethical decision making (see, e.g., Sherwin 1990, 24–29).

Ethical living, that is, living in the image of God, entails the enhancement of God's word, God's world, and the divine image implanted within each human person. Unethical acts, in contrast, not only diminish God's world, God's word and the divine image implanted within each human being, but they also diminish God. For example, a midrash states:

> Scripture tells us that whosoever spills blood, Scripture imputes it to him as if he has diminished the image of the King [i.e., God]. The matter is comparable to a king of flesh and blood who entered a city and erected icons and images and stamped coins [with his image upon them]. After a time, they pushed down the icons, smashed the images and destroyed the coins, and thereby diminished the image of the King. Therefore, whosoever spills blood, Scripture imputes it to him as if he had diminished the image of the King, as it is written, "whosoever sheds human blood . . . for in the image of God, God made humans." (Gen. 9:6) (*MRY,* sec. "*Yitro,*" chap. 8, 233 on Exod. 20:16; see also *GR,* chap. 34, sec. 14; note Heschel 1962, 220–21.)

From this text, one can elicit at least four theological assumptions endemic to Jewish ethics: (1) God exists; (2) the human being is created in God's image; (3) because the human being is created in God's image, certain actions against another person — in this case, murder, are morally wrong; and (4) because human beings are created in the image of God, an immoral act against another person is an affront to God, an act both against God's will and against God's person.

The boundaries of these assumptions were expanded by the Jewish mystics of the sixteenth- and seventeenth-centuries. These mystics maintained that not only is the human person created in the image of God, but that within each person there is an element of divinity, a part of God (*helek elohah mi-ma'al*), a spark of the divine (see, e.g., Jacobs 1966, 87–115). Hence, one ought to treat other human beings in a certain manner not simply because each person is in the divine image, but because God is a part of each person. In this view, how we relate to other human persons does not merely *reflect* how we relate to God. Rather, how we relate to other human persons and to ourselves *is* how we relate to God.

From what has been said, it should be apparent that Jewish ethics is a form of theological ethics in that it rests upon theological assumptions such as those just noted. Our attitudes toward and relationships with other human persons are inextricably linked to our relationship with God, and to our having been created in the divine image. An example of this is the well-known biblical verse, "You shall love your neighbor as yourself, I am the Lord" (Lev. 19:18). Rabbinic literature interprets this verse: "You shall love your neighbor as yourself *because* I am the Lord, because I have created him" (*ARN*, chap. 16, 64).

When asked what is the greatest principle of the Torah, Rabbi Akiva quoted the verse "You shall love your neighbor as yourself; I am the Lord" (Lev. 19:18) (*Sifra* 1947, sec. "*Kedoshim*," chap. 4, 89a). On another occasion, when someone asked him to teach "the whole Torah at once," Rabbi Akiva, like Hillel before him said, "That which is hateful to you, do not do unto your fellow human being" (*ARN*, Version B, chap. 26, 27a; for Hillel, see *Shab.*, 31a). Thus, two of the most venerable talmudic rabbis, Hillel and Rabbi Akiva, considered ethics to be at the core of Judaism.

In these texts attributed to Hillel and to Rabbi Akiva, the term used for "Judaism" is "Torah." For the talmudic rabbis and for classical Jewish literature, Jewish ethics is that which is taught by the Torah, by the sacred and significant texts of Judaism. Jewish ethics thus understood is the ethics of Judaism. In this view, Jewish ethics is neither defined nor determined by how a majority of Jews today or at other times may actually behave, or by what a majority of Jews today or at other times might consider morally correct. Rather, Jewish ethics and theology are the ethics and theology of Judaism as defined by the beliefs, practices, and sacred literature of Judaism. Consequently, various forms of secular morality detached from the theological underpinnings of Judaism, though affirmed by groups of Jews, may be the ethics of Jews, but cannot be considered representative of the ethics of Judaism (see, e.g., Liebman 1973, 135–59; Borowitz 1990, 17–36).

Beginning in the sixteenth century, the purview of Jewish ethics is defined as extending to three central areas of concern: the relationship of human beings to God, the relationships of human beings to one another, and the relationship of each individual human being to his or her own self. In the words of Judah Loew:

One must achieve the good which is one's purpose, thereby justifying one's existence, and when one's existence has been justified, the whole universe has been justified, since all hinges on man. . . . Therefore, a person should endeavor to cultivate good qualities. And what makes a person "good" so that one might say of him: What a fine creature he is? The first requirement is that one must be good in relation to one's own self. . . . The second category of good is that one be good toward the Lord who created man to serve God and to do God's will. The third category is that one be good to others. For a person does not exist by himself. He exists in fellowship with other people. . . . A person is not complete until he is completely pious vis-à-vis these three varieties of [human] perfection: with his Creator, with other people, and with his own self as well. Then he is completely perfect. (*DH*, chap. 1, sec. 2, 24 and "Introduction," 9; see also *HA*, 3:40; Edels on *BK*, 30a)

One area in which these three aspects of moral behavior coalesce is medical ethics, which is the subject of the chapter that now follows. As will be discussed there, concern with the care and cure of the human body is a way in which an individual can articulate his or her awareness of having been created in the image of God.

2

Health and Healing

THE DIVINE IMAGE relates not only to the will, soul and intellect, but to the body as well. The body is a mirror reflecting the image of God, as well as a receptacle that embodies the divine likeness: "A parable: There were two twin brothers who lived in a certain city. One was elected king while the other became a thief. At the king's command, the thief was hanged. But all who saw the thief hanging on the gallows said, 'The king is hanged.'" (*San.*, 46b).

Commenting on the biblical phrase, "in the image of God, God created human beings," a midrash tells (*LR*, chap. 34, sec. 3; *YS*, sec. "*Mishlei*," para. 947, 2:983; *ARN*, chap. 30, 33b):

> Hillel the Elder once completed his studies with his disciples who accompanied him from the academy. His disciples asked him, "Master, where are you going?"
>
> "To perform a religious duty," he responded.
>
> "Which religious duty?"
>
> "To wash in the bathhouse," said Hillel.
>
> "Is this a religious duty?"
>
> "Yes," replied Hillel. "If the statues of kings, which are erected in theatres and circuses, are scoured and washed by the person appointed to look after them, and who thereby obtains his maintenance through them . . . how much more I, who have been created in the image and likeness of God, for as it is written, 'for in the image of God, God made human beings'?" (Gen. 9:6)

As these texts plainly observe, the human body is portrayed as having been created in the divine "image and likeness."

13

As a creation of the divine in the image of God, the human body is a source of wonder, a manifestation of divine wisdom, an opportunity for profound gratitude.[1]

The following blessing, recorded in the Talmud, was later included in the liturgy Jews recite each day: "Blessed is God who created human beings with wisdom, and created in each of them many orifices and many cavities. It is fully known before the throne of Your glory that if one of them should be [improperly] opened or one of them closed, it would be impossible for one to stand before You. . . . [Blessed are You] who heals all flesh and who performs wonders" (*Ber.*, 60b). This blessing is to be recited after going to the bathroom. According to the commentaries to this text, the phrase "who heals all flesh" means that normal excretory function is a product of divine grace, that "evacuation is a healing for the entire body." I know of no comparable blessing recited on a comparable occasion in any other religious tradition. Here one encounters what the novelist George Eliot called Judaism's "reverence for the human body, which lifts the needs of the animal life into religion."[2]

To suggest that the human body or its natural functions are repulsive by nature is considered an affront to God's image and to divine wisdom. In themselves, bodily organs and functions are beautiful and good. Only when abused or misused do they become ugly and repulsive. According to the medieval ethical treatise *The Holy Letter:* "'God saw everything He had made and behold it was

---

1. Louis Jacobs classifies these three attitudes as each relates to physical gratification, as: thankful acceptance, ascetic, and puritanical. Jacobs correctly considers the first dominant in rabbinic literature, the second dominant among certain philosophers and in certain mystical trends (e.g., *Hasidei Ashkenaz*), and the third dominant among other philosophers (e.g., Bahya) and mystics (e.g., Hasidism). The first gratefully accepts the gift of creation and of the body. This view may be epitomized by the talmudic statement, "In the future one will have to render account for everything one saw but did not consume" (*PT. Kid.*, chap. 4, sec. 12). The second sets up a state of conflict between body and soul, and is expressed through ascetic practices. This approach is epitomized by the talmudic statement: "Whoever accepts the pleasures of this world is denied the pleasures of the world to come. And, whoever does not accept the pleasures of this world is granted the pleasures of the world to come" (*ARN*, chap. 28, 43a). The third teaches that pleasure — although legitimate — is not an end in itself (see Jacobs 1979, 157–58).

2. On evacuation of the bowels as an art of cosmic reparation (*tikkun*), see, for example, Hayyim Vital's *Pri Etz Hayyim* (1966, sec. "*Sha'ar ha-Tefilah*" chap. 5, 22; see also Givurtchav 1962, 1: 126).

very good' (Gen. 1:31). . . . Nothing in the human organs are created flawed or ugly. Everything is created with divine wisdom and is therefore complete, exalted, good and pleasant. But when one sins, ugliness becomes attached to these matters." (1976, 45, 48). Through the performance of sacred deeds, the body, which is good by nature, becomes holy by actions. According to Judah Loew, when an individual acts properly, one's body becomes sacred, expressing the image of God, but when one does not act properly, one's body is indistinguishable from that of any other animal (*NO*, sec. "*Netiv Koah ha-Yetzer,*" 2:130).

Like the Talmud, many of the medieval Jewish philosophers counseled contemplation of the body for the purpose of appreciating the *wisdom* of God. The cabalists, however, encouraged contemplation of the body as an entrée to the *knowledge* of God. In this regard, compare, for example, medieval Jewish philosophical and medieval Jewish mystical interpretations of the verse from Job (19:26), "From my flesh, I shall see God." Medieval philosophers such as Abraham bar Hiyya interpreted the verse to mean "from the nature of your flesh and the structure of your organs, you can comprehend the *wisdom* of your Creator" (1969, 38; see also Ibn Pakuda 1973, 160–61). Jewish mystics such as Judah Loew took this verse to mean, "When one contemplates the form of the human body, one is able to arrive at a *knowledge* of God" (*DH*, chap. 3, sec. 14, 143; see also, e.g., *Sefer ha-Temunah* 1892, 25a-b).

The Body Divine

The Jewish mystics perceived reality as folded over upon itself, as a constant flow of overlapping relationships, distinct from one another yet interpenetrating one another. One analogy they use is that of a nut. Each "world" in the organically linked structure of reality consists of a shell with substance within it. The substance of one world is the shell of another; the shell of one world is the substance of the other. At the core of all of reality is the *Deus Absconditus* — the *En Sof*, limitless divine essence, constantly gushing forth spiritual vitality to nourish the worlds, the spheres below.

Though self-contained and pristinely perfect, *En Sof* becomes manifest through a series of actions that are identified with ten divine attributes. These divine attributes are revealed in a symbolic configuration, known as the *sefirot*. This configuration of the *sefirot* is most often portrayed by the identification of each *sefirah* with one of the limbs of the body of *Adam Kadmon*, the "Primordial Man," also called *Adam Ilaya*, the "Supernal Man." The human person is created in the image of this configuration of the manifested divinity. The human being is the embodiment on earth of the spiritual entities that form the sefirotic realm. As Loew puts it, "this material world is like a garment for the spiritual world" (*DH*, chap. 3, sec. 14, 142).

According to the *Zohar*, the biblical verse "let *us* create man" refers to the interaction of the *sefirot* in the creation of human beings; "in our image" refers to the image of the *sefirot* (see *Zohar* 1883, 1:34a; see also Idel 1988a, 185).[3] While admonishing against taking literally what is meant to be understood figuratively and symbolically, the cabalists nevertheless insist that the biblical description of the human being in the divine image refers to the configuration of the *sefirot* in the form of a human body (see, e.g., *Zohar* 1883, bk. 1, 49b, 58b, 76a; see Tishbi 1961, 2:610). However, for the cabalists, it must be stressed, it is the human being who is in the image of God, and not God who is in the human image.[4]

This notion of the human being in the image of the *sefirot* reversed a trend in medieval Jewish thought of identifying the divine

3. There are three dominant attitudes to the human body in Jewish religious thought: positive, negative and neutral. All three are found in the *Zohar*. The positive view relates the body to the *sefirot*, and considers mundane acts performed in accordance with Jewish legal and moral requirements as virtual sacraments. The negative view sees the body as the product of the demonic "other side" (*sitra ahara*) and beyond repair. Ascetic practices are therefore encouraged to weaken the body's influence. The neutral view sees the body as redeemable through the performance of acts of virtue (see, e.g., Tishbi 1961, 2: 84–87).

4. The dimensions of each "limb" of the "divine body" are described in the ancient treatise, *Shi'ur Qoma* (1983). Though a number of scholars, most notably Gershom Scholem, maintain that the text describes the divine corpus in such gigantic terms so as to reject the notion of divine corporeality, there is no reason to make this assumption. The text should be taken at face value as a description of God's body. Why else would the author take such great pains at describing each limb of God's body unless he believed that God actually has a body? This more literal reading was also affirmed in a conversation with Professor Moshe Idel. Furthermore, that medieval scholars who affirmed the absolute incorporeal nature of God, such as Maimonides, took such offense at this work, would lead one to conclude that many medieval readers took the work seriously and literally. Maimonides, for example, considers it a dangerous foreign import into Jewish literature (see, e.g., 1948, 1: no. 117, 200–201; see also Scholem 1991, 15–56).

image exclusively with the intellect or the soul. Now, the divine image was identified with the ten *sefirot* or attributes of God, including intellect, mercy, justice, and with the first *sefirah*—will (*keter*). Whereas in earlier medieval Jewish thought, self-knowledge as the conduit to knowledge of God and the universe was primarily related to the human soul, now the human body became a vehicle not only for self-knowledge, but for knowledge of God, of the Torah, and of creation. With clear reference to the idea of the *sefirot*, Judah Loew writes, "When man considers the configuration of his body, he is able to reach an understanding of God" (*DH*, chap. 3, sec. 14, 143). The Delphic maxim—"Know Thyself"—was no longer restricted to knowledge of the soul, but now was also applied to the knowledge of the body (see Altmann 1969, 1–40).

Being modeled after the *sefirot*, the human body can be a gateway to the divine. Contemplation of the human body and its actions not only grants one knowledge of all worlds—of all dimensions of existence, but also indicates how physical actions can influence what happens in these worlds, including the divine world of the *sefirot*. In this typically cabalistic view, each human action, each physical gesture, has immense implications and influence. The physical life of the human being is therefore related not merely to the individual or social realm, but to the disposition of all that exists. From this perspective, the actions of the human body have transcendent and theurgic implications, effecting the Godhead itself. In a typical mystical text, the Hasidic master, Elimelekh of Lizensk, observed:

> The main reason man was created was to rectify his Root in the upper worlds. It is written, "For in the image of God, God made humans" (Gen. 9:6). God made humans in the form of the structure that exists on high, making each human being a precise counterpart of it. . . . The main human task is to rectify the divine structure (*shiur komah*). . . . Whenever a person sanctifies himself through a certain part of the body, that person rectifies the universes that correspond to that particular limb. (1787, 102b)

Through moral virtue and observance of the commandments, one provides a means for each limb of the body to articulate the spiritual through the physical, to make manifest the divine image embossed upon the human body. Thereby, the actual physical limitations and boundaries of the body may be overcome. The finitude of the body can be transcended through cohesion with transcendent deeds.

The sixteenth-century cabalist Moses Cordevero combines the analogies of action and ontology, and teaches that one must perform divine deeds in order to realize the divine image and likeness. In his ethical treatise, *The Palm Tree of Deborah* (*Tomer Devorah*), Cordevero wrote:

> It is proper for man to imitate his Creator, resembling Him in both likeness and image according to the secret of the Supernal Form. Because the chief Supernal image and likeness is in deeds, a human resemblance merely in body appearance and not in deeds debases that form. Of the man who resembles the form in body alone it is said, "A handsome form whose deeds are ugly." For what value can there be in man's resemblance to the Supernal Form in bodily limbs if his deeds have no resemblance to those of his Creator? (1965, 9; 1960, 46)

Without the body, the commandments cannot be performed, the moral virtues cannot be cultivated. Without the body, without a vehicle for giving spiritual deeds concrete physical expression, the "image of God" remains concealed, dormant, comatose (see, e.g., Tishbi 1961, 2:90–93). Through observance of the commandments and by means of the cultivation of the moral virtues, one makes manifest the image of God. Hence, the body is not an end in itself; it is a pathway, not a destination. Physical health provides a foundation for human beings to accomplish their spiritual mission.

Body and Soul

In a medieval "ethical will" attributed to Maimonides, the author wrote, "Perfection of the body is an antecedent to the perfection of the soul, for health is the key that unlocks the inner chambers. When I bid you to care for your bodily and moral welfare, my purpose is to open for you the gates of heaven" (Abrahams 1926, 105). But, a medieval Jewish philosopher observed, "What profit has one in his bodily health, if one's soul is ill?" (Ibn Falaquera 1976, 31). Since the limbs of the body are the instruments of the soul, a body in ill repair leaves the soul inoperative, the self spiritually immobile. However, if the soul is diseased, health of the body becomes a premise without a conclusion, a non sequitur.

Medieval Jewish writers such as Maimonides echoed Plato's observation that, "The cure of many diseases is unknown to the physicians . . . because they are ignorant of the whole [body and soul] which ought to be studied also; for the part can never be well, unless the whole is well. For all good and evil, whether in the body or in human nature, originates . . . in the soul, and overflows from thence . . . and therefore, if the head and body are to be well, you must begin by curing the soul; that is the first thing" (Plato, *Charmides*, secs. 156–57).

The primary concern of medical ethics is health; and ethics itself — the concern with how one ought to live, is a crucial component of health. For Maimonides, following Plato, the virtuous soul is the healthy soul; the healing of the soul relates to the inculcation of moral virtue:

> The improvement of the moral qualities is brought about by the healing of the soul and its activities. Therefore, just as the physician, who endeavors to cure the human body, must have a perfect knowledge of it in its entirety and its individual parts, just as he must know what causes sickness that it may be avoided, and must also be acquainted with the means by which a patient may be cured, so likewise, he who tries to cure the soul, wishing to improve the moral qualities, must have a knowledge of the soul in its totality and its parts, must know how to prevent it from becoming diseased, and how to maintain its health. (Maimonides 1912, chap. 1, 38; see also *MT — HD*, chap. 2, sec. 1)

It is not coincidental that Maimonides' younger contemporary, Joseph ibn Aknin, entitled his ethical treatise *Hygiene of the Soul* (see Halkin 1944). Neither is it surprising that Maimonides' immediate predecessor in the history of Jewish philosophy, Abraham ibn Daud (Abraham ben David), entitled his discussion of ethics "On the Healing of the Soul" (*Emunah Ramah* 1852, sec. 3, 98).

For the Jewish medievals, as for Aristotle, virtue constitutes the health of the soul. Just as doctors of the body are required for instruction regarding the maintenance of physical health, ethicists are necessary as "doctors of the soul" to provide instruction vis-à-vis moral health (see, e.g., *MT — HD*, chap. 2, sec. 1).

In his *Medical Aphorisms* Maimonides states, "It is a well-known assertion of philosophers that the soul can be healthy or diseased, just as the body is either healthy or diseased. These illnesses of the soul and their health which are alluded to by philosophers undoubt-edly refer to the opinions and morals of people. Therefore, I con-sider untrue opinions and bad morals, with all their different varieties, as types of human illness" (1971a, 2:203). As Maimonides further stated elsewhere, "The real duty of man is, that in adopting whatever measures he may for his well-being and the preservation of his existence in good health, he should do so with the object of maintaining a perfect condition of the instruments of the soul, which are the limbs of the body, so that his soul may be unham-pered, and he may busy himself in acquiring the moral and mental virtues" (1912, chap. 5, 71).

Nahman of Bratslav opposed treating illness on a purely physi-cal basis. In Hasidic thought, illness is often viewed as the outward manifestation of an inner spiritual disturbance. To treat the body alone might remove the symptoms but not their cause. For Nah-man, treating the corporeal aspect of a patient without attending to his or her spiritual dimension would inevitably prove faulty. Ac-cording to Nahman, the true healer cannot be a mechanic, but must be a person of spiritual depth in order for him or her to aspire to be a complete healer. Nahman described physicians who neglect the spiritual dimension either of their own selves or of their patients as a new variety of "sorcerer," trying to manipulate natural forces without recourse to the spiritual (see Green 1979, 234).

The verse in Deuteronomy (4:9), "But take utmost care and watch yourselves [or your souls] *scrupulously*" (Hebrew: *me'od*; liter-ally "very much") has been taken to mean that each individual must take primary responsibility for his or her own health. However, as the medieval commentaries explain, health is not restricted to physi-cal well-being but is also extended to moral and psychological well-being. Indeed, one commentator maintained that since the emphatic *"me'od"* is used in relationship to the care of one's soul in this verse, the obligation to maintain physical health is secondary to the obliga-tion to maintain moral and spiritual health (see, e.g., Lunshitz on Deut. 4:9). For the Jewish medievals, health of the body was a necessary but insufficient characteristic of a healthy person.

Understanding health as being both physical and moral rejects the conception of health as being limited to an absence of physical illness or to the presence of physical well-being alone. It rejects the "biomedical model" that has dominated the practice of medicine in our culture — an approach that understands the human being as a soulless machine to be repaired, rather than a person in need of care and cure (see Engel 1977). According to Jewish tradition, not only the healthy body but the healthy person is the goal. Just as a person is admonished not to neglect one's physical health, so is one advised to attend to one's moral and spiritual health. Indeed, the *Sefer Hasidim* equates neglect of one's spiritual and moral health to self-injury and even to suicide (*SH* 1960, nos. 675–76, 428–29).

As health focuses upon the whole person, medical treatment is understood to be treatment of the person who suffers from a disease, and not merely the treatment of the disease that afflicts the person. As Maimonides noted, quoting the Greek physicians, "the physician should not treat the disease but the patient who is suffering from it" (1963, 89).

Medieval Jewish literature posits a teleological understanding of the nature of health. The purpose of bodily health is to prepare the foundation for moral and spiritual health, whereby the human being may realize the qualities essential to being human, and to living in the image of God. Thus, the concern with health is, in the final analysis, a concern with how one lives the life divinely entrusted into one's care.

In Partnership with God

The dominant view in Jewish sources considers the physician to be a partner and a colleague of God in the act and in the art of healing (see Sherwin 1990, 68–70). No physician is a sole practitioner. Every physician practices with a senior partner — God. Medical practice presumes a covenantal relationship between God and the physician.

Although ancient Judaism had priests who were physicians, medieval Judaism considered the physician to be a priest, a servant of God, a vicar of God. God is the ultimate physician, and the human physician serves as God's agent, as God's partner. In sixteenth-century Poland, Moses Matt wrote, "The patient must trust in God, and must realize that everything is dependent upon God's will. The patient must continuously pray that God will help the physician so that the physician will not err in his treatment and so that the patient will be cured by the physician, for the physician is an agent of God" (1876, 110b).

In many of the "Physician's Prayers" found in medieval Jewish literature this theme is expressed. For example, the medieval Jewish philosopher, poet, and physician Judah ha-Levi wrote: "Not upon my power of healing I rely. Only for Your healing do I watch" (1924, 113; see also Sir. 13:1–2a). In his "Physician's Prayer," the seventeenth-century preacher and physician Jacob Zahalon wrote, "You [God] are the physician, not me. I am but clay in the Potter's hand, in the hand of the Creator of all things, and as the instrument through which You cure Your creatures" (see Friedenwald 1944, 1:274).[5]

The covenantal relationship between God and the physician is the premise of which the covenantal relationship between the physician and the patient is the corollary. In the words of Abraham Joshua Heschel:

> The doctor enters a covenant with the patient; he penetrates his life, affecting his mode of living, often deciding his fate. The doctor's role is one of royal authority, while the patient's mood is one of anxiety and helplessness. The patient is literally a sufferer, while the doctor is the incarnation of his hope. The patient must not be defined as a client who contracts a physician for services; he is a human being entrusted to the care of a physician. The physician is the trustee holding the patient's health in trust. In return, the patient's earnest is reliance, commitment. . . . [God's] chief commandment is, "Choose life" (Deut. 30:19). The doctor is God's partner in the struggle between life and death. . . . Medicine is prayer in the form of a deed. . . . The body is a sanctuary, the doctor is a priest. . . . The act of healing is the highest form of *imitatio Dei.* (1966, 31, 33)

Related to the view that the physician is a catalyst for divine healing is the claim that the physician is one whose task is not to effect a cure but to help Nature effect a cure. God creates Nature as the physician's tool, to be employed in the art of healing. The wise physician knows how to utilize this tool. In the words of the medieval Jewish physician and philosopher Isaac Israeli, "the physician

---

5. Zahalon's prayer influenced the celebrated "Physician's Prayer" ascribed to Maimonides, which was not written by Maimonides, but most probably by Marcus Herz, a nineteenth-century German-Jewish physician. An increasing number of medical schools are replacing the Hippocratic Oath with "Maimonides' Physician's Prayer" often because the Hippocratic Oath prohibits abortion (on the Hippocratic Oath, see, e.g., Edelstein 1943).

does not bring about the cure, but prepares the way for Nature; for Nature is the actual healer" (Quoted in Baron 1958, 8:260; see also Maimonides 1957, 44, 70; Ibn Falaquera 1976, 44).

Healing in partnership with God precludes the physician's acting as a sole practitioner. It also prohibits the patient from relying only upon the physician, to the exclusion of the physician's senior partner — God. This perspective is reflected in the biblical book of Chronicles: "In the thirty-ninth year of his reign [King] Asa suffered from an acute foot ailment, but ill as he was he did not turn to the Lord, but [only] to physicians. And Asa slept with his fathers, dying in the forty-first year of his reign" (2 Chron. 16:12–14). It is in this spirit that the medieval commentators interpret the Talmud's enigmatic statement, "the best doctors are destined for hell" (*M. Kid.*, chap. 4, sec. 14; *Kid.*, 82a; see *Sof.*, chap. 15, sec. 10). Rashi interprets this statement as a censure of the physician's tendency to disavow his or her reliance upon God, his or her partner, in the process of healing.

Commenting on this talmudic passage, Judah Loew explains that medical practice, though sanctioned, must also be sanctified. It must embody elements of the natural and the supernatural; it must articulate the human application of the divine power to heal. The physician who is solely a naturalist, who denies the spiritual dimension, is deficient and is therefore destined for the realm of deficiency and negation: hell. Further, the physician who treats only the body and neglects the soul wallows in the physical world, denies human nature as a composite of the spiritual and the material, and is therefore denied entrance into the spiritual realm, being assigned instead to its opposite: to hell (*NY*, chap. 30, 142; *HA*, 2:153 on *Kid.*, 82a).

In his commentary to the talmudic passage "the best of physicians are destined for hell," Samuel Edels interpreted this text to mean that the physician who considers himself or herself the best of physicians is destined to reside in hell as a punishment for two interrelated sins: pride and murder. Edels explained that the haughty physician will mistakenly rely on his or her own prowess in complex life-threatening situations rather than adequately study the case and consult fellow physicians. Such an arrogant physician is likely to mistreat the patient, which would endanger the life of the patient. The death of the patient would then be the result of negligence, and the physician would be guilty of homicide. From this perspective, the practice of medicine is spiritual brinkmanship. Both the life of the patient and the soul of the physician are constantly at risk.

The Sanction to Heal

In classical Jewish sources, the sanction to heal is affirmed by means of four primary methods: (1) exegetical analysis of Scripture; (2) reasoned analysis; (3) legal analysis; and (4) reflection upon the claim that there exists a divine-human partnership in "the work of creation" (*Shab.*, 10a).

The locus classicus in rabbinic literature for the sanction of medical practice is a talmudic commentary on the scriptural verses "When men quarrel and one strikes the other with stone or fist, and he does not die but has to take to his bed — if he then gets up and walks outdoors upon his staff, the assailant shall go unpunished, except that he must pay for his idleness and his healing" (Exod. 21:18–19). From the obligation of the assailant to pay the medical costs of his victim, the sanction to heal is inferred. The school of Rabbi Ishmael inferred from the term "his healing" (literally: "and to heal he shall heal") that "permission [*reshut*] was granted [by God] to the physician to heal" (*BK*, 85a).

A second exegetical tradition curiously relates the obligation upon the physician to treat the sick to the biblical injunction requiring the return of lost property to its owner (Deut. 22:2). The Talmud extends the obligation to rescue one's property to a further obligation to rescue one's fellow person from danger (*BK*, 81b). Maimonides applied this biblical injunction to the obligation to render medical care (*CM, Ned.*, chap. 4, sec. 4).

Nahmanides, himself a physician, related the sanction to heal to the generic verse, "You should love your neighbor as yourself" (Lev. 19:18). However, he also tied the sanction to heal to the verse "Do not stand [idly] by the blood of your brother" (Lev. 19:16), which is invoked by the Talmud to require one to aid an imperiled individual, in this case, an individual imperiled by illness (1964, 2:42).[6]

Nahmanides, in his Commentary on Leviticus (26:11), drew a

6. The obligation of coming to the aid of an imperiled party is a requirement of Jewish law (see, e.g., *San.*, 73a; *MT—LM*, chap. 1, secs. 14–16; *AT—HM*, para. 426; see also Kirshenbaum 1976).

bizarre distinction between the physician's obligation to heal and the patient's obligation to seek medical care. Nahmanides affirms the obligation of the physician to heal but denies the correlative obligation of the patient to seek a medical cure, since there is no specific scriptural sanction in that regard (1960, 2:185–86; see also Arama 1522, in sec. "*Va-Yishlah*"). Nevertheless, the logical weakness of his argument is rebutted by subsequent commentators who have pointed out that without an affirmation of the patient's entitlement to be healed, the scripturally sanctioned obligation of the physician to heal would be meaningless (Cf. Ben Samuel ha-Levi on *SA — YD*, para. 336, sec. 1).

After rejecting Nahmanides' position, the eighteenth-century commentator Hayyim Joseph David Azulai states:

> Nowadays one must not rely on miracles, and the afflicted individual is duty bound to conduct himself in accordance with the natural order by calling on a physician to heal him. In fact, to depart from the general practice by claiming greater merit than the many saints [of past] generations who were themselves cured by physicians is almost sinful on account of the implied arrogance and the reliance upon miracles when life is threatened. . . . Hence, one should adopt the ways of all people and be healed by physicians. (1843, 85b, on *SA — YD*, para. 336)

Moses Maimonides, the greatest medieval Jewish philosopher and physician, considered the sanction to heal to be logically self-evident. In his *Mishneh Torah*, Maimonides categorically stated the obligation to heal without recourse to any proof text, a phenomenon that surprised some subsequent commentators (*MT — HN*, chap. 6, sec. 8, apparently following al-Fasi on *BK*, 81a; cf. *CM*, Ned. chap. 2, sec. 4).

Echoing a statement found in Maimonides' medical writings, Jacob Zahalon wrote that, just as it is unreasonable for an individual to argue that belief in divine providence should lead one to deny oneself food, so it is equally unreasonable for one to argue that belief in divine providence should lead one to deny oneself medical care. As Zahalon wrote, "It is not viable for a healthy person who has a desire to eat, to say that if life has been decreed for me by God I shall live without food, and if death has been decreed, I shall die, because such a person would be guilty of suicide. . . . Similarly, the sick person who refuses to avail himself of medical care because he or she believes God has either already decreed life or death, is also guilty of suicide" (1683, "Introd."; see also Friedenwald 1944, 1:272).

A similar argument, grounded in the assumption that God provides the raw materials for human beings to develop their own sustenance, is expressed in the following late midrashic text:

> It occurred that Rabbi Ishmael and Rabbi Akiva were strolling in the streets of Jerusalem accompanied by another person. They were met by a sick person. He said to them, "My masters, tell me by what means I may be cured." They told him, "Do thus and so until you are cured." He asked them, "And who afflicted me?" They replied, "The Holy One, blessed is He." [The sick person] responded, "You have entered into a matter which does not pertain to you. [God] has afflicted and you seek to cure! Are you not transgressing God's will?"
>
> Then Rabbi Ishmael and Rabbi Akiva asked him, "What is your occupation?" He answered, "I am a tiller of the soil and here is the sickle in my hand." They asked him, "Who created the vineyard?" He answered, "The Holy One, blessed be He." Rabbi Akiva and Rabbi Ishmael said to him, "And you enter into a matter which does not pertain to you! [God] created [the vineyard] and you cut God's fruits from it." He said to them, "Do you not see the sickle in my hand? If I did not plow, sow, fertilize and weed nothing would sprout." They said to him, "Foolish man! Have you never in your life heard that it is written, 'As for man, his days are as grass; as grass of the field, so he flourishes' (Ps. 103:15). Just as if one does not weed, fertilize and plow, the trees will not produce [fruit] and if fruit is produced but is not watered or fertilized it will not live but die, so with regard to the body. Drugs and medicaments are the fertilizer and the physician is the tiller of the soil." (*Midrash Samuel* 1893, 54; *Midrash Temurah* in Eisenstein 1915, 2:580–81)

Despite the assumption that illness might be an affliction from God as punishment for sin, Jewish tradition considers the practice of medicine as an act of virtue aimed at fulfilling God's will rather than an act of contention aimed at the subversion of God's will. As David ben Samuel ha-Levi noted in his commentary to the legal code, *Shulhan Arukh* (*SA — OH*, para. 230, sec. 4), true healing comes only from God. Nevertheless, God has given human creatures the sanction and the ability to heal. God's supernatural healing and human beings' natural healing are not mutually exclusive; they are mutually inclusive (see Ibn Pakuda 1973, 247). When divine healing is not forthcoming, even when the patient is presumed to be suffering from a divinely afflicted malady, human medical intervention is not only permitted but appropriate. For instance, Numbers (12:8–11) describes Moses' sister, Miriam, as having been afflicted with leprosy by God as punishment for the sin of slander. Commenting on this text, a midrash states, "When Moses saw what befell his sister . . . Moses said: 'Master of the Universe, already long ago You granted me the power to heal. If you will heal her, it is well, but if not, I will heal her'" (*DR*, chap. 6, sec. 13; see also Judah Ashkenazi on *SA — OH*, para. 230, sec. 4).

The Nature of the Sanction to Heal

The very existence of a scriptural sanction to heal was taken by the medieval Jewish commentators as an indication that healing cannot be considered an enterprise aimed at subverting God's design (*Tos. BK*, 85a). Nonetheless, the nature of, and the boundaries governing the sanction to heal were and continue to be debated and discussed. As in any covenant, the covenants between God and the physician and between the physician and the patient are defined by certain limitations, which are open to various interpretations.

The talmudic text states that "permission" (*reshut*) is granted to the physician to heal (*BK*, 85a). The use of the term "permission" provoked a debate among the medievals about whether the sanction to heal is a "permission," wherein it is optional, or whether it is an unqualified "obligation" (*hovah*), an unequivocal "covenantal imperative" (*mitzvah*).

Most sources claim that the "permission" to heal constitutes an obligation upon the physician to heal. This position is linked to the assumption that saving life, rescuing an imperiled person, is an obligation by which one is scripturally enjoined. As the legal code *Arba'ah Turim* puts it, "The Torah gave permission to the physician to heal; moreover, it is a religious obligation, and it is included in the obligation to save life" (*AT — YD*, para. 336, sec. 1 and Karo's commentary there; see also Nahmanides 1964, 2:41).

This obligation to save life (*pikuah nefesh*) is virtually unequivocal in Judaism. Hence, relating healing to the obligation to save life made healing an indisputable obligation. Indeed, Jewish law went so far as to set aside other religious obligations, such as Sabbath observance, when life is threatened. In this regard, the Talmud observes that the commandments of the Torah were given to "live by" (Lev. 18:5) but not to die because of (see *Yoma*, 85b; see also *Yoma*, 83a; *Git.*, 9b; *SA — OH*, para. 329, secs. 1–3).

A physician who refuses to render medical care in life-threatening situations is condemned as a potential murderer by the medieval legal codes, as is a physician who renders less than the best possible available medical care (*AT — YD*, para. 336, sec. 1; *SA — YD*, para. 336, sec. 1). Along similar lines, the sixteenth-century chronicler and physician Solomon ibn Verga explained the talmudic phrase "the best of physicians is destined for hell" to mean that the physician should picture hell as being open to receive him for neglecting a patient in his care (1955, chap. 41, 113).

According to Jewish law, a person whose actions bring about the death of another, even accidentally, is liable for manslaughter. In this regard, the Talmud and the medieval codes observe that one reason a specific sanction to heal is afforded the physician is to free him or her from liability for manslaughter in cases of medical practice or even in cases of medical malpractice where criminal negligence is absent (see, e.g., *T. Git.*, chap. 4, sec. 6; *AT — YD*, para. 336, sec. 1; *SA — YD*, para. 336, sec. 1; Nahmanides 1964, 2:41).

According to Jewish law, a person should not be compensated monetarily for religious observance. Since the physician's obligation to heal is considered a religious injunction, the question of whether the physician is entitled to be paid for his or her services is discussed in Jewish religious literature. Although some sources deny the physician's right to be compensated for his or her services, most of the sources accept the propriety of paying the physician for medical care (see, e.g., *SA — YD*, para. 336, sec. 2; see also Jakobovits 1959, 222–31). Indeed, the Talmud itself observes that "a physician who charges nothing is worth nothing" (*BK*, 85a).

Though the patient is obliged to pay the physician for medical care, the physician is admonished against being primarily motivated by a pecuniary interest in the rendering of medical care. Many of the commentators on the talmudic statement "the best of physicians are destined for hell" observe that this phrase refers to the physician who places economic concerns before medical concerns (see, e.g., Rashi to *Kid.*, 82a; Ibn Falaquera 1976, 49). Jewish law further restricted the charging of fees to those patients who could afford them (*Ta'anit*, 21b).

According to Jewish tradition, the primary tasks of the physician are not pathology and curing those persons already sick: they are pedagogy and preventive medicine. In this regard, the medieval pietist text *Sefer Hasidim* describes the wise physician as one who instructs patients on how to prevent illness (*SH* 1960, para. 592, 385).

As a pedagogue, the physician is encouraged not only to teach his or her patient how to preserve health but to serve as a "role model" for the patient. As the medieval Jewish physician and scholar Judah ibn Tibbon wrote to his son, also a physician, "There is no more disgraceful object than a sick physician." He then quoted Ben Mishle (Samuel the Prince) who said: "How shall he heal the malady who himself suffers from its pain" (see Abrahams 1926, 76; see also Plato, *Laws*, bk. 9, para. 857).

The Jewish medievals understood the physician to have two therapeutic tasks: "to maintain health if it be present, and to restore it if it be absent" (Abrahams 1926, 136; Ibn Falaquera 1976, 43; Maimonides 1963, 84). Of these two tasks, preservation of health is considered paramount, because it is better for a person to avoid becoming ill than to become ill and then have to be cured.

For Maimonides, the physician who is aware of the patient's healthy state is better equipped to diagnose a patient when the patient becomes ill. In this vein, Zahalon advised the physician to instruct a patient who has recovered from an illness on how to conduct himself so that the illness would not return (see Friedenwald 1944, 2:273). Maimonides states that only fools believe that medical care relates to times of illness but does not relate to the preservation of health (1957, 44). Maimonides further recommends that, since the scope of medical knowledge is so vast, it is best to rely upon the advice of one's colleagues in difficult cases. For this reason, Maimonides advocated group medical practice, so that a pool of knowledge, drawn from various specialists, could be utilized both in treatment and in diagnosis (1963, 99).

Patient: Heal Thyself

In the New Testament, Jesus refers to a proverb that was apparently popular in his day, "Physician, heal thyself" (Luke 4:23). Rabbinic and medieval Jewish tradition might have coined a correlative proverb, "Patient, heal thyself." The latter proverb would articulate the view that the patient (and not the physician) is primarily responsible for his or her own health and that the initiation of required medical care is primarily the responsibility of the patient (see Ibn Attar on Exod. 21:19; see also Sirkes' commentary on *AT — YD*, para. 336, sec. 1). Furthermore, a person who refuses to seek medical care is compared to an individual who deliberately walks through fire with the foolish expectation that reliance upon God would provide protection from injury (see Ayash 1683, commenting on *SA — YD*, para. 336, sec. 1).

Medieval Jewish ethical treatises taught that a person's physical and moral vices can engender physical ailments (see, e.g., Ibn Gabirol 1901, introduction, 84–85). Consequently, responsibility for preventing illness and for engendering health should rest primarily with the patient and only secondarily with the physician. A midrashic text puts it this way: "Rabbi Aha said: It depends upon a person himself that diseases should not come upon him. What is the proof? For, said Rabbi Aha, Scripture states, 'The Lord will keep away [from you] all sickness' (Deut. 7:15); this means it is from you [i.e., dependent upon you] that disease should not come upon you" (*LR*, chap. 16, sec. 8).

In his *Treatise on Asthma*, Maimonides listed six "obligatory regulations" that one should observe in order to preserve one's own health. These obligations are (1) clean air to breathe, (2) proper diet, (3) regulation of emotion, (4) moderate bodily exercise, (5) proper sleep, and (6) proper excretion (1963, 6).

Regarding clean air, Maimonides observed that "the concern for clean air is the foremost rule in preserving the health of one's body and soul" (1963, 36, 73–74; 1957, 67–68).

For Maimonides, proper diet is a religious obligation, since "improper diet is like a fatal poison. It is the basis for all illness." Maimonides particularly cautioned against the hazards to health that derive from overeating. For Maimonides, gluttony is a moral vice that inevitably results in physical illness (*MT — HD*, chap. 4, sec. 15). Elsewhere Maimonides observed, "I have seen gluttons who throw their food and poke it back into their mouths like ruminating beasts. This is one of the biggest causes of disease" (1963, 24; see also 1957, 31–43; 1971a, chap. 20). Still elsewhere, Maimonides advised that it is a general rule of the preservation of health, and a specific rule with regard to proper diet, that "if a person took as good care of himself as he does of his animals, he would be saved from many illnesses" (1957, 31). Relating earlier Greek, Arabic, and Jewish sources, the twelfth-century poet and physician Joseph ben Meir Zabara observed:

> Galen was asked: What is the greatest cure? Moderation in food and drink. And a certain sage has said: Who diminishes his eating will lengthen the time of his eating and will abide in health. . . . And our sages of blessed memory have said: Diminish your eating and you will diminish your disease. . . . And when Galen was asked: Why do you stint on your food?, he replied: My purpose is to eat to live; the purpose of others is to live to eat. . . . He that fills his belly each day undermines his health. (1932, 116–18)

For regulating the emotions, many of the Jewish medievals advocated the "golden mean" (see, e.g., *MT—HD*, chap. 1, secs. 2–4; Maimonides 1912, chap. 4, 54–55). Of special concern were the physical and moral dangers posed by worry and depression. In this regard, Joseph ibn Aknin quoted an earlier proverb, "Sickness is the prison of the body, and worry is the prison of the mind" (see Halkin 1944, 111).

In his discussion of the beneficial effects of exercise, Maimonides states that it should relate to "exercise of the soul," that physical exercise should lead one to the development of an emotional and psychological state of happiness, joy, and contentment (1971a, chap. 18, 51). Physical exercise is considered an essential element in the health regimen of any individual. The *Mishneh Torah* says: "If one leads a sedentary life and does not take exercise, neglects the calls of nature, or is constipated—even if he eats wholesome food and takes care of himself with medical rules—he will, throughout his life, be subject to aches and pains, and his strength will fail him" (*MT—HD*, chap. 4, sec. 14). In his *Treatise on Asthma*, Maimonides claims that "inactivity is as big an evil where preservation of health is aimed at as moderate exercise is a great boon to it" (1963, 25).[7]

7. Although physical exercise is not prohibited but is encouraged, the rabbinic disapproval of sports during the Hellenistic period articulates the rabbis' objection to making the body an end in itself. In this regard, Saul Lieberman wrote, "The physical care of the body played a prominent part in everyday life of the Gentile, and undoubtedly it began to occupy an important place in Jewish life also. The Rabbis, of course, felt a deep contempt for the one who pays excessive attention to the development of the body, but there is no Biblical law forbidding physical train-

The normal functioning of the urinary tract and of the bowels was considered an expression of divine grace and a condition that one should strive to maintain. After attending to nature's call, a blessing is to be recited (see *Ber.*, 60b). Further, the rabbis recommend leisure in the bathroom. The Talmud observes, "A person who prolongs his stay in the privy, prolongs his days and years" (*Ber.*, 55a). Maimonides relates proper excretory functioning to a happy and healthy life. In the *Mishneh Torah*, he insisted that "one should not neglect the call of nature, but should respond immediately." He further observed that, "It is a leading principle of medicine that if there is constipation or if the bowels move with difficulty, grave disorders result" (*MT—HD*, chap. 4, secs. 1, 13).

Maimonides summed up a number of the features of his health regimen with these words:

> A great principle of hygiene, as physicians say, is as follows: As long as a person takes active exercise, works hard, does not overeat, and keeps his bowels open, he will be free from disease and will increase in vigor. . . . Whoever lives in accordance with the directions I have set forth has my assurance that he will not be sick until he grows old and dies; he will not be in need of a physician . . . unless his constitution be congenitally defective or he has acquired bad habits . . . or if the world should be visited by pestilence and drought. (*MT—HD*, chap. 4, secs. 14, 20)

Maimonides' concern with the deleterious effects of bad habits is sprinkled throughout his works (see, e.g., *GP*, bk. 3, chap. 12, 445). For Maimonides and other medieval Jewish philosophers and pietists, bad habits pose a serious threat to one's moral health as well as to one's physical well-being. In their view, bad habits are morally dangerous because they undermine the very premise upon which ethics rests: the availability of moral volition. Rather than the person having the habit, the habit has the person, restricting moral choice, inviting spiritual illness. In this regard, Moses Hayyim Luzzatto observed, "He who has thus become a slave to habit is no

---

ing. The Rabbis did not miss the opportunity to condemn sport as an occupation" (1965, 92). On moderate exercise as a boon to health, see, for example, Maimonides, (*MT—HD*, chap. 4, sec. 14). Maimonides' medical aphorisms discuss the effects of exercise on the emotions and the soul. Exercise leads to joy, happiness and contentment (1971a, chap. 18, p. 51).

longer his own master, and cannot act differently, even if he should want to do so. He is held in bondage by certain habits which have become second nature to him" (1966, 122).

The patient's primary responsibility for the preservation of his or her own health is related by Jewish law to two legal prohibitions, which are exegetically derived from the verse in Deuteronomy (4:9), "But take utmost care and watch yourselves scrupulously." These two prohibitions are (1) not to take any action that might endanger one's own life (see, e.g., *SA — YD*, para. 116, sec. 5, and, Isserles's gloss there), and (2) to remove any obstacle considered dangerous to one's life. Both of these laws rest upon a theological assumption that presumes that life is a gift of God, a trust, that each person maintains as a steward and trustee of God. In the words of the Talmud, "Let God who gave me my life take it away, but no one should injure oneself" (*AZ*, 18a). Thus, the concern with health is, in the final analysis, a preoccupation with how one cares for the life God entrusts to him or to her. According to Ibn Falaquera, the preservation of health is an act of worship, an expression of divine service. In Ibn Falaquera's words, "a person must care for his body, like an artisan for his tools. For the body is the instrument through which one serves one's Creator" (see Chodos 1938, 193).[8]

Despite all efforts to maintain health and to sustain life, death inevitably comes to us all. How to die is the ultimate challenge to the individual human person. Contemporary developments in medi-

8. To be sure, there are adequate Jewish sources that advocate asceticism as part of a spiritual discipline. The body-soul dualism that is at the root of the ascetic posture is not at all foreign to Judaism. Once the body and soul are set against one another, it logically follows that the suppression of one results in the enhancement of the other. Since the soul was considered essential, eternal, and spiritual while the body was considered tangential, transient, and material, the denial of the body, or even the destruction of the body for the development of the soul — to use Maimonides' phrase, is a logical corollary. The puritanical approach that dominates much of the medieval Jewish ethical literature and Hasidic literature would certainly be perceived by moderns — particularly by Americans — as being "ascetic" in the popular understanding (though not in the technical understanding) of the term. In this view, advocated by Bahya ibn Pakudah among others, the goal of human existence is spiritual development. This cannot occur if the body is weakened. As the "instrument" of the soul, the body cannot be debilitated. However, in this view, only minimal physical requirements to ensure the health and well-being of the body need be attained. Anything more is considered superfluous and undesirable.

cal technology have exacerbated the age-old problem of how to die. With an aging population, end-of-life problems in bioethics are rapidly becoming urgent issues of social policy and ethical decision making. Foremost among them is euthanasia. The problem of euthanasia, from the perspective of Jewish ethical and legal sources, is the topic of the chapter that now follows.

3

Euthanasia

IT IS TOLD that when the Hasidic master, Rabbi Bunam of Przysucha, was on his deathbed, his wife and his disciples wept bitterly. When Rabbi Bunam noticed it, he said to them, "Why do you cry? All my life I have been learning how to die."

For Judaism, the problem of dying well is not how to die in a state of grace, but how to die gracefully. The challenge is not how to escape death, but how to sanctify life. The purpose of life is how to live a life of purpose that would make one's death a catastrophe.

How we view death is very much affected by how we view life. And, the converse also seems true: how we view life reflects our understanding of death. The theologies we affirm, the philosophies we embrace, and the cultural assumptions we presume, serve as a foundation, as a framework for the attitudes we articulate about life and death, for the type of care we render the dying, for the rituals we observe when dealing with death and dying, and for the inevitable confrontation with our own individual mortality. In addition, how we view life *after* death also influences how we view life and how we view death. If there is life after death, then death is a point of transition. If there is no life after death, no perpetuation beyond the grave, then death might signify obliteration, a final terminal in the flight of life. Furthermore, how we view the body impacts upon our views of life, death, and afterlife. If all that we are is a body, death might signify an ending. If, as Plato suggested, the soul is imprisoned in the body, then death would entail a joyous liberation (*Phaedrus*, 250). If, as some Jewish sources suggest, the body is a temple (see, e.g., Ben Asher 1892, sec. "*zenut*," 80) — then death is a

35

tragedy, a destruction of the temple. Yet, death may still be a prelude for the ascent of the soul, the holy of holies of the temple, to another realm of existence.

Judaism's attitudes toward death and dying are responses to the mystery of existence, to the confrontation with the reality of our own mortality, and to the hope of some kind of self-perpetuation beyond the grave. Though many modern Jews have jettisoned belief in a life after death, Judaism never has done so (see, e.g., Jacobs 1964, 398–454; 1973, 301–22).

Though death is a fact of life, there is a natural human proclivity to avoid it. Both novelists and psychologists have observed that it is virtually impossible for a person to contemplate his or her own death. For example, the German author Goethe wrote, "It is entirely impossible for a thinking being to think of its own non-existence, of the termination of its own thinking and life." According to Freud, there is an intrinsic human proclivity to repress death and the thought of dying (On Freud and Goethe, see Edwards 1972). A similar perspective is found in one of the most significant modern literary works on death and dying; namely, Leo Tolstoy's, "The Death of Ivan Ilych."

Given the difficulty if not the impossibility of contemplating one's own death, one should not be surprised that an historically pervasive attitude toward death has been and continues to be escapism, an attempt to deny death's reality. Euphemisms are often used to disguise death. For example, the deceased is referred to as "departed," or as one who "passed on." The grave is called a "resting place" for one who is "asleep" or "on a journey." Funerals are conducted in "parlors."

The early-twentieth-century Jewish philosopher Franz Rosenzweig reads philosophy as an elegant mind-game aimed at avoiding the reality of human mortality. In Rosenzweig's words, "All cognition of the All originates in death, in the fear of death. Philosophy takes upon itself to throw off the fear of things earthly, to rob death of its poisonous sting, and Hades of its pestilential breath. . . . It bears us over the grave which yawns at our feet with every step. . . . [Philosophy attempts] to distract us from its [death's] perennial dominion." However, concludes Rosenzweig, "A person's terror, trembling before the inevitable sting of death condemns the compassionate lie of philosophy as cruel lying" (1970, 3–5).

Jewish tradition confronts rather than avoids the inevitability or the reality of death. At the very beginning of the Hebrew Scriptures, we are told, "dust you are and to dust you return" (Gen. 3:19). Ecclesiastes (3:1–2) forthrightly states, "A season is set for everything, a time for every experience under heaven: a time for being born, and, a time for dying." Ecclesiastes (7:2) further counsels that "it is better to go to a house of mourning than to a house of feasting: for that [i.e., death] is the end of every person, and the living one should take it to heart."

The awareness of human finitude found in Hebrew Scripture is amplified in rabbinic literature. For example, the Talmud recounts that "when Rabbi Jonathan finished the Book of Job, he used to say: the end of man is to die, and the end of a beast is to be slaughtered, and all are doomed to death" (*Ber.*, 17a).

A verse in Psalms (144:4) reads, "One's days are like a passing shadow." On this verse, a midrash comments: "What kind of shadow? If life is like a shadow cast by a wall, it endures. . . . Rabbi Huna said in the name of Rabbi Aha: Life is like a bird that flies past, and its shadow flies past with it. But Samuel said: Life is like the shadow of a bee that has no substance at all" (*ER*, chap. 1, sec. 1).

While rejecting an escapist attitude toward death, and while advocating a frank confrontation with death and dying, Jewish tradition considers the encounter with human mortality to be an invitation neither to morbidity nor to nihilism. The attitude satirized by the prophet Isaiah (22:13), "Eat, drink and be merry, for tomorrow we die," finds no resonance in Jewish thought. Rather, the candid awareness of human mortality is treated by Jewish religious literature as an opportunity to confront the quest for and the question of human purpose and meaning. Since life is a blind date with an uncertain future, each moment is considered a summons to begin or to continue the project of creating the ultimate work of art — one's own existence. Commenting on Hillel's famous statement, "If not now, when?" (*PA*, chap. 1, sec. 14), a medieval Jewish writer observed that Hillel did not say, "If not *today*, when?" but "If not *now*, when?" because "even today is in doubt regarding whether one will survive or not, for at any instant one can die." Consequently, "one cannot wait even a day or two to exert oneself in the pursuit of human [moral] fulfillment" (Gerondi 1971, 115).

A candid confrontation with death can compel one to examine and to improve the moral quality of life. This sentiment is often stated in talmudic literature. For example, "Rabbi Eliezer said: Repent one day before your death. His disciples asked him: Does then one know on what day he will die? Then all the more reason to repent today, he replied, lest he die tomorrow" (*Shab.*, 153a). Another text advises: "One should always incite the good inclination to fight against the evil inclination. . . . If he subdues it, well and good. If not, let him study the Torah. . . . If he subdues it, well and good. If not, let him recite the *Shema*. . . . If he subdues it, well and good. If not, let him remind himself on the day of death" (*Ber.*, 5a).

Although never obfuscating the reality of death, Judaism is not a death-centered religion. Unlike the cults of death that characterized ancient Egyptian religion, and unlike the Babylonian Gilgamesh who vainly strives to escape death, the primary directive of Hebrew Scriptures is the challenge of sanctifying life. Reflecting on death soon after an almost fatal heart attack, Abraham Joshua Heschel encapsulated the Jewish attitude as follows: "Life's ultimate meaning remains obscure unless it is reflected upon in the face of death. . . . [Judaism's] central concern is not how to escape death but rather how to sanctify life" (1996a, 366).

Each life hovers between two parentheses indicated by the biblical verses: "Choose life" (Deut. 30:19) and "There is a time to die" (Eccles. 3:2). A conflict between these imperatives now often ensues because of the accelerating collision between developments in medical technology and the inevitable end of life. As our population ages, as our medical technology further develops, as our health care resources diminish, new and challenging ethical problems about the process of dying increasingly come to the fore. Public debate on euthanasia and other end-of-life issues may soon eclipse public debate over abortion and beginning-of-life issues.

Framing the Question

The increasing relevance of the problem of euthanasia offers a poignant challenge to the contemporary Jewish ethicist: Can the moral and halakhic resources of the past effectively address the choices that health care professionals, patients, families of patients, and hospital "ethics committees" are being called upon to make on a daily basis? Can ancient and medieval texts offer informed guidance regarding this life-and-death decision that has become exacerbated by developments in medical technology and pain management, by the lengthening of human life expectancy, and by growing economic restrictions on the use of medical resources? Dealing with the problem of euthanasia serves as a critical example of how the methodology of the ethicist-halakhist operates in applying the textual resources of the past to the ethical challenges of the present (see, e.g., Newman 1995, 140–60).

As will become immediately apparent, the manner in which Jewish legal discourse frames ethical questions differs from how other forms of ethical and legal discourse do so. For example, Anglo-American legal discourse usually begins with rights: What and whose rights are involved, what to do when there is a conflict of rights, and so forth? With specific regard to euthanasia, Anglo-American legal discourse tends to frame the issue in terms of whether an individual has a right to choose his or her own death, and whether to implement that choice. As in the case of abortion, so in the case of euthanasia, the right of the individual to determine the disposition of his or her own body, often is presumed. Indeed, in our society, moral and legal debates increasingly seem to presuppose that no discussion of ethical issues can proceed unless they can be couched in the language of rights (see, e.g., Beauchamp and Childress 1979, 47–53). Furthermore, a strong proclivity of Anglo-American jurisprudence has been to relegate ethical behavior to the private realm, unencumbered by social or legal regulation, as long as one's chosen actions do not impinge on the rights of others (see, e.g., Devlin 1965).

For Jewish law and ethics, the starting point is altogether different. This is not only because Jewish ethics rests upon theological assumptions, such as those noted above (chap. 1), but also because certain terms and concepts crucial to other forms of moral discourse, such as Anglo-American discourse, have no resonance in classical Jewish texts. For example, whereas discussion of euthanasia and abortion in Anglo-American law might presume that the individual has a variety of "property rights" over one's body, as will be noted below, Jewish law presumes that a person's body ultimately belongs to God, that one's own body is a variety of bailment from God. Consequently, one cannot do whatever one wishes with it. However, more crucial is the fact that the idea of rights, as it is generally understood in Anglo-American jurisprudence, has no meaning in Jewish legal or moral literature. There is neither a term for, nor a concept of, rights in classical Jewish law. Jewish law does not frame ethical issues in terms of rights. In Jewish ethical and legal discourse, issues are framed in terms of obligations that purport to fulfill the will of God (see, e.g., Silberg 1973, 66–70). "Rights" is an almost meaningless term in Jewish jurisprudence just as a term like "King of the United States" would be meaningless in American constitutional discourse.

Jewish ethics and Jewish law are intertwined (see, e.g., Silberg 1973, 61). There is in Judaism no realm of private morality detached from legal (halakhic) concerns. When applied to particular ethical concerns such as abortion and euthanasia, the question that initiates discussion is not: Is there a right to have an abortion or to practice euthanasia, and if so, in which circumstances can that right be exercised? Rather, for Jewish law the primary question is: What am I obliged to do or not to do? This question may be amplified, using a variety of categories endemic to Jewish law, to include questions such as: Is this action a religious commandment (*mitzvah*)? Is it a halakhic obligation, prescribed by Jewish law (*hovah*)? Is it proscribed or forbidden (*assur*) by Jewish law? Is it permitted (*reshut*) in certain circumstances by Jewish law, and which are those circumstances? Consequently, in the following discussion of euthanasia from the perspective of Jewish ethics and law, the question of whether there is a human right or a constitutional right to choose to end one's life is not addressed. Rather, the discussion focuses upon the questions of what one is obliged, forbidden, and permitted to do in certain circumstances as human life draws to its inevitable conclusion. The discussion begins by considering which tenets and texts may be utilized as precedents for dealing with this type of life-and-death decision.

Talmudic Precedent

As a rule, Judaism forbids a human being to kill another human being, and for a human being to kill his or her own self. Yet, there are exceptions. One is killing in self-defense (see, e.g., Exod. 22:1; *San.*, 72a-b). Another is slaying an enemy in a justifiable war. Still another is the execution of certain types of criminals. (In this regard, it should be noted that in classical Jewish law it is not the "state" or the "people" who executes a criminal, but the witnesses upon whose testimony he or she has been convicted.) Furthermore, in Jewish law, it is permissible to kill a potential murderer in order to ensure the safety of his or her intended victim (see, e.g., *San.*, 73a). These and other forms of "justified homicide" have been sanctioned as "necessary evils" by Jewish legal and moral tradition (see, e.g., Cohn 1971, *EJ*, 8:944–46).

Whereas in various situations killing another human person may be justifiable and permissible according to Jewish law, in instances where martyrdom is indicated, killing oneself, allowing oneself to be killed, or killing another person, may be *required* by Jewish law. Precisely because martyrdom represents the ultimate expression of human sacrifice to God (*Kiddush ha-Shem*), it has been considered throughout most of Jewish history to be the most exalted virtue — transcending the obligation to preserve human life at any cost. According to the Talmud, for example, there are occasions when a Jew is obliged to sacrifice his or her life rather than to transgress the commandments of the Torah (e.g., *San.* 74a; *Yoma*, 82a). There are recorded examples of Jews who not only martyred themselves and who allowed themselves to be martyred, but who also killed others — including their own wives and children, rather than allowing them to become apostatized (see, e.g., Spiegel 1967). For many, even during the Holocaust, martyrdom was considered not a tragedy, but a privilege, an ultimate opportunity for serving the divine (see, e.g., Shindler 1973, 88–105). In this view, killing oneself, killing another, or allowing oneself or another to be killed as a martyr are not "necessary evils," but are desirable outcomes. It is therefore significant that many posttalmudic sources referenced a talmudic text that describes martyrdom as a precedent for discussing euthanasia. The text reads (*AZ*, 18a):

> It was said that within but few days Rabbi Jose ben Kisma died and all the great men of Rome went to his burial and made a great lamentation for him. On their return, they found Rabbi Hanina ben Teradion sitting and occupying himself with the Torah, publicly gathering assemblies, and keeping a scroll of the Torah in his bosom. Straightaway they took hold of him, wrapt him in the scroll of the Torah, placed bundles of branches around him and set them on fire. They then brought tufts of wool, which they had soaked in water, and placed them over his heart, so that he should not expire quickly. His daughter exclaimed, "Father, that I should see you in this state!" He replied, "If it were I alone being burnt it would have been a thing hard to bear; but now I am burning together with the scroll of the Torah, God who will

have regard for the plight of the Torah will also have regard for my plight." His disciples called out, "Rabbi, what do you see?" He answered them, "The parchments are being burnt but the letters are soaring high." "Open then your mouth" [said they] "so that the fire enter into you." He replied: "Let God who gave me [my soul] take it away, but no one should injure oneself." The executioner then said to him, "Rabbi, if I raise the flame and take away the tufts of wool from over your heart, will you cause me to enter into the life to come?" "Yes," he replied. "Then swear unto me" [he urged]. He swore unto him. He thereupon raised the flame and removed the tufts of wool from over his heart, and his soul departed speedily. The executioner then jumped and threw himself into the fire. And a *bat kol* [a heavenly voice] exclaimed: "Rabbi Hanina ben Teradion and the executioner have been assigned to the world to come." When Rabbi heard it he wept and said: "One may acquire eternal life in a single hour, another only after many years."

Modern philosophers often distinguish between two kinds of euthanasia: active and passive. This distinction is relevant to how posttalmudic literature interpreted the preceding talmudic passage. Active euthanasia refers to an action that causes or accelerates death. Passive euthanasia refers to the withdrawal of life support, usually applied by others to the patient. In addition, a distinction is also often made between "voluntary" and "involuntary" euthanasia. In voluntary euthanasia, the individual whose life is in question takes an action that brings his or her own life to an end. In involuntary euthanasia, an action to end the patient's life is taken without his or her explicit consent to end his or her life. Thus, euthanasia may take a variety of forms: active-voluntary, passive-voluntary, active-involuntary, and passive-involuntary. To be sure, the distinction among these four forms of euthanasia is helpful, but it is also often hazy. For instance, is "pulling the plug" passive or active euthanasia; does it remove an action, that is, is it the cessation of "heroic measures," or is it an action aimed at accelerating death?

The preceding talmudic text was interpreted by later authorities as having established the following principles:

1. Martyrdom is exempted from the prohibition against suicide.

2. An individual's life belongs not to himself or herself but to God.

3. Active-voluntary euthanasia is prohibited, but passive-voluntary euthanasia *may* be permitted. When the rabbi is encouraged to open his mouth so that the fire may enter and end his agony (i.e., active-voluntary euthanasia), he refuses. But, when the executioner offers to remove the soaked tufts of wool artificially prolonging his life (i.e., an artificial life-support system), the rabbi gives him permission (i.e., passive-voluntary euthanasia).

As discussed later in this chapter, the views on euthanasia that are drawn from this talmudic text are reiterated in subsequent Jewish literature.

Active Euthanasia Is Prohibited

The *Sefer Hasidim* states: "If a person is suffering from extreme pain and he says to another: 'You see that I shall not live [long]; [therefore,] kill me because I cannot bear the pain,' one is forbidden to touch him [the terminal patient]." The text continues and based upon the Talmudic description of the death of Hanina ben Teradion proscribes the terminal patient from taking his or her own life:

> "If a person is suffering great pain and he knows that he will not live [long], he cannot kill himself. And this principle we learn from Rabbi Hanina ben Teradion who refused to open his mouth [to allow the fire to enter and take his life]. (*SH* 1924, no. 315, 100)

In one of the "minor tractates" of the Talmud, we read, "A dying man [*goses*] is regarded as a living entity in respect to all matters in the world. Whosoever touches or moves him is a murderer [if by so doing his death is accelerated]. Rabbi Meir used to say: He may be compared to a lamp which is dripping [going out]; should one touch it, one extinguishes it. Similarly, whoever closes the eyes of a dying man [thereby accelerating his death] is considered as if he had taken his life" (*Sem.*, chap. 1, sec. 1). This prohibition against practicing active euthanasia is reiterated by the medieval codes of Jewish law. It extends to the patient, the attending physician, the family and friends of the patient, and to all other individuals (see, e.g., *Shab.* 151b; Isserles' gloss to *AT — YD*, para. 339, sec. 1; Schrieber 1883, no. 326).

In his legal code, the *Mishneh Torah*, Maimonides wrote: "One who is in a dying condition is regarded as a living person in all respects. . . . He who touches him [thereby accelerating his death] is guilty of shedding blood. To what may he [the dying person] be compared? To a flickering flame, which is extinguished as soon as one touches it. Whoever closes the eyes of a dying person while the soul is about to depart is shedding blood. One should wait a while; perhaps he is just in a swoon" (*MT — LM*, chap. 4, sec. 5).

The fourteenth-century code of Jacob ben Asher is called the *Arba'ah Turim*. In many ways, it served as the model for Joseph Karo's sixteenth-century code, the *Shulhan Arukh*. Echoing earlier texts, Jacob ben Asher wrote, "A dying man is to be considered a living person in all respects . . . [therefore] anyone who hastens the exiting of the person's soul is a shedder of blood" (*AT — YD*, para. 339). The *Shulhan Arukh* reads, "A patient on his deathbed is considered a living person in every respect . . . and it is forbidden to cause him to die quickly . . . and whosoever closes his eyes with the onset of death is regarded as shedding blood" (*SA — YD*, para. 339, sec. 1).

The nineteenth-century *Kitzur Shulhan Arukh* by Solomon Ganzfried embellishes a bit on the earlier sources: "Even if one has been dying for a long time, which causes agony to the patient and his family, it is still forbidden to accelerate his death" (1860, sec. *Yoreh De'ah*, para. 194, sec. 1).

From these and similar texts, one can adduce the following premises upon which classical Jewish views regarding active euthanasia are based:

1. An individual's life is not his or her own "property" but God's, and therefore God has the final disposition over it. In other words, each person serves as God's steward for the life given into his or her care. As Hanina ben Teradion put it, "Let God who gave me my soul take it away" (*AZ*, 18a).

2. Jewish law does not dwell on the issue of quality of life. Rather, Jewish law maintains that each moment of life is inherently valuable in and of itself, independent of its quality. Life being sacred — each moment of life being intrinsically valuable — every effort must be made to preserve each moment of life, even to the moment of death. For example, according to Jewish law, "even if they find a person crushed [under a fallen building] so that he can live only for a short time, they must continue to dig," and if this has

occurred on the Sabbath, one is *required* to violate the Sabbath even if it means granting the victim only "momentary life" (*Yoma*, 84–85).

3. An individual is prohibited from inflicting self-injury, particularly the ultimate self-injury — suicide, which is generally defined as self-homicide (see, e.g., *BK*, 91b; *AZ*, 18a; *MT — LM*, chap. 2, sec. 3).

4. Since "there is no agency for wrongful acts," and since murder is a wrongful act, one cannot act as the agent of a person who desires death and bring about or accelerate that person's death, even at that person's explicit request (see, e.g., *Kid.*, 42b; *GR*, chap. 34, sec. 14). In this regard, the physician is explicitly enjoined from employing medical intervention for the intention of accelerating death (see, e.g., Shabbatai ben Meir's gloss on *SA — YD*, para. 336, sec. 1).

Passive Euthanasia May Be Permitted

As noted, the talmudic case of Hanina ben Teradion is used by posttalmudic sources as a precedent for the permissibility (but not necessarily as a requirement) for passive euthanasia. The rabbi permitted the tufts of wool that were "artificially" sustaining his life to be removed. This would seem to permit both voluntary and involuntary passive euthanasia, either on the part of the patient (voluntary) or on the part of another party (voluntary or involuntary), such as a physician. To be sure, Jewish law would not permit the removal of all life-support mechanisms. For example, it generally would not permit withholding insulin from a diabetic (see, e.g., Telushkin 1961, 20–24; Steinberg 1978, 30–31). The story of Hanina ben Teradion clearly relates to an individual who has no chance of survival in any case.

In many of the same sources noted above that proscribe active euthanasia, one finds material that permits passive euthanasia. For example, *Sefer Hasidim* observes, "One may not [artificially] prolong the act of dying. If, for example, someone is dying and nearby a woodcutter insists on chopping wood, thereby disturbing the dying person so that he cannot die, we remove the woodcutter from the vicinity of the dying person. Also, one must not place salt in the mouth of a dying person in order to prevent death from overtaking him" (*SH* 1924, no. 315, 100). This view is adapted and is quoted almost verbatim in subsequent codes of Jewish law. Moses Isserles, in his gloss to the *Shulhan Arukh* (*SA — YD*, para. 339, sec. 1), wrote, "It is forbidden to cause one's death to be accelerated, even in the case of one who has been terminally ill for a long time . . . *however,* if there is some factor which is preventing the exit of the soul such as a nearby woodchopper or salt placed under his tongue — and these things are impeding his death — it is permissible to remove them because in so doing one actively does nothing but remove an obstacle [preventing his natural death]." Again, echoing the *Sefer Hasidim* (*SH* 1924, no. 316, 100; *SH* 1960, no. 723, 443), the *Shulhan Arukh* states, "One must not scream at the moment at which the soul [of another] departs, lest the soul return and the person suffer great pain. That is to say, it is not simply permitted to remove an obstacle to one's [natural] death, but one cannot lengthen the pain and suffering of the patient" (*SA — YD*, para. 339, sec. 1).

In this regard, Isserles interpreted the view of the *Sefer Hasidim* as meaning that "it is certain that for one to do anything that stifles the [natural] process of dying [of a dying person] is forbidden" (Isserles' gloss to *AT — YD*, para. 339, sec. 1). Similarly, the sixteenth-century Italian rabbi Joshua Boaz referred to the *Sefer Hasidim* as being the basis of his own view that "it is permissible to remove any obstacle preventing [death] because so doing is not an action in and of itself" (Boaz's supercommentary to al-Fasi's commentary to *MK*, 16b; see also *SH* 1924, no. 316, 100). Furthermore, in a seventeenth-century responsum by Jacob ben Samuel (1696, no. 59), the author takes the controversial view that any medical or pharmacological intervention that impedes the natural process of dying should not be introduced (Cf. Reischer 1860, sec. 3, no. 13; Eiger's commentary to *SA — YD*, para. 339, sec. 1).

While most of the sources allow the removal of external impediments to the process of dying, there is considerable disagreement regarding the removal of treatment that has been initiated. The classic reference in the *Sefer Hasidim* refers to the removal of things like the sound of wood being chopped, which would disturb a patient in a death swoon (*SH* 1924, no. 315, 100). Again here, the application of a medieval precedent about wood chopping to a contemporary situation like the removal of a respirator is an example of halakhic creativity and innovation (see, e.g., Newman 1995, 140–60).

On the basis of this text from *Sefer Hasidim,* many contemporary authorities sanction a decision not to introduce artificial life-support systems, but prohibit their removal once introduced. In the same text, *Sefer Hasidim* prohibits "placing salt in the mouth of a dying person to prevent death from overtaking him or her." In a case in which salt already has been placed, most authorities prohibit its removal. Such action is proscribed as an act of active euthanasia, which would cause the patient to be touched or moved, that is, an action that would actively accelerate death (see, e.g., *SA — YD*, para. 339, sec. 1 and commentaries of Isserles, Shabbatai ben Meir, and David ben Samuel). However, in his note on this text, Zevi ben Azriel of Vilna (1733) maintained that removal of the salt is in keeping with the principle that the removal of any impediment to the process of dying is not an action at all and hence permissible. In so doing, he cautioned, the patient must not be moved. He, therefore, interpreted the prohibition of the earlier authorities as being related to the apprehension over moving the patient and not to an absolute prohibition against the removal of the salt. According to this view, if translated to contemporary parlance, the introduction of heroic measures to treatment of a terminal patient is not encouraged and may be prohibited. However, if heroic measures have been introduced, they may be removed (see also C. D. Halevi 1987, 147–55).

Commenting on the phrase in Ecclesiastes (3:2), "There is a time to die," the *Sefer Hasidim* observes that Ecclesiastes does *not* also state that "there is a time to live." The reason for this, according to the *Sefer Hasidim*, is that, when the "time to die" arrives, it is not the time to extend life. Consequently, the *Sefer Hasidim* prohibits efforts to resuscitate a terminal patient on the grounds that extending the process of dying by resuscitation would cause the patient continued unnecessary anguish and pain (*SH* 1960, no. 234, 208). This text might serve as the basis for justifying a DNR (Do Not Resuscitate) order for terminal patients whose condition has reached the point of death and whose resuscitation through heroic measures would only prolong their death and extend their agony. Just as some sources consider active euthanasia to be a presumption of God's authority over life and death, the *Sefer Hasidim* insists that extending the process of dying, when the terminal patient is in severe pain, is also a presumption of God's authority over life and death and a presumptive rejection of the scriptural view that "there is a time to die."

Removal of natural hydration and food from a terminal patient to hasten death is specifically proscribed, probably because such withdrawal is considered cruel (see, e.g., *San.*, 77a; *MT – LM*, chap. 3, sec. 10; Greenwald 1947, 21). However, according to the *Sefer Hasidim*, the removal of food and water are required in two kinds of cases. One is in the case in which nutrition or hydration would harm or cause pain to the patient. The second is in the case of a terminal patient where death is imminent. Such a patient must be made comfortable, for example, by keeping his or her lips and mouth moist, but such a patient must not be fed, lest the process of dying be prolonged and painful agony be unduly lengthened (*SH* 1960, no. 234, 208; see also Dorff 1991, 27–28).

From the literature reviewed to this point, it would appear that the Jewish view of euthanasia is that active euthanasia is prohibited, but passive euthanasia may be permissible and even desirable; for while classical Jewish sources place great value on saving and prolonging human life, they put no premium on needlessly and artificially prolonging the act of dying (see, e.g., Feinstein 1963, 2:174; see also Feinstein 1996, 39). However, the sources seem uncompromising in the view that active euthanasia, under any circumstances, is a form of suicide or murder and is therefore prohibited. Immanuel Jakobovits, in his seminal work *Jewish Medical Ethics*, summarizes the Jewish position on euthanasia as follows:

> It is clear, then, even when the patient is already known to be on his deathbed and close to the end, any form of *active euthanasia* is strictly prohibited. In fact, it is condemned as plain murder. In purely legal terms, this is borne out by the ruling that anyone who kills a dying person is liable to the death penalty as a common murderer. At the same time, Jewish law sanctions, and perhaps even demands, the withdrawal of any factor — whether extraneous to the patient himself or not — which may artificially delay his demise in the final phase. (1959, 123–24; see also, Federbush 1952; Haliburd 1978; Saltzman 1982; Rosner and Bleich 1969, 33, 253–331)

Despite the apparent consensus on the matter, a number of contemporary scholars have attempted to discover and to formulate a basis for the permissibility of active euthanasia under certain circumstances. This reevaluation of the sources has been prompted by certain medical and pharmacological developments and by the proliferation of terminal cancer cases brought about by the lengthening

of the average human life span, as well as by the current proliferation of other degenerative diseases such as AIDS.

Active Euthanasia Reconsidered

There seems to be unanimity of opinion in Judaism that life is
intrinsically precious, even "momentary life." This assumption
makes moot any discussion regarding the quantity of life versus the
quality of life. This claim also serves as a foundation for the con-
demnation of murder and suicide, of killing and self-killing. However, as noted above, certain exceptions to the prohibition against
killing and self-killing were condoned by classical Jewish tradition.
These exceptions to the rule indicate that the value of life itself is
not *always* considered absolute. The permissibility, even the desirability, of martyrdom assumes that there are occasions when life
itself may be set aside because the preservation of life is not always
an absolute moral imperative.[1]

While it is true that the dominant view of Jewish tradition is
that life itself is of intrinsic value, there exists an alternative view
that relates both to cases of martyrdom and to cases of pain and
anguish. For example, there is a talmudic text that maintains that a
life of unbearable pain, a life coming to an inevitable and an excruciating end, is not a life worth continuing, that such a life is like
having no life at all. This passage describes an individual who suffers from a severe physical affliction as one "whose life is no life"
(*Beitzah*, 32b). Similarly, a nineteenth-century commentary on the
Mishnah observes that "great pain is worse than death." And
though "a dying person [*goses*] is like a living person in all respects,"
the Mishnah in effect "devalued" the monetary worth of a dying
person who wished to vow the equivalent of his monetary worth as
a donation to the sanctuary (Lipschutz 1830, on *M. Yoma,* chap. 8,
sec. 3; see also *Arakhin,* 6b; *Sem.,* chap. 1, sec. 1).

---

1. In the Talmud (*AZ,* 27b) and in the codes (e.g., *SA — YD,* para. 155, sec. 57
and Eisenstadt's commentary there), one finds the view that sometimes it is preferable, particularly in the case of a terminal patient, to choose death rather than to be
treated by a gentile physician who may try to entice the Jewish patient to apostasy
or who may use "idolatrous" practices to effect a cure. In such instances extending
"momentary life is not considered." This clearly indicates that the preservation of
life in itself was not always of paramount importance or consideration. On suicide
in Jewish law, see, e.g., Reines 1961, 161–70.

A further examination of classical Jewish sources related to martyrdom reveals that life in and of itself was not always considered of ultimate value. Such an examination also reveals precedents for taking one's own life and allowing oneself to be killed rather than to endure the physical torture that was frequently a martyr's fate. What proves intriguing is the pertinence and the applicability that instances in which martyrs chose to accelerate their own death rather than to withstand physical agony may have to the problem of euthanasia in general, and to the problem of active euthanasia in particular.

Talmudic literature records many instances of martyrdom. One, noted above, is the case of Rabbi Hanina ben Teradion (*AZ*, 18a). Another text describes how four hundred Jewish children drowned themselves at sea to avoid submitting to rape at the hands of Romans (*Git.*, 57b). In a medieval commentary to the tale of the children, a reference is made to the case of Hanina ben Teradion. The two cases taken together are interpreted by Jacob Tam as meaning that, to avoid sufferings certain to result in death, it is permitted to take one's own life, and in such an instance it is required to violate the injunctions against injuring oneself (*Tos. Git.*, 57b). In this regard, the death of King Saul proves pertinent.

The case of King Saul's death provoked considerable discussion in classical Jewish literature that concerned itself with suicide. Wounded in battle, Saul asked to be killed rather than to be handed over to his enemies. According to one version, Saul killed himself by falling on his sword (1 Sam. 31:1–6). According to a second version, he asked a youth to kill him: "Stand over me and finish me off, for I am in agony and barely alive" (2 Sam. 1:9), and the Amalekite youth complied. King David subsequently had this youth executed for killing God's "anointed" (2 Sam. 1:13–17).

Commentators debate whether the youth was justified in killing Saul, whether David was justified in killing the youth, and if so, on what grounds? The biblical text suggests that David had the youth executed not because he put Saul out of agony but because he presumed to slay God's anointed king. In any case, Saul was found justified in his action by some rabbinic authorities because he chose death, martyrdom, rather than to be abused by the enemies of Israel, a precedent followed throughout Jewish history. What is particularly relevant to euthanasia is the comment of the twelfth-century biblical commentator David Kimhi (Radak) on this episode.

Kimhi commented (to 2 Sam. 1:9) that Saul's statement means: "I suffer so severely from my wound, and my soul is yet in me; therefore, I want you to accelerate my death." Thus, according to Kimhi, Saul's motive was to choose death rather than to continue to suffer, rather than to choose death to escape being abused by his enemies. If both Saul's action and his motive (according to Kimhi) are considered justifiable, then this text could serve as a precedent for active euthanasia (cf. Sirkes' and Karo's glosses to *AT—YD*, para. 157).

Some primary texts and some commentaries stress the notion that like King Saul (according to Kimhi), one can take one's own life to avoid sufferings certain to result in death. However, others stress the idea that death is only preferable when that suffering will lead to such sins as sexual sins (as in the case of the children) or to apostasy (see, e.g., *Ket.* 33b). Others claim that these instances are not applicable to euthanasia since here the affliction is the result of human oppression, whereas in cases of euthanasia the affliction is from illness which may be the will of God. Nevertheless, it is noteworthy that the language of the deathbed confessional of a dying person is remarkably reminiscent of that of a martyr. In one version of the confessional, the patient says, "I surrender my life, my body and my soul for the unification of the Divine Name." Here there is a clear parallel between the martyr and the dying person.

Although suicide is proscribed by Jewish law, the prohibition against suicide was clearly set aside in cases of martyrdom. In other sources, suicide was redefined so that killing oneself was not always defined as suicide.[2] One such source is a controversial eighteenth-century responsum by Saul Berlin.

Berlin's responsum maintains that an individual who takes his or her own life because of mental or physical pain and anguish is not to be considered a suicide. According to Berlin, the earlier halakhic regulations prohibiting suicide were primarily intended for cases where the act resulted from a pessimistic view of life. However, Berlin asserted, a person who takes his or her own life to

---

2. On the initial question of whether mourning for a suicide is prohibited, see the uncharacteristically "liberal" view of Moses Schreiber where Schreiber holds that relatives of a suicide should indeed observe mourning rites (1883, no. 326; see also Eisenstadt's commentary to *SA—YD*, para. 345, sec. 2 where suicide is virtually defined out of existence; Greenwald 1947, 319–20).

avoid continued pain and anguish is not to be considered a suicide (1793).[3]

The controversial and unprecedented nature of Berlin's responsum and the possibly tenuous analogy between cases of martyrdom and cases of euthanasia, while suggestive, still do not adequately defend an option for active euthanasia within Jewish tradition. Consequently, it is necessary to look further.

In a late midrash on Proverbs, the text tells us:

> It happened that a woman who had aged considerably appeared before Rabbi Yose ben Halafta. She said: "Rabbi, I am much too old, life has become a burden for me. I can no longer taste food or drink, and I wish to die." Rabbi Yose answered her: "To what do you ascribe your longevity?" She answered that it was her habit to pray in the synagogue every morning, and despite occasional more pressing needs she never had missed a service. Rabbi Yose advised her to refrain from attending services for three consecutive days. She heeded his advice and on the third day she took ill and died. (*YS*, sec. "*Mishlei*," no. 943, 980)

This text may be interpreted as a reinforcement of the view that passive euthanasia is permitted by Jewish law under certain conditions. The woman's withholding of her prayers removed the cause of the extension of her life. Similarly, the removal of life-support systems from a patient to whom—like this woman—life has become a burden, would be permissible. Nevertheless, it may be argued that this case underscores the inability always to make a clear-cut distinction between passive and active euthanasia. Her discontinuance of her prayers or a physician's or nurse's "pulling the plug" may be considered a deliberate action aimed at precipitating an accelerated death. Once the line between passive and active

3. In some subsequent editions of Berlin's collection of responsa, the responsum on suicide has been eliminated by the printer. No doubt the reason is because Berlin's view, which, in effect, redefines "suicide," is without precedent in halakhic literature.

Berlin claimed that *Besomim Rosh* was written by the famous fourteenth-century halakhic authority, Asher ben Yehiel, known by the acronym "Rosh." Actually, these responsa were written by Berlin himself. The book was attacked as a forgery soon after its first publication (see Jacobs 1975, 347–52; Siemet 1972–73, 509–23).

euthanasia becomes so blurred, one may attempt to cross the line with care and with caution. For if the woman's withholding of her prayers is a sanctioned action deliberately designed to accelerate her own death, then other actions designed to hasten the death of those to whom life has become an unbearable burden might also be eligible for the sanction of Jewish tradition.

The underlying assumption of this midrashic text is the efficacy of prayer in attaining particular results. Here, the woman effected those results (her own death) by withholding prayer (see the statement of Rav Dimi and the commentaries on it in *Ned.*, 40a). For this woman, prayer was a "life-support system." But, what about a case in which one actively prays for death to avoid enduring pain and suffering?[4] The woman's withholding of her prayers caused her *own* death, but what about a case in which prayer is aimed at bringing about the death of another? It would seem to reason that if the rabbis permitted one actively to pray for one's own death and even for the death of another, rather than have one endure pain and suffering, then a basis of an argument could be made for a rabbinic precedent where both voluntary and involuntary active euthanasia are concerned. In the Talmud one finds such a precedent:

> On the day that Rabbi Judah was dying, the rabbis decreed a public fast and offered prayers for heavenly mercy [so that he would not die]. . . . Rabbi Judah's handmaid ascended to the roof and prayed: "The immortals [the angels] desire him [to join them] and the mortals desire him [to remain with them]; may it be the will [of God] that the mortals may overpower the immortals [i.e., that he would not die]." When, however, she saw how often he resorted to the privy, painfully removing and replacing his *tefillin* [in terrible agony], she prayed: "May it be the will [of God] that the immortals may overpower the mortals." The rabbis meanwhile continued their prayers for heavenly mercy. She took a jar and threw it down from the roof to the ground. [For a moment,] they stopped praying, and the soul of Rabbi Judah departed. (*Ket.*, 104a)

4. On praying for one's own death, see, for example, 1 Kings 19:4, Jon. 4:3, *Ta'anit* 23a. On praying for the death of another person, see, for example, *BM*, 84a. Steinberg refers to a specific prayer for another to die to free him or her from pain. Without noting a specific citation, Steinberg refers to such a prayer in Isaac Lampronti's *Pahad Yitzhak* (1978, 36).

Some interpret this text to mean that the death of Rabbi Judah was caused by the rabbis' cessation of their prayers when they were startled by the noise of the shattering jar. Others interpret this text to mean that his death was caused by the handmaiden's active prayer aimed at bringing about Rabbi Judah's death in order to alleviate his substantial suffering. It is in this latter sense that the text was interpreted by the fourteenth-century talmudic commentator, Nissim (Ran) (on *Ned.*, 40a): "Sometimes one must request mercy on behalf of the ill so that he might die, as in the case of a patient who is terminal and who is in great pain." According to Israel Lipschutz, the handmaiden's praying for the death of Rabbi Judah relates not only to this case but to any case because "great suffering is worse than death." Lipschutz does claim, however, that taking any action other than prayer that accelerates death is prohibited (1830, on *M. Yoma*, chap. 8).

The question of whether one may pray for the death of a patient in agonizing continuous pain is discussed in a lengthy responsum by the nineteenth-century Turkish rabbi Hayyim Palaggi. In this case, a woman has been suffering for many years with a degenerative terminal disease. She has been afforded the best available medical treatment. Her family has provided constant and loving care. Hope for a remission has been abandoned by the patient, by the family, and by the attending physicians. Her condition progressively has deteriorated. Her pain has become constant and unbearable. Her illness has left her an invalid. She has prayed to God to die, preferring death to life as a liberation from pain. She has asked her family to pray for her death, but they have refused. Palaggi has been asked whether there are any grounds for prohibiting prayers asking that she might find rest in death.

In a long and complicated argument, the details of which need not be restated here, Palaggi ruled that, while family members may not pray for her death, others may do so. In the course of reaching this conclusion, Palaggi quoted a number of earlier sources, including the previously cited statement of Nissim. Thus, Palaggi reaffirmed the earlier view that active prayer for the death of a terminal patient in pain, whose life has become a self-burden, is both permissible and even desirable. It is noteworthy that Palaggi did not even question the woman's right to pray for death on her own behalf.

Among Palaggi's reasons for refusing the patient's family permission to pray for her death was the possibility of their actions being motivated by less than honorable motives. Palaggi specifically considered the possibility of the patient's spouse wishing her death so as to remarry someone already in mind. Palaggi also reflected on the possibility that the members of the patient's family may have desired her death — consciously or subconsciously — to free themselves from the burden of her care and support. This insightful psychological observation should be considered in cases of involuntary euthanasia, where the patient's family is confronted with the decision — even at the patient's request — to bring about the patient's accelerated death either by active or by passive euthanasia. As Palaggi noted, consideration for the patient is the only consideration. The financial or psychological condition of family members must not be the determining factor in such discussions. The establishment of ethics committees in many hospitals has helped to relieve patients' families of the anguish of such decisions and of the future guilt that may be precipitated by the realization that a decision to accelerate death might have been because of conscious or subconscious ulterior motives. As Palaggi noted, "strangers" cannot be held under suspicion of ulterior motives.

What is also significant about Palaggi's responsum is the manner in which he dealt with the endemic conflict of principles embodied in any examination of euthanasia from a Jewish perspective. These conflicting principles are preserving life and relieving agony. Palaggi attempted to obviate this apparently unresolvable conflict by reframing the question. According to Palaggi the question is: to what point is one morally obligated to continue life? By stating the question in this manner, Palaggi found a loophole in the categorical imperative to continue preserving life. He was therefore able to conclude that, in certain instances, such as the one at hand, it is both permissible and even desirable to take positive action that will liberate a terminal patient from agony by accelerating his or her death.

To be sure, Palaggi did not explicitly advocate active euthanasia in the sense of performing concrete medical or other intervention other than prayer to accelerate the death of a terminal patient in agony. Nevertheless, Palaggi established the viability of an attitude that would recommend active euthanasia in particular instances. And, although it was not his intention to do so, his view might be extended a step further to serve as the basis for advocating active euthanasia in cases similar to that of the woman described in his responsum (Palaggi 1840, no. 50, 1:90a–91a; see also Haas 1985, 59–85; Freehof 1960, 120–21; Greenwald 1947, 20, no. 14).

A further basis for a possible justification for active euthanasia from classical Jewish sources may be posited by combining precedent with a form of argument characteristic of Jewish legal discourse. The precedent is the talmudic text in which the term "euthanasia" — an easy, good, or quick death — occurs (Hebrew: *mitah yafah*). The form of argument is a fortiori (Hebrew: *kal vahomer;* literally: "the light and the weighty"). An example of this form of inference would be, "Here is a teetotaler who does not touch cider; he will certainly refuse whiskey." The acceptability of applying this form of argument to legal issues is stated in the Talmud (see, e.g., *Nid.*, 19b).

The term *mitah yafah* is used in the course of talmudic discussion concerning the execution of criminals convicted of capital offenses. In one text, the verse "You should love your neighbor as yourself" (Lev. 19:18) is interpreted to mean that the criminal is to be given a *mitah yafah;* the pain usually inflicted by the various types of death sentences is to be reduced both in time and in degree by administering a painkilling drug (see *San.*, 45a, 52a; *BK*, 51a; *Pes.*, 75a). In his commentary to the Talmud, Rabbi Jacob Emden stated that this practice of giving a painkilling drug to a criminal about to be executed was practiced so that the pain of execution would not hamper the exit of the soul and extend the person's pain and anguish (Emden on *San.*, 43a). At this point, one may argue either from one comparable case to another or from the "weighty" to the "light" case.

1. The terminal patient is compared by the Talmud to a criminal condemned to death in that his or her case is hopeless (*Arakhin*, 6b). From this equation one might argue that the terminal patient ought to be given at least the same consideration as a criminal about to be executed for having committed a capital offense. One may further argue that if a criminal, guilty of having committed a capital offense is shown such consideration, how much more should consideration be shown the terminal patient, innocent of any capital offense.

2. One may extend these lines of argument to a further consideration of how cases of martyrdom, that is, cases of "justified" self-homicide, might be extended to cases of active euthanasia. As noted earlier in this chapter, some sources maintain that it is permissible

in cases of martyrdom to allow oneself to be killed quickly or to take one's own life rather than to endure prolonged suffering and anguish (see, e.g., *SSR*, chap. 2, sec. 7). One may maintain that, if such cases of martyrdom are not to be considered suicide or self-homicide, so cases in which an individual suffering agony takes his or her own life should similarly not be condemned as suicide, and that certain cases of accelerating one's own death, to be free of excruciating pain, may be justifiable.

3. Jewish law forbids self-harm. Jewish law further prohibits an individual from intentionally placing himself or herself in a harmful or a potentially harmful or dangerous situation. Yet, even though Jewish legal authorities recognize the potentially hazardous nature of various types of medical, pharmacological, and surgical intervention, they nevertheless sanction such intervention. Therefore, the rule against potential danger may be set aside where such treatment is concerned. Consideration of the following halakhic precedents in this regard leads to further conclusions regarding possible justification of various forms of active euthanasia within the framework of Jewish law.

According to some halakhic authorities, when conventional therapies have been exhausted, experimental therapy may be introduced by a competent physician. This approach is sanctioned even if death were to result from such experimental therapy, especially where a terminal patient is involved. As long as even the most remote possibility of remission exists, hazardous therapy, even life-threatening therapy, may be employed. Using such therapy, though it is known in advance that it might immediately end the patient's life, would be a form of active euthanasia that would not be proscribed by Jewish law.

The prohibition against placing oneself in danger may be also set aside when a medical or surgical procedure potentially endangers the life of a patient whose life is not clearly endangered by his or her medical condition. Specifically, if the purpose of the procedure is to reduce or eliminate substantial pain, such a procedure is permitted, even when the patient's condition is not life threatening, despite its potential threat to the life of the patient (see, e.g., Meiri 1965, 85a; Greenwald 1947, 21, no. 16; Nahmanides 1964, 2:42–43; Lipschutz 1830, on *M. Yoma*, chap. 8; see also Rosner and Bleich 1969, 32–34). From this perspective, as from that of Palaggi, the imperative to reduce or to eliminate pain is given precedence over the obligation to sustain life at all costs. One may extend this argument to a conclusion that would sanction the administering of painkilling drugs or procedures, even if it is known in advance that the patient might die as a result of such action. Hence, active euthanasia employed with the specific primary intention of alleviating unbearable pain would be an acceptable moral option, even if, in the act of alleviating pain, the death of the patient resulted.

In this case, as in those previously discussed, an *a fortiori* argument can be made: if administering a painkilling drug or undertaking a pain-alleviating procedure that may accelerate the patient's death can be done in cases in which death is not imminent, then it should be permissible to administer a painkilling drug or a painkilling procedure that may accelerate the patient's death in cases in which death is certainly imminent. From this basis one may argue that, if there is a choice between prolonging the process of dying, where death seems imminent and certain, and taking action that will alleviate pain but that will also accelerate the process of death, where death is imminent and certain, then the latter option is both morally viable and legally permissible.

Not only may one make a case for active euthanasia in Jewish law, one may also argue that in certain circumstances the killer is not to be considered a murderer. To consider an act as murder, according to Jewish law, two of the conditions that must be satisfied are premeditation and malice (see Exod. 21:14) (see Cohn 1971, 944–46). Rabbinic literature specifically exonerates a physician who kills his patient, even if he acted with willfulness, when malice is not also present. Though the medieval codes link premeditation with malice, there is no logical or psychological reason to do so. The rabbinic precedent may stand on its own (see Rashi on Exod. 21:14, *MRY*, sec. "*Mishpatim*," 263). Thus, under certain circumstances, according to this minority view, the physician may be legally (but not necessarily morally) blameless for practicing active euthanasia.

One specific case in which active euthanasia by patient, agent, or physician may be more justifiable than others, according to some of the literature, would be that in which the patient is afflicted with a terminal disease, such as cancer. Talmudic law distinguishes between *goses*, that is, one terminally ill, and *tereifah* (literally, torn), that is, one terminally ill, for instance, as the result of irreparable organic damage (e.g., as the result of liver cancer; as the result of an automobile crash).[5] Apparently, in the former case, recovery is at least theoretically possible, whereas in the latter case, recovery is altogether impossible. One who kills a *goses* is considered a murderer by the Talmud and the codes. But one who kills a *tereifah* may not be guilty of murder (see, e.g., *San.*, 78a; *MT—LM*, chap. 2, sec. 8). Since the 1970s, a number of scholars have utilized this significant distinction between "*goses*" and "*tereifah*" to argue for the permissibility of active euthanasia according to Jewish religious law in certain very specific types of situations (see, e.g., Sherwin 1974; Sinclair 1989, 19–70; Dorff 1991, 19–26. See also the intriguing argument by Werner 1976, 40, that claims that active euthanasia is not prohibited to Gentiles.)

Though the majority view found in classical and contemporary Jewish literature condemns active euthanasia, this chapter's discussion and the sources noted herein indicate the viability and the defensibility of a minority view supporting active euthanasia in certain circumstances when the primary motive is to alleviate pain and suffering, especially in cases where death is certain and imminent and where there is irreparable organ damage. Indeed, a number of contemporary rabbinic decisions and views affirm this position. For example, David Shohet, writing in *Conservative Judaism* as early as 1952, came to this conclusion after a review of the classical Jewish sources on the matter. He states that an adequate defense can be made to "support the contention that to bring a merciful end to intolerable suffering to a patient who has no longer any hope of recovery and his death is imminent, is an act which may be considered lawful and ethical in Jewish law" (1952, 1–15; see also Knobel 1995, 27–59).

Conclusion

Continued developments in medical technology, increased life expectancy, and the rapid "graying" of the American people all

5. *Goses* usually refers to a patient with a terminal disease who is likely not to survive beyond seventy-two hours (for definitions and discussion of *goses*, see, e.g., *ET,* 5: 393–403). Rashi and Maimonides differ on their definition of a *tereifah*. According to Rashi (on *San.*, 78a), the definition of a *tereifah* is the same for an animal and a human being in terms of the deterioration of internal organs. Maimonides distinguishes between animals and humans in this regard and defines a human *tereifah* as one with (presumably irreparable) internal injuries or degeneration (*MT-LM*, chap. 2, sec. 8).

point to an inevitable collision of events that have made, and will continue to make, the problem of euthanasia ever more severe in the foreseeable future. For the American Jewish community, with its median age already substantially higher than that of the American population as a whole, the problem of euthanasia is of particular and immediate pertinence.

It is only reasonable for Jewish patients, families, medical professionals, social workers, clergy, and those involved with the Jewish hospice movement to look to Jewish tradition — particularly to Jewish law and bioethics — for direction and for guidance in dealing with life's challenges and crises, especially those that come at life's end, such as the process of dying and the problem of euthanasia.

Jewish sources have developed a variety of concrete attitudes and views regarding the attempt to resolve the inevitable conflict between a commitment to valuing life and a commitment to mitigating pain and suffering during the process of dying. What emerges from a consideration of a vast number of classical sources is that Jewish tradition puts a high premium on extending life, but it recognizes that prolonging the process of painful death is not necessarily desirable. Therefore, it endorses passive euthanasia in most cases where death is imminent and inevitable, where further treatment is medically futile, and where the process of dying is accompanied by considerable and unbearable suffering and anguish. This attitude, as noted above, also relates to the introduction of heroic measures. In some instances, when death is near and certain and where considerable pain will ensue, heroic measures, or resuscitation, are not encouraged and, according to some authorities, are proscribed.

The preceding discussion outlines the dominant view in Jewish sources prohibiting active euthanasia of any kind. However, in view of contemporary realities, I have felt it necessary to defend a position within the framework of classical Jewish sources that would justify active euthanasia in at least certain circumstances. I believe that patients, families of patients, physicians, health care workers, and social service professionals, who deal with the death and dying of individuals — whose last days are overwhelmed with unbearable agony, who have no hope of recovery, who have irreparable organ damage, and who have exhausted all medical remedies — should be able to advocate and to practice active euthanasia without feeling that they are criminals, without being burdened with great guilt for actions that they sincerely consider merciful, without feeling that they have transgressed divine and human laws, and without feeling that they have rejected the teachings of Jewish tradition. To be sure, Judaism instructs us to "choose life" (Deut. 30:19), but Judaism also recognizes that "there is a time to die" (Eccles. 3:2). In each case in which the problem of euthanasia presents itself, each person involved must decide which verse applies and how the fulfillment of that verse may best be implemented. Scripture says, "You should love your neighbor as yourself" (Lev. 19:18), which the Talmud takes in certain circumstances to mean, "Therefore, choose an easy death for him" (*Pes.*, 75a).

4

In Adam's Image

IN GENESIS (5:1–3) we read, "This is the book of the generations of Adam. — When God created man, God made him in the likeness of God; male and female God created them. And when they were created, God blessed them and called them 'Adam.' — When Adam had lived 130 years, he begot a son in his likeness after his image, and he named him Seth." From this passage it would appear that Adam was created in the image and likeness of God, whereas Adam's progeny are created in the image and likeness of Adam. Indeed, this view is found in the Mishnah: "If a person strikes many coins from one mould, they all resemble one another, but the Supreme King of Kings, the Holy One, blessed be He, fashioned every human being in the stamp of the first human being [i.e., Adam], and not one resembles another" (*M. San.,* chap. 4, sec. 5). Consequently, Adam's nature has direct relevance to our understanding of human nature. In a number of texts, Adam is described as a Golem.

In the Gemara's explication of the just cited mishnaic text, an "hour-by-hour" account of God's creation of Adam on the sixth day of creation is provided: "Rabbi Johanan ben Hanina said: The [sixth day of creation] consisted of twelve hours. In the first hour his [Adam's] dust was gathered; in the second it [the dust] was made into a shapeless mass [Hebrew: *Golem*]; in the third his limbs were extended; in the fourth a soul was infused into him; in the fifth he arose and stood on his feet; in the sixth he gave [the animals] their names" (*San.,* 38b).

In various midrashic variants of this text, the sequence is reported differently. In the first hour, God conceives of creating hu-

62

mans; in the second, God takes counsel with the angels regarding whether humans should be created; in the third, God assembles the dust; in the fourth, God kneads the dust; in the fifth, God shapes the form; in the sixth, *God makes him into a Golem;* in the seventh, God breathes a soul into him (*LR,* chap. 29, sec. 1; see textual variants, e.g., *MP,* chap. 92, sec. 3, 202; *PRE* 1852, chap. 11; *ARN,* 3a; *PR,* chap. 46, 187b; see also Ginzberg 1955, 5:79). In this midrashic version, unlike the talmudic version, the Golem already has a human form — Adam's form. The Golem is not a formless mass, but a manikin; human in shape but not in essence. Thus, this text describes the state of "Golem" as soulless, but *with* human form.

The term *Golem* means an "unformed mass." A form of the word *Golem* appears only once in the Bible (Ps. 139:16): "Your eyes saw my unformed mass [*galmi*], it was all recorded in Your book." The following midrash interprets this verse as Adam saying to God: Your eyes saw my Golem, that is, God saw Adam as a Golem:

> Rabbi Tanhuma in Rabbi Banaya's name and Rabbi Berekiah in Rabbi Eliezer's name said: God created him [i.e., Adam] a Golem and he lay stretching from one end of the world to the other, as it is written, Your eyes saw my Golem (Ps. 139:16). Rabbi Judah ben Simon said: While Adam lay as a Golem before God who spoke and the world came into being, God showed him every generation and its sages, every generation and its scribes, interpreters and leaders. Said God to him: Your eyes saw My Golem [i.e., the eyes of the Golem have seen My unformed world]; the unformed substance [i.e., the Golem's potential descendants] which your eyes have seen is already written in the book of Adam — [as it is written] "This is the book of the generations of Adam." (Gen. 5:1) (*GR,* chap. 24, sec. 2; cf. *Exod. R.,* chap. 40, sec. 3, *MP,* ch. 139, sec. 6, 265b; *YS,* sec. "*Tehillim,*" para. 885, 967; *Yalkut ha-Makiri* 1900, 135a-b.)

This midrash tells us that humans are not only the descendants of Adam but of a Golem as well. Perhaps, as the biblical verse indicates (Ps. 139:16), God saw Adam as Golem. In other words, God sees Adam — the human being — as essentially a Golem, who becomes human only when realizing his or her potential, which is symbolized in the text as the potential offspring of Adam-Golem. Otherwise, why would God show Adam his potential while still in golemic form rather than in his completed form?

The moral challenge to each human being is to emerge from the golemic state to attain fulfilled human status as a being in the image of God. The task is to evolve the self from the primitive status of Golem to the actualized human status of intellectual discernment and moral rectitude (see e.g., Maimonides' *CM* on *PA,* chap. 5, sec. 6). As Rabbi Mendel of Kotzk said, "Judah Loew created a Golem, and this was a great wonder. But how much more wonderful it is to transform a person of flesh and blood into a *hasid* [a pious person]?" (see Buber 1948, 2:285; Idel 1990, 281).

Creating Golems

According to the Talmud, humans not only evolved from a Golem, but humans are also capable of creating Golems. Unlike the previously discussed text that describes the Golem as a creation of God, the following talmudic text describes the Golem as a creation of human beings:

> Rava said: If the righteous desired it, they could create a world, for it is written "Your iniquities have been a barrier between you and your God" (Isa. 59:2). Rava created a man and sent him to Rabbi Zera. Rabbi Zera spoke to him [the artificially created man], but received no answer. Thereupon, he [Rabbi Zera] said to him [the artificially created man]: "You are from the pietists. Return to your dust." Rabbi Hanina and Rabbi Oshaia spent every Sabbath eve studying the *Sefer Yetzirah* (*The Book of Creation*), by means of which they created a third-grown calf which they ate." (*San.,* 65b)

Rava's statement introduces two important concepts. First, human beings are capable of creating worlds and life. Second, sin prevents humans from fully manifesting the creative abilities that they potentially share with God. Rava seems to be saying that the feature that we share with God is our creative ability. We strive for *imitatio Dei.* When we are creators, we are most like God; we are most clearly in the divine image.

For Rava, the creation of worlds and the creation of artificial life is not a usurpation of God's role as creator; it is instead a fulfillment of the human potential to become a creator. Whereas other religious traditions have considered the creation of artificial beings by human beings to be demonic, Jewish tradition embraced, and even encouraged, such creative activity. The talmudic account of the creation of an artificial man and an artificial calf is reported in a matter-of-fact manner. It is surprisingly never subjected to the dialectic analysis characteristic of talmudic debate and disputation.

The term *Golem* is not found in our text; nevertheless, the text represents the first Jewish record of a creation of a Golem by a human being, and it was so understood by later commentaries.

Hasidut (piety) was the central concern among the *Hasidei Ashkenaz*, the Jewish pietists of medieval Germany. One clear indication of having achieved piety, they believed, was the ability, inherent in the truly pious, to create life. Therefore, among them, the creation of the Golem came to be viewed as a mystical rite of initiation. By creating a Golem the initiate validated his status as one of the pious and demonstrated his mastery over the esoteric truths reserved for the pious. Creation of the Golem became a ritual of initiation into the mysteries of creation. For the *Hasidei Ashkenaz*, a magical ritual served as an entrée to mystical communion with the divine. By penetrating the mystery of creation, by becoming a creator, one came to experience the mystical rapture of oneness with *the* Creator. The creative experience thus became a conduit to mystical ecstasy.

Like Rava, the *Hasidei Ashkenaz* required piety and righteousness from the potential creator of a Golem. This prerequisite infused ethical virtue into the endeavor of creating artificial life. The creator of the Golem had to demonstrate moral qualities as well as technical skills. For Rava and for the *Hasidei Ashkenaz*, something as precious as life itself is too delicate to be surrendered to the moral novice. For them, the use of technical skills assumed the prior mastery of ethical insight and behavior (see Scholem 1965, 178–80).

While the human being is encouraged to develop his or her creative potentialities, various versions of the Golem legend nonetheless warn that there are physical, moral, psychological, and spiritual dangers inherent in the creative process. In a number of versions of the Golem legend told about Judah Loew of Prague, the Golem runs amok and destroys part of the city of Prague (see, e.g., Rosenberg 1909; Bloch 1925; Winkler 1980). In versions told about Rabbi Elijah of Chelm, the Golem either harms or kills its creator.

The message is that what we create to help and to protect us, may elude our control, and may harm or even destroy us.

According to a medieval legend, the biblical character Enosh learned that God had created Adam from the earth. Enosh then took some earth, kneaded it into a human form, and blew into its nostrils to animate it as God had done to give Adam life. Satan then slipped into the figure and gave it the appearance of life. Enosh and his generation worshipped the figure and, hence, idolatry began (see Scholem 1965, 181).

According to another medieval legend, the prophet Jeremiah and his son Sira created a Golem. After studying the *Sefer Yetzirah* for three years, they undertook the creation of a Golem through the use of letter permutations and combinations. On its forehead they wrote the phrase, "the Lord God is truth [*emet*]." But once the Golem became vital, it took the knife with which Jeremiah carved these words on its forehead, and it scratched out the letter *alef.* Now the phrase read, "the Lord God is dead [*meit*]." Jeremiah then asked the Golem why it did what it did. The Golem replied with a long parable. The message of the parable is that, once human beings become creators, they are in danger of forgetting *the* Creator. Once the creature becomes a creator, impressed by his or her own achievements, he or she may act as if God is dead and he or she is now God. "What solution is there?" Jeremiah asked of the Golem. The Golem advised Jeremiah to destroy it by reversing the letter combinations used to create it. Jeremiah did so, and the Golem returned to the elements from which it had been created (see Scholem 1965, 180; Idel 1990, 66–69).

The moral of these medieval stories is that psychological and spiritual dangers are inherent features of the enterprise of human creativity, that in forgetting the divine creator, the human creator can readily forget that he or she is a creature of God. Untempered by moral restraints, infected with arrogance engendered by creative success, the human creator's pride might easily evolve into idolatry — the rejection of God, and the worship of his or her own self and the products of his or her creative endeavors.

Spin-Offs of the Golem Legend

One would be challenged to identify a postbiblical Jewish legend that has been more influential than the legend of the Golem. Its echoes are found throughout world literature (see, e.g., Goldsmith 1981; Sherwin 1985, 1–2). There is evidence, for example, that the legend of the Golem influenced the composition of Mary Shelley's *Frankenstein* and its many spin-offs in literature and film. Influences can also be detected in Goethe's ballad, "The Sorcerer's Apprentice" (see, e.g., Scholem 1965, 154) and its spin-offs such as scenes in the Disney film *Fantasia*. It stimulated: drama by Rudolph Lother, the Capek brothers (1961) and H. Leivick (1927); poetry by Hugo Salus and Jorge Luis Borges; an opera by Eugene d'Albert; a ballet, "The Golem Suite," by Joseph Achron; novels by Gustav Meyrink (1964), Max Brod, Abraham Rothberg (1970), and Cynthia Ozick (1982); children's books by Isaac B. Singer (1982), Elie Wiesel (1983) and David Wisniewski (1996); short stories by David Frischmann and Y. L. Peretz. For decades, science fiction writers such as Avram Davidson have been intrigued by the Golem (see, e.g., Davidson 1974). In comic books, the presence of the Golem abounds. For example, Superman occasionally must encounter "The Galactic Golem." From the earliest days of film, the Golem has appeared on the silver screen, beginning in 1914 with director Paul Wegener's now classic silent film, *The Golem* (for a filmography, see Sherwin 1985, 55).

The Past Meets the Present

In 1972, Ananda Chakrabarty, a microbiologist, filed a patent application for a humanly engineered bacterium capable of breaking down multiple components of crude oil, a property found in no naturally occurring bacteria. This bacterium was believed to have particular value in the treatment of oil spills. While the U.S. Office of Patents and Trademarks granted a patent for the *process* of producing the bacterium, it denied Chakrabarty a patent for the bacterium itself on the grounds that microorganisms are "products of nature" and that as living entities they are not patentable.

Chakrabarty appealed the denial of a patent for the bacterium to the U.S. Court of Customs and Patent Appeals, which affirmed Chakrabarty's right to a patent. The court held that live organisms were not outside the scope of patentable inventions. On March 17, 1980, arguments on the case of *U.S. Commissioner of Patents and Trademarks (Sidney Diamond) v Ananda Chakrabarty* (447 U.S. 303, 1980) were presented before the U.S. Supreme Court. On June 16,

1980, in a five-to-four decision, the Supreme Court affirmed the decisions of the U.S. Court of Customs and Patent Appeals permitting Chakrabarty a patent on the bacterium. Speaking for the majority, Chief Justice Burger held that "a live, human-made, microorganism is patentable subject matter under statute providing for issuance of patent to a person who invents or discovers 'any' new or useful 'manufacture' or 'composition of matter.'" Four hundred years after Judah Loew is described by Jewish legend as having created the Golem — almost to the day, March 20, 1580 — the U.S. Supreme Court was hearing arguments related to the propriety of the creation of artificial life, the risks of the creation of artificial life-forms, the ownership of artificially created life-forms, and the legal status of such creations (see Kass 1985, 128–53). Four days after the Supreme Court announced its decision, a letter was sent to President Jimmy Carter from the General Secretaries of the National Council of Churches, the U.S. Catholic Conference, and the Synagogue Council of America. The letter stated:

> With the Supreme Court decision allowing patents on new forms of life — a purpose that could not have been imagined when patent laws were written — it is obvious that these laws must be reexamined. The issue goes far beyond patents. New life-forms may have dramatic potential for improving human life. . . . They may also, however, have unforeseen ramifications, and at times the cure may be worse than the original problem. . . . Those who would play God will be tempted as never before. . . . Given all the responsibility to God and to our fellow human beings, do we have the right to let experimentation and ownership of new life-forms move ahead without public regulation? These issues must be explored, and they must be explored now. (President's Commission 1982, 95–96)

In response to this appeal, President Carter asked the President's Commission for the Study of Ethical Problems in Medicine and Biomedical and Behavioral Research to undertake a study of "the social and ethical issues of genetic engineering with human beings." In November 1982 the Commission issued its findings in a work entitled *Splicing Life*. In this report, one finds the following observation:

Like the tale of the Sorcerer's apprentice or the myth of the Golem created from lifeless dust by the 16th century rabbi, Loew of Prague, the story of Dr. Frankenstein's monster serves as a reminder of the difficulty of restoring order if a creation intended to be helpful proves harmful instead. Indeed, each of these tales conveys a painful irony: in seeking to extend their control over the world, people may lessen it. The artifices they create to do their bidding may rebound destructively against them — the slave may become the master. (President's Commission 1982, 95–96)

Apprehension that the Golem-slave would become the master of its creator was not simply a concern of the Commission, nor is it merely a restatement of the master-slave dialectic developed by Hegel. That the Golem will enslave its master is a common theme in the literary spin-offs of the Golem legend. For example, in the Capek brothers' famous play *R.U.R.*, we read, "Mankind will never cope with the Robots, and will never have control over them. Mankind will be overwhelmed in the deluge of these dreadful living machines, will be their slave, will live at their mercy" (1961, 28).

The report of the presidential commission notes a study done by the National Science Foundation (NSF) that found that most Americans opposed most restrictions on scientific research in all areas but one — creation of new life-forms and genetic engineering with human beings. While the commission concurred that there are valid reasons for this apprehension, it also asserted that much popular opposition to genetic engineering was based upon fear grounded in a lack of awareness of the nature of genetic engineering and of the potential benefits it holds forth. While the commission was sensitive to the possible moral abuses of genetic engineering, it also indicated that it might be unethical to stifle the potential benefits that genetic engineering may bring to many people. For example, drugs could be produced in large quantities at comparatively little cost that could help treat diseases and genetic defects that otherwise either would not be treated or could be treated only at extraordinary cost. Furthermore, because of natural or humanly induced climatic or other changes in our environment, genetic engineering can forestall extensive catastrophe. For instance, if a sudden shift of climate were to occur, the use of genetic engineering to alter quickly the genetic composition of agricultural plants can save whole populations from mass starvation.

The commission observed that gene splicing occurs regularly within bacteria, and it concluded that "the basic processes underlying genetic engineering are thus *natural* and not revolutionary. Indeed, it was the discovery that these processes were [naturally] occurring that suggested to scientists the great possibilities and basic methods of gene splicing. What is new, however, is the ability of scientists to control the processes" (President's Commission 1982, 31–32). Similarly, Judah Loew and others described the creation of artificial life as an action in consonance with the natural order of creation (see, e.g., *BG*, chap. 2, 27–28). In other words, such acts are essentially "natural" and do not represent a contravening of the natural order.

That artificially created organisms might endanger human life was found by the commission to be a largely unfounded fear, grounded in the public's lack of knowledge about the controls under which such activities were conducted. It found both scientific and governmental controls upon such experimentation to be more than adequate. Seymour Siegel, a preeminent Jewish theologian who was a member of the commission, reported the following in an address to the Rabbinical Assembly:

> The National Institute of Health has formulated guidelines to be followed by laboratories sponsoring DNA research. These guidelines have reduced the danger of these experiments to practically zero. . . . I can testify personally, as a member of the Biohazards Committee of the giant pharmaceutical firm, Hoffman-LaRoche, as to the exquisite care which is taken in the protection of the environment and the researchers involved in DNA experiments. . . . Thus it seems obvious to me that the potentially great benefits to mankind in carrying on these researches far outweigh any possible harm. (1978, 165)

Although the commission decided that genetic engineering is currently monitored adequately in the United States, it recommended that such careful monitoring continue. It also reinforced a popular apprehension regarding the dangers of genetic engineering in a nondemocratic political setting, or for use in developing pathogenic microorganisms for biological warfare or for terrorism. Furthermore, the commission warned that the hubris of the scientist that might lead him or her to create artificial beings without regard to the potential physical and moral dangers of such action had to be controlled. It denounced as outrightly unethical certain possible uses of genetic engineering, such as the creation of a genetically engineered slave population of partly human and partly animal beings. In short, the commission, in general, and the theologians on the commission, in particular, felt that in itself genetic engineering is good, that it articulates the biblical view that human beings are cocreators with God. However, it also maintained that genetic engineering, like any human activity, can express itself as a misuse of human freedom with concomitant harmful results (see also Ramsey 1970; Jonas 1974, 141–67; Kass 1985, 43–157; Shannon 1976, 295–373; Goodfield 1977). The commission concluded that the creation of artificial life should be permitted, even encouraged. However, such activities must be done with expert care and with a keen awareness of the potentially harmful consequences of such actions (see, e.g., novels by Crichton [1969] and Saul [1982]; see also Piller and Yamamoto 1988).

As noted, the creation of artificial life is generally sanctioned by Jewish religious tradition, albeit with certain caveats. A similar approach has been taken by various governmental agencies and by private industry. Ancient and medieval Jewish thinkers as well as contemporary ethicists, scientists, theologians, and philosophers have recognized that human creativity is a double-edged sword, that the creative process is replete with dangers and risks. However, the consensus seems to be that, once certain controls and safeguards are applied, the potential benefits of the creation of artificial life outweigh the dangers. Furthermore, the President's Commission echoed traditional Jewish teachings when it affirmed that the human being is most human as a creator, that through creativity the human being expresses his or her most Godlike qualities, that human creativity is *imitatio Dei.*

While both classical Jewish literature and contemporary popular literature confront the substantial dangers related to the creation of artificial life, it would seem that Jewish literature puts much-needed emphasis upon the psychological, spiritual, and moral risks attached to this undertaking. More than contemporary literature, classical Jewish literature stresses these features of the creative act. Jewish literature requires rigorous moral, technical, and intellectual prerequisites of one who would deign to create life. Furthermore,

Jewish literature refuses to sever creature from creator. Not only is the creator responsible for what the creature does but the creator is responsible for what the creature becomes. The creature reflects not only the technical skill but also the moral nature of its creator. Conversely, the nature of the creator is also affected by the nature of the creature and by the psychological risks that characterize the act of creation itself. Though creativity can be an entrée to spiritual rapture, it can also be an invitation to spiritual disaster.

For the traditional religious mentality, the greatest spiritual danger is heresy (the rejection and negation of God). The risk of "playing God" is inextricably related to the possibility of rejecting God. Impressed by his or her own creations, the individual may replace worship of God with self-worship. Technological advances — as Jeremiah was told by his Golem — threaten to lead us to the conclusion that "God is dead." Indeed, this is one of the lessons the rabbis elicit from the biblical story of the Tower of Babel (Gen. 11).

The Tower was the first great technological achievement of humankind, according to the Bible. For the talmudic rabbis, however, it also marked the inception of idolatry. Having dispensed with God and having built the Tower, the people now unabashedly worshipped the products of their own hands, their own artifices (see, e.g., Ginzberg 1955, 1:77–81, 5:200–208). For the rabbis, a further risk of technological achievement is the devaluation of human life, the rejection of the inherent preciousness of human life, and the valuating of human artifacts over human beings. According to a midrash when the Tower reached an extraordinary height, bricks had to be hoisted from the ground to the top of the Tower. At that point, "if a worker fell off the Tower and died, no attention was paid. However, if a brick fell off, everyone sat down and wept and said: Woe to us, when will someone else come in its stead" (*PRE* 1852, chap. 24).

By nature, a Golem is an artifact. It is therefore in danger of becoming an idol. In technological achievement as in idolatry, the temptation, the spiritual danger is the same — that one might worship the products of one's own hands, that one might attribute divine powers to one's own creation. In such a case, illusion is substituted for reality and an exercise in deception ensues (see, e.g., Kochan 1990, 157). Furthermore, the spiritual risks endemic to technological achievement also relate to art. Before Hegel, art was largely considered to be an imitation of reality. With Hegel, art became artifact, an entity in itself. Before Hegel, aesthetics mostly focused on the beautiful in nature and on art as an imitation of natural beauty. With Hegel, the focus of aesthetics shifted to a concern with beauty in artistic products of human expression (see, e.g., Barrett 1986, 98–99).

The historically uneasy relationship between Jewish tradition and representational art, especially sculpture, articulates the dangers inherent in the artistic process. There is an apprehension that the artifact may replace that which it represents, that the importance of the contrived entity might supersede the significance of the natural being, that the artistic product might become an object of veneration supplanting the attention that might otherwise be paid to that which it purports to represent, that the enchantment offered by the wonders of "virtual reality" could engender a deception in which a fabricated "fiction" might be treated as verified fact (see, e.g., Kochan 1990, 157–59). From this perspective, the greater the appeal of the artifact, the greater its potential spiritual danger.

When the product of artistic creativity is mistakenly identified with its creator, whether this entails equating nature with God or an artifact with what it represents, a fraud is being perpetrated. According to Judah Loew, the reason a Golem can never attain human status is because a creature or an artifact cannot acquire the status of its creator. Just as human beings created in God's image should not be confused with God, so should a human artifact, such as a humanly created Golem, not be construed to be truly human. In Loew's words, "For he [i.e., Rava] was a human being himself; and, how would it then be possible for him to create a complete person like himself? Just as it is impossible to conceive that God, who is supreme over everything, would create one like Himself" (*HA*, 3:166–67).

Golems and Machines

The description of the ritual for the creation of a Golem by Eleazar Rokeah — one of the leading personalities of the *Hasidei Ashkenaz* — indicates that separate letter permutations are required for the creation of a female Golem from those required for the creation of a male Golem. The idea that a Golem may be female or male is found in a number of sources. Most noteworthy in this regard is a legend concerning Solomon ibn Gabirol.

Because he was afflicted by a severe skin disease, the medieval Jewish philosopher, Solomon ibn Gabirol lived in isolation. According to a legend, he created a woman to keep house for him. When what he did became known, Ibn Gabirol was reported to the authorities. Because it was assumed that he had created her by magic, possibly for lewd activities, he was ordered to dismantle her. He did so, reducing her to the wood and hinges from which she was created (see, e.g., Scholem 1965, 199; Bin Gorion 1976, 752).

That a female Golem was created is not unique in the Jewish literature about the Golem. What is distinct is that Ibn Gabirol's Golem was not made from earth or clay but was made of wood and hinges. Here one finds the roots of the portrayal of the Golem as a mechanical being, as an automaton, as a robot.

The relationship between humans and machines is explored in *God and Golem, Inc.* by Norbert Wiener, the father of cybernetics (1964, 71, 95). Wiener identified the relationship between people and machines as the central problem of our society. Wiener described the machine as "the modern counterpart of the Golem" and depicted the problem of the relationship between people and machines as having been anticipated by the Golem legend. One of the most significant works of world literature that explores the dangers that mechanized and intelligent artifacts pose to their creators is the 1920s Czech play *R.U.R.* by the brothers Capek.

It is reasonable to assume that the Capek brothers, who were from Prague, were influenced by the Golem legend when they wrote *R.U.R.* It is in this work that the term "robot" was coined. "Robot" derives from a Slavic root meaning a "worker." *R.U.R.* is the abbreviation for "Rossum's Universal Robots." The play takes place at an R.U.R. factory that manufactures robots. In the course of the play, the robots take over both the factory and the world. After the robots have all but annihilated the human race, Alquist, a clerk at the R.U.R. factory, asks the robots, "Why did you murder us?" Radius, one of the robots, replies, "Slaughter and domination are necessary if you want to be like man. Read history, read the human books. You must domineer and murder if you want to be like men" (Capek and Capek 1961, 94).

Artificially created beings only reflect their creators. The evil a machine may do only reflects its creators. The artificial beings we create can tell us more about human nature than about the nature of technology or of machines. Their creation is not only an expression of human achievement but an exercise — sometimes a horrify-ing one — in human self-understanding. As philosopher William Barrett has observed "the computer only gives us back ourselves. It is a faithful mirror that reflects the human traits that are brought to it. . . . there could be other human faces that the computer might give back to us — the face of arrogance, of ruthlessness, of the lust for power" (1978, 103). According to Barrett, fear of the results of our technological achievements is simply a reflection of our fear of ourselves. This fear may not be unjustified. The threat of nuclear or biochemical warfare, or of computers running amok, indicates in a shockingly real way that the Golems we create to serve and defend us may ultimately harm or destroy us.

It was the great scholar of Jewish mysticism, Gershom Scholem, who perceived the computer as a modern manifestation of the Golem (1971, 335–40; see also Rosenfeld 1966, 23–26). As Scholem well knew, many cabalistic descriptions of the creation of the Golem maintained that the Golem was created through the per-mutations of the letters of the Hebrew alphabet, each of which also represents a number (see, e.g., Scholem 1965, 185–86). Scholem also must have realized that computers operate through the permu-tations of a binary numerical system. A version of the cabalistic method of letter and number permutations (*zeirufei ha-otiot*) is what animates computers, as it animated the Golem. And, just as the power of the Golem created by Judah Loew cascaded out of con-trol, and just as the force of Elijah of Chelm's Golem fell back upon him causing him injury, potential harm and destruction from the products of our own creativity continues to haunt us today.

The explosion of technology since the Industrial Revolution may indicate to us that, the more exposure to machines we experi-ence, the more we may tend to define ourselves and to think of ourselves as machines. Machines may not only reflect human pro-clivities, they may cause us to alter the manner in which we think of human nature, of ourselves.

The tendency in modern Western thought to define the human being as a kind of machine and, conversely, to grant human status to certain kinds of machines is based upon a mechanistic and physi-calist view of reality that is reductionistic in nature and in approach. This philosophy tends to obscure the spiritual dimension of the hu-man creature and to treat the category of human uniqueness as a superfluous theological bother. Precisely because this attitude has become so deeply ingrained in modern Western thought, it bears some discussion (see Barrett 1986).

One of the traits unique to human beings is self-definition. Only human beings define themselves. How we define ourselves reflects what we think of ourselves, how we view ourselves. Beginning in the eighteenth century, it became fashionable to define the human being as a kind of machine. Once internalized, this philosophical position becomes a determining factor in human behavior. Once accepted by the individual, this philosophical assumption becomes a psychological presupposition.

In the seventeenth century, the eminent philosopher René Descartes introduced a distinction between "thinking beings" and "extended beings." He classified human beings as uniquely self-conscious thinking beings. For Descartes, animals were "extended beings." Descartes described animals as automata. In the eighteenth century, the French philosopher Julien Offray de La Mettrie rejected Descartes's position out of hand. According to de La Mettrie, human beings are machines. In his work, *Man, A Machine* (*L'homme-machine*), de La Mettrie described the human body as "a machine that winds its own springs" (1912, 21, 93; see also Geduld and Gottesman 1978, 31).

De La Mettrie's view was expanded by mechanist and materialist philosophers and thinkers who came after him. For example, in the nineteenth century, the American atheist philosopher Robert Ingersoll observed that "man is a machine into which we put what we call food and produce what we call thought." In other words, humans are thinking machines. The novelist Isak Dinesen went further by writing, "What is man when you come to think about him, but a minutely set, ingenious machine for turning, with infinite artfulness, the red wine of Shiraz into urine?" In the early twentieth century, an American philosopher defined the human being as "an ingenious array of portable plumbing."

It is all but inevitable that once internalized, the conception of the human being as a variety of machine would influence our behavior. Even our daily colloquial speech has been influenced. For example, we speak of ourselves as being "turned on" and "turned off." We "tune in" and "tune out." We provide "input" and "output." We go on vacations to "recharge our batteries." We "gear ourselves up" and "get our motors running" at the beginning of a day. By the end of a day, we are "wound up," so we must "unwind." By thinking of ourselves in mechanistic terms, we become machine-like. As Karl Marx warned: as machines become more like humans, humans will become more like machines. With advances in technology, the lines of demarcation between humans and Golems tend to become blurred.

If a machine is a type of Golem, then destroying it would not be murder. However, what would be the case if the killed victim had been part human and part machine, that is, a cyborg? This last question has been raised in science fiction literature. For example, in his story *Fires of Night*, Dennis Etchison asks whether killing a person with artificial limbs or organs would be murder. At what point would such an individual cross over the line from being a human to being a machine? When would such an individual stop being a human who is part machine and become merely a machine that is part human? (see, e.g., Kurzweil 1999, 52–54, 135–45). Discussion of this issue is amplified by Martin Caidin in his novel *Cyborg* (1972), which became the basis for the television program, "The Six-Million-Dollar Man." In this story, an American astronaut crash-lands. His destroyed limbs are replaced by bionic limbs. He is now literally half-human, half-machine.

With the rapid pace of developments in bionics and computer science, and the use of artificial organs and implanted microchips, questions originally raised by science fiction writers currently fall under the domain of medical ethics. Although these issues have not yet been adequately treated by the American courts, they have at least been anticipated by classical Jewish literature regarding the Golem.

The Golem's Legal Status

In the eighteenth century, Zevi Ashkenazi wrote a curious responsum about whether a Golem may be included in a quorum for prayer, a *minyan*. The complete text of this responsum follows in translation:

> I became doubtful [concerning the resolution of the following question]: Is [the case of] a man, created by [means of magically employing] the *Sefer Yetzirah* identical [to the case] reported in the *Tractate Sanhedrin?* Namely, "Rava created a man [and sent him to Rabbi Zera. Rabbi Zera spoke to him but received no answer.

Thereupon he said to him — You are a creature of magicians. Return to your dust.]" So it has also been asserted concerning my ancestor, the Gaon, our Master and Teacher, Rabbi Elijah, chief rabbi of the Holy Community of Chelm. Who is allowed to be counted as one of ten [a quorum for prayer] in matters which require ten, i.e., [recitation of such prayers as] *Kaddish, Kedushah*, for it is written, "I [God] will be sanctified amidst Israel" (Lev. 22:32)? Do we include [such an individual as the artificially created man] or do we say that since it is taught in *Sanhedrin*, "He who raises an orphan in his home, Scripture ascribes it to him as though he had begotten him"? For it is written "Five sons of Michal, the daughter of Saul whom she bore to Adriel" (2 Sam. 21:8). "Did not Merab bear them? Yes, but Michal raised them [and they are therefore called her sons]" [see *San.*, 19a]. In the present case as well [the artificially created man is considered a child of the one who created him; therefore a regular human being; therefore he can be counted].

Since the workings of the hands of the righteous is involved, he is to be included, for the works of the hands of the righteous are their progeny [see Rashi on Gen. 6:9 based on *GR*, chap. 30, sec. 6].

But it seems to me that as a result of meeting Rabbi Zera who said: "You are the work of magicians, return to your dust," he was killed. And do you not think that if there would have been a need to include him amongst a quorum that Rabbi Zera would have "cast him from the world"?

[It thus appears that] there is no prohibition of murder concerning him. [Otherwise Rabbi Zera would be guilty of murder.] For Scripture remarks — and I know there are other possible explanations: "Whosoever sheds a *man's* blood, by man shall his blood be shed [for in the image of God made He man," Gen. 9:5.] [That is to say,] only a *man* formed within a human being; that is, only [killing one who was] a fetus formed within his mother's womb [is counted as murder]. Nevertheless, since he [the artificially created man] has a purpose, he [Rabbi Zera] should not have cast him out of existence. But it is certain that he [the artificially created man] is not counted amongst the ten needed for holy deeds. (Ashkenazi [1767] 1970, no. 93; see also Sherwin 1985, 21–22; Idel 1990, 217–18)

This responsum is curious in that it is not a responsum at all. A responsum is a legal opinion offered by a rabbi in response to a question put to him. This "responsum" is a discussion of a problem the author put to himself. That Ashkenazi raised the question of whether a Golem may help form a *minyan* and that he and others treated it as a viable halakhic issue demonstrates the seriousness with which the Golem was taken (see Shapira 1967, 1/2:38–39, n. 11; Idel 1990, 213–31). Though Ashkenazi addressed the particular question of whether a Golem could be included in a *minyan*, he also implicitly raised a general question that becomes pertinent to a discussion of contemporary moral implications of the Golem legend: What is the legal status of a Golem? Whereas Adam began as a Golem, but developed into a human being created in the image of God, the question remains of whether a Golem created by Adam's descendants can evolve into a person bearing the image of God?

Defining the legal status of a "person" is a problem addressed by many legal systems. By asking whether a Golem can be included in a *minyan*, and by querying the propriety of Rabbi Zera's action in "killing" Rava's Golem, Ashkenazi's responsum focuses attention on the legal status of the Golem. Ashkenazi implicitly asks whether the Golem can claim personhood, with its attendant obligations, privileges, and legal protections. Though for Ashkenazi, the Golem has no claim on human personhood, left unanswered, however, is the question of the legal status of this "artificially" created entity that has human form. If the Golem cannot be assumed to have the status of personhood, then what status might it have?

Jewish law does not recognize "artificial persons" as having the status of legal persons. American law, however, recognizes two categories of persons: "natural" and "artificial." A natural person is an individual human being. An example of an artificial person would be a corporation. Like a Golem, such an artificial person is a human creation. The very word "corporation" derives from the Latin *corpus*, meaning a body. Like a Golem, a corporation is a body without a soul (see, e.g., Blackstone 1765, 455–73; *Black's Law Dictionary* [1891], s.v. "Person," 1299–3000). The dominant approach of Jewish law to corporations is not to treat them as persons, but as "limited partnerships" formed by natural persons. Human partners can be expected to act morally, and to be ethically and legally accountable for their actions, whereas artificial persons such as corporate Golems cannot always be expected to do so (see, e.g., Phillips 1992, 435–59).

Certainly, corporations cannot meet the criteria for legal and moral responsibility that are applied to human persons. For example, by its very nature, a corporation could not be punished for a breach of law or morality in the same manner as could a human being (such as imprisonment or capital punishment). For instance, a corporation that releases carcinogenic wastes or poisonous industrial substances into a lake from which people derive their drinking water might be only liable for a nominal statutory fine, while an individual person causing deliberate harm to other human beings in an identical manner might be liable to fines and imprisonment. Indeed, recognizing the legal status of artificial persons such as corporations might encourage corporate officials to seek personal legal protection by hiding behind a "corporate shield."

By excluding the Golem from the *minyan*, Ashkenazi reaffirms the proclivity of Jewish law not to accept the legal category of "artificial person." In view of the moral problems generated by the acceptance of artificial persons in American law, this approach seems prudent. Yet, the question of the status of the Golem in Jewish law still remains unanswered by Ashkenazi. If the Golem cannot claim the status of personhood, even artificial personhood, then what status can it claim? By raising the issue of the propriety of Rabbi Zera's action via-à-vis the Golem, Ashkenazi opens an avenue of discussion for further consideration of the status of the Golem.

Because Ashkenazi did not consider Rava's Golem to be human, Rabbi Zera could not then be liable for murder for having destroyed it. Ashkenazi simply could not imagine a talmudic sage such as Rabbi Zera as being guilty of cold-blooded murder. Nonetheless, Rabbi Zera's action may not have been blameless. If the Golem had the status of a living creature, for example, an animal, then it could not be killed without reason. Furthermore, even if the Golem is a lifeless artifact, created for some purpose, its destruction would hardly be justified (see, e.g., Zadok of Lublin 1903, 91–92). Ashkenazi's claim that Rabbi Zera was not guilty of murder because the Golem was not a natural person fails to address the question of whether Rabbi Zera might be culpable for a lesser offense such as destruction of property, wasting resources (*ba'al tashhit;* see, e.g., Deut. 20:19), or, the senseless killing of an animal. Completely exonerating Rabbi Zera from any culpability would mean that the Golem has no legal status, and consequently no legal protection from abuse of any kind.

An interesting observation on this issue of "Golem abuse" was made by the sixteenth-century cabalist Isaiah Horowitz (1960, sec.

"*va-yeishev*," 3:65a). According to the biblical text, Joseph was a tattletale who reported his brothers' wrongdoings to his father, Jacob (Gen. 37:3). Some of the commentaries to this passage relate that one of the items Joseph reported was that his brothers were engaged in illicit sexual activities. Horowitz claims that such was the appearance but not the reality. According to Horowitz (who quotes the text from *Sanhedrin* regarding Rava's artificially created man), Joseph's brothers were not engaged sexually with a human woman but with a female Golem. Horowitz further reports that Abraham wrote the *Sefer Yetzirah* and passed it down to his son, Isaac, who then passed it down to his son, Jacob. Jacob, in turn, passed it down to his sons, Joseph's brothers. Jacob's sons used the *Sefer Yetzirah* to create a female Golem with which they enjoyed sexual relations. But, since it was not human, these actions could not be considered sinful.

Zevi Hirsch Shapira commented on Horowitz's discussion. According to Shapira, the female Golem lacked the powers of speech and intelligence and, therefore, should be excluded from the category of being human (1967, 1/2:38–39). But, what if the female Golem had intelligence? Would Jacob's sons have been guilty then for abusing her? What if Rava's male Golem had intelligence? Would Rabbi Zera have been guilty then of murder?

According to the *Sefer ha-Bahir* (1951, no. 196, 89), Rava's Golem did not have the power of speech because it was not created by the completely righteous. However, had it been so created, it would have had the power of speech and would have been intelligent. Hence, the inability to create an intelligent Golem reflects a flaw in the creator of the Golem that is reflected in the Golem he created (see Idel 1990, 128–29).

The daring late Hasidic master Gershon Hanokh Lainer of Radzyn, in his controversial *Sidrei Taharot* went even further than the *Sefer ha-Bahir*. Gershon Hanokh stated that if an intelligent Golem had been created, "he would have the legal status of a true man . . . even as regards being counted in a *minyan* . . . and he would be the same as if God had created him." Thus, Gershon Hanokh admitted the possibility of considering an artificially created being, who had all the normal human traits, including intelligence, as a human being. Gershon Hanokh would grant human personhood to such an "artificially" created human being (Lainer 1903, 5a). Destroying such a Golem, it would follow, would be murder. If Joseph's brothers had sexually abused such a female Golem, Gershon Hanokh would hold them liable for rape. Furthermore, killing Adam, who was neither conceived nor born like other humans, and who had once been a Golem according to the midrashic account, would certainly have been murder. Whatever its origins, a Golem that achieves human status must be treated as a natural person.

In making his claim that a Golem might be considered human, Gerson Hanokh articulated his disagreement with the position of Judah Loew and others, who maintained that a Golem could never have all of the essential human characteristics, and, hence, could never be considered a human being. For Judah Loew, and for others previously noted, a human artifact could never be a human being. However, Gershon Hanokh is willing to eradicate any absolute distinction between humans and Golems. For Gershon Hanokh, a Golem that meets certain criteria can be considered human (see Idel 1990, 224–28). Judah Loew, in contrast, would insist upon a firm line of demarcation between humans and Golems. For Loew, a Golem by definition cannot be considered a human (*HA*, 3:166–67).

This collision of views between Judah Loew and Gershon Hanokh finds contemporary expression in the vast literature on the question of whether machines that appear to have human traits can be considered human in any sense. If, for example, one considers intelligence to be the cardinal characteristic in determining whether one is human, could an intelligent machine then be considered human? Gershon Hanokh might answer in the affirmative, while Judah Loew would answer in the negative. Like Judah Loew, some contemporary philosophers and scientists maintain that a machine, even an intelligent machine, could not be considered human because it always would lack some essential human trait. Some thinkers of this school would further maintain that human intelligence, like human nature, is sui generis and that, just as a machine must always be distinguished from a human being, so must mechanical intelligence or artificial intelligence be distinguished from human intelligence. Other thinkers of this school might argue that, while intelligence is an essential human trait, the possession of intelligence by a nonhuman being, for example, an extraterrestrial or a dolphin, would not ipso facto qualify such a being for human status. Nor would the absence of a normal degree of human intelligence (e.g., an imbecile) disqualify a human person from the status of being human.

Philosophers and theologians who refuse to grant human status or human intelligence or both to Golems and machines rest their argument upon a fundamental presupposition — the unique nature of the human being. Where these thinkers may disagree is on the question: What is it that makes human existence sui generis? What quality is it that makes human beings human? Some maintain that the very fact that each human being is different from every other human being is itself adequate evidence for affirming the unique nature not only of the human person but of each and every human person (see, e.g., *San.*, 37a). Machines and Golems can be duplicated; human beings cannot. Others hold that ensoulment is what makes the human being unique. The Golem, by definition, is a soulless, though not necessarily a lifeless, being. Thus, to speak of a "human Golem" in this view would be a contradiction in terms, a linguistically meaningless statement. Still others hold that such qualities as the ability to laugh, to create, to be embarrassed, to express emotion, to love, to carry on a telephone conversation, to be self-conscious, to act freely and spontaneously, to have hopes and dreams, to be inconsistent and unpredictable, are peculiarly human and cannot be found in machines. Furthermore, even if such paradigmatically "human" characteristics were apparently present in machines, such machines still would not qualify for human personhood because those traits would merely be a reflection of the characteristics of the designer of the machine. The logic of Judah Loew's thinking applies here: just as the human person though created in God's image is not God, so a Golem or a machine into which certain human characteristics have been programmed would not be considered a human being (see e.g., Scholem 1971, 335–41; Rosenfeld 1966, 15–26; Rosenfeld 1977, 58–74).[1]

Four positions regarding the status of a Golem emerge from the previous discussion:

1. Rosenfeld's writings are startling in that he anticipated many problems in the 1970s that were to become particularly relevant in decades to come. For example, his writings on gene therapy and genetic engineering (1972), on cryonics (deep freezing of human tissue) (1967) and on the implications of the Golem legend for bioethics and for issues of human identity are striking in their previsaging of future problems (see, e.g., 1966, 1977). Furthermore, to my knowledge, Rosenfeld was the first halakhic scholar to advocate the permissibility in Jewish law of cloning human beings. Like the current discussion, he links his view to reflection on the Golem in classical Jewish literature (1977).

1. A Golem has no legal status. It is simply an artifact. As such, it can be used (and abused) in any manner, and even be wantonly destroyed.

2. Though an artifact, a Golem cannot be destroyed (or abused) without a reason, since it was presumably created for a purpose. However, once that purpose has been fulfilled, it may be destroyed. According to Zadok of Lublin (1903, 91–92), Rabbi Zera was permitted to destroy Rava's Golem because he discerned that the purpose for which the Golem had been created already had been fulfilled in that Rava wanted to demonstrate that such a being could be created by him. Similarly, Rabbi Hanina and Rabbi Oshaia were permitted to eat the calf they created artificially because providing themselves with food for the Sabbath meal was the purpose the calf was created by them in the first place. Nonetheless, destroying an artifact without reason, would be a culpable offense.

3. A Golem cannot have human status, but as a living creature, it can have animal status. As Ashkenazi's own son, Rabbi Jacob Emden put it, Rava's Golem is "just like an animal in the form of a human" (1884, 28a). Such a Golem would therefore have all of the legal protections that an animal might have. Hence, destroying a Golem with purpose might be compared to the justifiable act of killing an animal, whereas destroying a Golem without any reason would be analogous to an unjustified act of killing an animal. To this observation, one may add that since animals may be a variety of property, the two categories of "property" and "animal" might be collapsed into one insofar as liability is concerned. For example, the U.S. Patent and Trademark Office currently grants patents on genetically altered "new" animals, which implies that such "artificially" created animals are legally being defined as the property of the holder of the patent. The first such patent was issued in 1988 to Harvard University for a genetically altered mouse that can effectively be used in testing substances used to treat or prevent cancer in humans.

4. A Golem can have or can acquire human status. Though created through the employment of "artificial" means, once "born" a Golem who is human in every respect (and not just in appearance) is no longer a Golem at all, but a human being. For example, since a person brought into being "artificially" (e.g., through the employment of various means of reproductive biotechnology) would be indistinguishable at birth from other human beings, such an individ-

ual would have every claim on human personhood. Like Adam (according to various *midrashim*), who progressed from a golemic to a human status, such an individual would be no less human than Adam or any other human being. In fact, as Lainer claims, if Ashkenazi's criteria were applied to the first human being, that is, Adam, then Adam—who was created in a different manner than other human beings, could "legally" have been murdered. Since such a conclusion is patently absurd, Lainer concludes that the nature of the individual, rather than the "process" by means of which that individual was conceived and gestated, is the critical factor in determining human personhood.

As the midrash implies, like Adam, each human being has evolved from the golemic to the human stage. However, not all Golems do so. In this regard, it should be noted that in modern Hebrew the term *Golem* means "cocoon" (Even-Shushan 1969, 1:179), and in medieval Hebrew it can mean "embryo" or even "sperm" (see, e.g., Idel 1990, 300; cf. Scholem 1965, 161). In at least one medieval Hebrew text, *Golem* denotes not simply a fertilized ovum, but an embryo with distinctly identifiable limbs (see the poem of the ninth-century Italian Jewish poet Amitai ben Shefatiyah in David 1975, 16). This observation has certain moral implications with regard both to abortion and to the employment of a variety of methods in reproductive biotechnology such as artificial insemination, in vitro fertilization, artificial embryonization, parthenogenesis, and cloning (see below, chap. 6).

In 1978, shortly after the birth of the first "test-tube baby," Judah Gershuni discussed the implication of in vitro fertilization from a halakhic perspective. Although most of his discussion focuses upon the question of the permissibility of masturbation on the part of the sperm donor, Gershuni—almost as an afterthought, briefly draws an analogy between the "test-tube baby" and the Golem, with specific reference to the responsum of Zevi Ashkenazi. The basis of this analogy is that the "test-tube baby," like the Golem, is not conceived in vivo (1978, 21). This observation asks one to consider how the various steps in this process—from conception to birth—are linked to halakhic and theological implications of the Golem. Furthermore, considering an "artificially" created embryo as having the status of a Golem can serve as a basis for the adjudication of cases relating to the status and to the disposition of such entities. One such example is the Tennessee case of *Davis v Davis* where the disposition of frozen embryos had to be decided as part of a property settlement in a divorce case.

In the initial trial, the judge framed the issue in terms of whether the embryos were human beings or property. Since the judge could not accept their designation as property, he ruled that the "children" are human beings (*Davis v Davis v King*, 1989). This decision provoked extensive discussion among bioethicists. One prominent American bioethicist maintained that the judge was incorrect in framing the issue in terms of whether embryos are "people or products." He recommends (as do others) placing embryos in a third category altogether. However, he does not define the status of beings in such a category (see Annas 1989, 20–22). In contrast, writing a number of years before the Davis case, a leading American authority on the legal implications of reproductive biotechnology maintained that in order legally to protect and to ensure the rights of individuals (i.e., sperm and egg "donors"), "extracorporeal body parts" must be considered as the property of the individuals who provide them (see Andrews 1986, 28–39; cf. *Del Zio v Manhattan's Columbia Presbyterian Medical Center*, 1978; see also Breitowitz 1997, 155–86).

From Ashkenazi's responsum, it is clear that destroying a Golem is not murder. Hence, destroying a frozen embryo, or aborting (even a viable) embryo conceived in vitro though gestated in vivo, would not be murder, as some suggest. These include advocates of a "pro-life" position who identify the attainment of human personhood with ensoulment at conception (see, e.g., *Catechism of the Catholic Church* 1994, paras. 2270–75, 547–49, paras. 2373–77, 571; cf. Feldman 1968, 268–71). Furthermore, according to some Jewish sources, while destruction of a human embryo may not be an act of murder for Jews (cf. Bleich 1977, 326–39), it may be considered an act of murder for non-Jews, that is, for Noahides (see, e.g., Feldman 1968, 254–62). The identification of the embryo with the Golem may be a way of circumventing the equation of destruction of an embryo with murder as far as non-Jews are concerned (cf. Bleich 1991, 93–97).

From this perspective, embryos that are the product of certain "artificial" procedures used in reproductive biotechnology could have the status of "Golem," and it would therefore be permissible to destroy them under certain circumstances (see below, chap. 6). Upon birth, however, the child would assume the status of a natural person, of a human being, with all legal protections afford to human beings (see, e.g., *M. Ohalot*, chap. 7, sec. 6; on the Golem and reproductive biotechnology see also Sherwin 1995a, 314–24).

Conclusion

At a time when Golems populate our daily lives, the challenge before us is not how to build bigger and better Golems but how to prevent ourselves from becoming Golems and from having our lives controlled or even harmed by the Golems we have created. Gustav Meyrink's novel, *The Golem*, warns of the danger of "humans to dwindle to soulless entities as soon as was extinguished some slight spark of an idea" (1964, 26). Meyrink and others offer a warning while they pose a challenge. The warning is that if we conceive of ourselves as golemic machines, then we become like machines — devoid of freedom, creativity, and spontaneity; we become soulless, mechanical entities. We regress from the status of human beings back to the golemic state; we choose thereby to evolve backwards. For these writers, and for others, the pressing problem is not so much whether Golems can be considered humans but how to prevent humans from becoming like Golems. The challenge they pose is the pressing need for human beings to intensify their quest to realize and to manifest those essentially human qualities that ultimately distinguishes us from the Golems we have created. In this view, the omnipresence of Golems in our daily lives offers us a challenge to become more intensely human, to accentuate those characteristics that make us peculiarly human and that can promise to liberate us from the protohuman golemic state to which we have a tendency to regress. The moral choice is whether to devolve back to the golemic or to evolve in the image of God.

In *The Golem*, Gustav Meyrink wrote (1964, 41): "The Golem? I've heard of it a lot. What do you know about the Golem . . . ? Always they treat it as a legend, till something happens and it turns into reality once more."

5

Parent-Child Relations

THE GREAT FIGURES of the Bible were great in many ways, but not as parents. For example, the first parents, Adam and Eve, raised two boys in the best of all possible environments, and we know what one did to the other. Abraham, the father of the three Western faiths, was a terrible father. He expelled one of his sons from his home, and he almost killed the other as a sacrifice to God. Moses is remembered for his greatness as a liberator, a prophet, a leader, and a lawgiver but not as an effective father. King David, the eventual father of the Messiah, had irreconcilable differences with his own son, Absalom. The parents of the Jewish people, biblical role models who are revered for so many things, were mostly failures as parents. Consequently, the lives of the great figures of Scripture provide little insight in how to parent well. However, such insights may be gleaned from the writings of the talmudic rabbis, and the medieval philosophers, moralists, mystics, and legalists.

Postbiblical Jewish religious literature is grounded in Hebrew Scripture. Because the relationship of children to their parents is discussed numerous times in Scripture, it can only be expected that this relationship would preoccupy postbiblical literature to a considerable degree. The relationship, particularly the legal duties, of parents toward their children is hardly discussed in Hebrew Scripture. Consequently, little discussion of this relationship is found in postbiblical Jewish literature. For example, the fifth commandment of the Ten Commandments relates to the obligations of children toward their parents, while none of the Ten Commandments deals with the relationship of parents toward their children. The greater attention paid in this chapter to child-parent relations than to parent-child relations reflects this imbalance in the classical sources.

It may be further noted that unlike other traditions, Jewish tradition recognized childhood and adolescence as distinct stages in human physical, social, and psychological development. In premodern Europe, for example, childhood was not recognized as a distinct stage in human development with its own unique traits. Rather, children were often understood simply as miniature adults. Consequently, children were usually expected to behave and to dress like little adults. In classical Jewish literature, however, children were supposed to behave, to play, and to dress like children. Unlike other premodern cultures, ancient and medieval Jewish culture keenly recognized adolescence as a transitionary period between childhood and adulthood (see, e.g., Kraemer 1989, 65–80).

In Jewish law, the status of the child was that of a "minor" (see, e.g., Lebinger 1915–16; B. Cohen 1966, 2:1–9). Not only was adolescence considered a distinct stage in human development, but the onset of puberty — especially among females, was recognized as a substage of adolescence (see, e.g., Bamberger 1961, 281–94). During the Middle Ages, the bar mitzvah developed as a standardized life-cycle ritual for recognizing the Jewish male's transition out of childhood status (see, e.g., Sherwin 1973, 53–65; 1990, 150–68). Not earlier than the nineteenth century a female counterpart to bar mitzvah, bat mitzvah, developed (see, e.g., *EJ*, 4:246). Relationships between parents and their children in Jewish tradition presumed that which other traditions failed to acknowledge; namely, that childhood and adolescence are particular and discrete stages in human physical, intellectual, psychological, and social development.

Why Honor Parents?

The fifth commandment of the Ten Commandments obliges a child to honor his or her parents. Of the Ten Commandments, a reason for observance is provided only here. No rationale is offered for the other nine commandments. No reason is given, for example, for why one should not murder or steal or covet. According to the text, one should honor one's parents "[so] that you may long endure on the land which the Lord your God is giving you" (Exod. 20:12, Deut. 5:16). In other words, longevity is the promised reward for observing this commandment, while a curtailed life is the threatened punishment for its violation (see *MRY*, sec. "*Yitro*," chap. 5, 232).

Some of the medieval Jewish biblical commentators took the promise of reward at face value. To the biblical assurance of longevity, they added the promises of prosperity and of spiritual rewards in the afterlife (see, e.g., Ben Asher 1892, 107a). Other commentators perceived the promise of reward either as being an inadequate motivation or as being too mercenary a basis for observance, so they offered alternative and supplementary reasons and motivations for why a child ought to honor his or her parents.

Unlike many of the other commandments of the Torah, honoring parents has not been an activity limited to Jews. It always has been widely practiced in many cultures, Eastern and Western. Such diverse figures as Plato and Confucius taught that a child should honor his or her parents. Because honoring parents was perceived as a universal human trait, Jewish thinkers like Judah Loew maintained that the inclination of a child to honor his or her parents is a feature of human nature, that it is natural for a child to honor his or her parents (see, e.g., *GA*, 5:36 on Deut. 5:16). In this view, the primary motivation for honoring one's parents is not the promise of reward or the fear of punishment. One honors one's parents because it is natural to do so. A hint that the talmudic rabbis also considered honoring parents a universal moral trait may be detected in rabbinic accounts of Gentiles, who went to extremes in honoring their parents, and in rabbinic texts that predicate a Gentile appreciation of Judaism upon the Jewish emphasis of filial responsibility (see, e.g., *Kid.*, 31a; *PR*, chap. 23/24, 122).

That Jews have no monopoly on the virtue of honoring parents is also found in a responsum by Benjamin Ze'ev ben Matityahu, who flourished in sixteenth-century Turkey. This responsum was written to answer the question of why a blessing accompanies the performance of virtually every commandment, while no blessing is prescribed with regard to honoring parents. His answer is that "one only recites a blessing when performing deeds that distinguish us from non-Jews, that is, in those deeds that non-Jews do not perform at all. However, with regard to those deeds that even non-Jews occasionally perform, we recite no blessing, because in performing them, we are not more holy than are they, since they observe them as do we. An example of this is honoring one's parents" (1539, no. 169; see Abramowitz 1971, 116).

In his commentary on the Bible (to Exod. 20:12), Abraham ibn Ezra expanded upon the notion that honoring parents is an innate human quality. According to Ibn Ezra, it is both natural and rational for an individual to express gratitude toward those who have been generous toward him or her. Foremost among those deserving of gratitude are one's parents. Honoring one's parents is therefore a natural and a rational reciprocation on the part of a child for the benefits he or she has received from his or her parents. Acts of generosity by the parent toward the child should evoke acts of honor and gratitude by the child toward the parent (Ibn Ezra on Exod. 20:12; see also Bekhor Shor 1956, 1:92 on Exod. 20:12; note Blidstein 1975, 8–19).

Ibn Ezra's view that roots filial duty in filial gratitude for parental generosity appears in numerous other sources. An example is the anonymously written thirteenth-century ethical-legal treatise, *Sefer ha-Hinukh,* traditionally ascribed to Aaron ha-Levi of Barcelona. Here we read:

> At the root of this commandment [to honor parents] is the notion that it is proper for an individual to acknowledge and to treat with loving-kindness another person who has treated him with goodness, and he should not be a scoundrel, an ingrate who turns a cold shoulder [to him] — for this is an evil quality, utterly vile before God and humankind. It is for a person to realize that his parents are the cause of his being in the world; hence, it is truly proper for him to give them every honor and every benefit that he can, since they brought him into the world and then labored through many troubles over him when he was young. (1978, no. 33, 180–83)

By attempting to discover a humanistic basis for the obligation to honor one's parents, Ibn Ezra and others tried to fortify and to justify on the basis of humanistic criteria that which was believed to have been conveyed through an act of divine revelation. By so doing, they attempted to root ethical behavior both in a human and in a divine source. They maintained that what has been granted by means of revelation may be further justified by means of human intellect and human intuition. This approach, however, was not universally accepted by Jewish scholars. Some felt that it is adequate to ground ethical behavior in revealed commandments, that the attempt to seek additional justifications or motivations for moral action is superfluous and potentially dangerous. From this perspective, rationality is too precarious a foundation upon which to predicate ethical action. That the only viable foundation for Jewish ethics in general, and for filial duty in particular, is divine revelation is asserted by Don Isaac Abravanel in his commentary on the Bible. Abravanel writes:

> God wanted to explain to you that it is improper to base these worthwhile virtues and qualities upon the human intellect. Rather they should be observed because it was commanded by God to follow them, so that one might cleave to God and achieve fulfillment and to goodness. Their observance cannot be justified from any other perspective, such as rational legal ethics . . . even though human reason establishes that a man will revere his parents from his youth, your motivation in revering your parents and in observing the commandments should be because I [God] commanded you regarding it. For this reason the text states: "I am the Lord your God" (Exod. 20:1), that is, that your motivation derives from God's commandment rather than from another motivation. (1964, 2:109–11 on Lev. 19:3)

Ibn Ezra assumes that that which is rational and natural is that which is moral. However, an alternate approach to ethics perceives the moral task to be the regulation and even the suppression of one's natural instincts, such as tendencies toward violence, promiscuity, excessive acquisitiveness, gluttony, and so forth. Some sources further observe that it is precisely because it is sometimes unnatural for an individual to want to care for his or her parents, especially if they are very elderly, ill, or senile, that makes a discrete requirement to honor and to care for one's parents necessary. In this view, if honoring and caring for parents were instinctual, then to command filial duty would be superfluous and unnecessary (see, e.g., Hafetz 1914, 148b on Deut. 5:16).

Just as there are those who deny the existence of a natural proclivity on the part of children to honor their parents, so there are those who reject the assumption that it is rational for children to honor their parents in reciprocity for parental generosity. The expectation for filial gratitude assumes that the recipient is grateful to his or her benefactor. However, when gratitude is absent, the rationale of gratitude as a basis for honoring parents collapses. For example, there are those like Jeremiah (20:14–18), Jonah (4:3, 8) and

Job (3:11–12) who perceived life itself as an imposed burden rather than as a gift. Even those who consider life to be good are not obliged to accept their existence as a product of parental generosity. Although many parents have children out of love, not all do so.

According to some medieval sources, if gratitude toward parents is relevant, it is because of the effort the parent expends in raising a child and not because of their having engendered the child. Conceiving the child might simply be the result of lust or personal pleasure, whereas efforts expended in nurturing and in teaching a child require constant care and deliberation. In this regard, the fourteenth-century scholar Israel ibn al-Nakawa wrote, "A person should honor his parents more for the moral instruction they gave him than for their having brought him into this world. For in bringing him into this world, their own pleasure was their motive" (1931, 4:18). A more extreme view than that of Ibn al-Nakawa is offered by Bahya ibn Pakuda. Bahya claims that parental generosity cannot be assumed, that a parent's care for his or her children may be only an extension of his or her own self-interest. Bahya wrote:

> It is clear that the parent's intention is to benefit himself through the child, for the child is part of the parent, who places great hopes in him. Remark how he gives preference to the child in food, drink, and clothing, how he guards him against all misfortunes and finds all the pain and trouble involved in safeguarding his peace a trifle, so strong is mercy and compassion toward his children impressed on a parent's nature. Nevertheless, both the Torah and reason oblige the children to obey, honor, and fear their parents. (1973, 177)

A final objection to the attempt to ground filial devotion primarily upon humanistic criteria is the view that the commandment to honor one's parents is not an end in itself but a means to higher ends. In this view, ethical behavior toward one's parents serves as a conduit to the worship of God, the divine parent; the ethical is a prolegomenon to the theological. Honoring one's parents is a first step toward the recognition that no human being is self-caused. Even the gratitude one might express toward one's parents is only preparation for expressing gratitude to God for one's existence (see, e.g., *Sefer ha-Hinukh* 1978, no. 33, 183).

The biblical text describes the Ten Commandments as having been written on two tablets of five commandments each. According to a subsequent tradition, the first five commandments, inscribed on the first tablet, deal with human obligations toward God, while the second set of five commandments treats interpersonal relations. It would then seem that the fifth commandment, which deals with honoring parents, that is, the last commandment on the first tablet, appears misplaced. In his commentary to the Ten Commandments (on Exod. 20:12–13), Nahmanides attempted to resolve this apparent difficulty by maintaining that, because honoring parents is a first step to honoring God, it properly belongs on the first tablet. In his view, giving honor to a human parent serves as a prelude to and as a preparation for honoring God, the ultimate parent.

The *Zohar* derives the honor of parents from the honor due God. Following the Talmud (*Nid.*, 31a; see also *Kid.*, 30b), the *Zohar* describes God as providing a person with his or her soul, while one's parents provide a person with his or her body. Because the soul is the most essential part of the person, God is considered the primary parent and, consequently, the parent first deserving reverence and respect (see, e.g., 1883, 1:49; 3:19b). The *Zohar* states, "As one must honor and revere God for the soul that he infused within us, so one must honor and revere one's parents for the body they provided, for one's parents are partners with God and they provide the body. As they are partners in the act of one's creation, so they should be partners in the receipt of reverence and of honor" (1883, 3:83a, sec. "*Raya Mehemna*").

By acknowledging God as the primary parent and as the ultimate source of one's existence, and by acknowledging one's own parents as the most direct source of one's own being, one is led to the inescapable conclusion that no one is the source of his or her own being. Filial duty derives from an awareness of that which transcends us, of that from which our very existence and our personal identity derive. This view maintains that one should honor one's parents because this commandment evokes the awareness that each of us is a creature of God, the Creator; a child of parents; a member of a family; and an heir to a tradition. Theologically, this means that honoring parents entails honoring the divine parent. Sociologically, this means that honoring parents indicates an awareness of one's membership in a family unit that both includes and transcends the self. Historically, this means that, by honoring one's parents, one thereby commits oneself to the perpetuation of the moral values of one's forebears and to the tradition that they have conveyed.

The sociopolitical implications of filial duty were discussed by Maimonides and Gersonides (Levi ben Gershon). According to Maimonides, the family unit is the foundation upon which society rests. In fact, Maimonides considered the "government of the household" to be a branch of political science. Following Plato (*Laws*, para. 790), Maimonides observed that, when the family structure is weak, society inevitably becomes destabilized (*GP,* bk. 3, chap. 41, 562).

Gersonides considered the family the basic political unit upon which larger political entities, such as cities and states, were based. When the parent-child relationship functions properly, the larger society can function better. When the family serves as a conduit for moral values, the larger society is strengthened, the society's future becomes more assured. In his commentary on the Torah, Gersonides wrote, "Through this [commandment of honoring one's parents] proper family government can be established. This represents the beginning of how proper state government is attained; a consensus among its citizens will occur, and the young will accept moral instruction from their elders" (1547, 1:80b–81a, on Exod. 20:12).

Besides stressing the political implications of honoring parents, the fourteenth-century Gersonides, like the fifteenth-century Albo and the sixteenth-century Abravanel, emphasized its meaning for history and tradition. For Gersonides, Albo, and Abravanel, the family functions as the conduit through which tradition is conveyed from ancestors to descendants, from the past to the future. In their view, the very existence of Judaism itself is vested in the willingness of children to accept and to convey the moral and the religious values of their forebears. Honoring parents is thereby a means to an end that transcends both the individual family and the individual self; namely, the perpetuation of Jewish life, thought, and tradition. According to Albo and Abravanel, observance of the commandment to honor one's parents profoundly affects the very continuity of Judaism as a living tradition (Albo 1930, 3:251–52; Abravanel 1964, 2:190–91 on Exod. 20:12).

How to Honor Parents

Scripture is not very forthcoming about *how* the obligation to honor parents ought to be performed. The fifth of the Ten Commandments requires a child to honor his or her parents, but it does not delineate the nature of honor, or the kinds of actions it might entail. Similarly, a verse in Leviticus (19:3) requires a child to "fear" or to "revere" his or her parent, but it does not inform us about the implications or requirements of this command. While Scripture demands specific attitudes, it does not adequately delineate the actions that are to articulate those attitudes. That task falls to postbiblical Jewish tradition (see Blidstein 1975, 37–60).

The tradition is reluctant to specify and to quantify filial obligation. It prefers to expect unlimited filial devotion rather than to legislate specific minimally required duties. Ideally, the honor and devotion due one's parents is "beyond measure" (*PT. Pe'ah*, chap. 1, sec. 1; *DR*, chap. 6, sec. 2; see also Eliezer of Metz 1837, no. 56, 49b). In this regard, the following talmudic story is typical: "Rabbi Tarfon had a mother. When she wished to mount into bed, he would bend down to let her ascend [by stepping on him, and when she wished to descend, she would do so by stepping on him]. He went to the academy and boasted of his observance of filial piety. [Whereupon] his colleagues said to him: You have not yet even reached half the honor [due her]" (*Kid.*, 31a). Similarly, in his discussion of the duties owed by a child to a parent, Maimonides observed that "the obligations a child owes his parents are too numerous to list, and a discussion of them would be overly long" (*CM, Kid.*, chap. 1, sec. 7, 197; see also *SM*, nos. 210–11, 166).

Despite the inclination of the talmudic and medieval sages to consider filial duty as having an infinite scope, those who translated sentiment into statute were obliged to focus upon clearly defined acts of obligation. Maimonides, who in his commentary to the Mishnah described filial obligations as being innumerable, nevertheless provided specific circumscribed duties in his legal code, the *Mishneh Torah*. By so doing, Maimonides and others gave notice that one who enacts all of the specifically required duties of filial obligation is deemed as having only partially satisfied an obligation of infinite demands (*MT—LR*, chap. 16, sec. 14).

The Bible requires that a child honor and revere his or her parent. The Talmud proceeds to describe what constitutes honor and reverence: "Our rabbis taught: What is 'reverence' and what is 'honor'? 'Reverence' means that one must neither stand in his [parent's] place nor sit in his place, nor contradict his words, nor tip the scales against him [in a scholarly dispute]. 'Honor' means that he [the child] must give him [the parent] food and drink, clothe and cover him, lead him in and out" (*Kid.*, 31b; see *PT. Kid.*, chap. 1, sec. 1; *Sifra* 1947, 87a, sec. "*Kedoshim*," beginning). Furthermore, these sources maintain that a child is obliged to honor and revere both parents equally and that the obligation to honor parents falls equally on a son and on a daughter (*Kid.*, 30b; *MRY*, sec. "*Yitro*," chap. 8, 233).

Underlying the specific duties imposed upon the child is the expectation not only of their performance but of their performance in a certain manner. Attitude as well as action is demanded. For example, the Talmud records a case of a person who was deemed reprehensible not because he failed to fulfill his obligations toward his father but because of the attitude that accompanied his actions: "A man once fed his father on pheasants [which were very expensive]. When his father asked him how he could afford them, he answered: What business is it of yours old man, grind [chew] and eat. . . . A man once fed his father fatted hens. Once the father asked: Son, where did you get these hens? The son answered: Old man, eat and be quiet; just as dogs eat and are quiet" (*PT. Kid.*, chap. 1, sec. 7; see also Rashi on *Kid.*, 31a-b).

Honor and reverence relate to attitudes as much as to deeds. The aim of the deed is to articulate the attitude. When the attitude is absent, the deed is crippled. Doing the right thing from the wrong motivation can be counterproductive. If honoring one's parents requires one to help ensure the parent's sense of dignity and of self-worth, if it aims at showing the parents that children are concerned with their well-being, then fulfilling the attitudinal requirement becomes as important as the deed.

For some of the sources, the attitudinal requirements incumbent upon the child must include love to be complete. According to Rashi (on *Kid.*, 32a), for example, love should be the motivation behind a child's desire to support his or her parent financially. The medieval mystical-ethical treatise *Sefer Hareidim* perceives love of parents to be a natural outgrowth of a child's gratitude for his or her parents' generosity toward him or her. This text refuses to endorse an attitude of quid pro quo. Instead, it insists that a child honor his or her parents by manifesting a "powerful love as they have loved him" (Azikiri 1987, chap. 9, nos. 36–38, 68–69). In this passage, *Sefer Hareidim* quotes the *Zohar* (1883, 3:281a–b): "one ought to do all for his parents and love them more than himself, and everything he possesses ought to be considered as nought in his zeal to do their will."

The Talmud and the medieval legal codes require a child to honor a parent throughout that parent's life and afterward as well. Specifically, the child is obliged to mourn his or her parents and to speak of them with honor and respect after they have died (*Kid.*, 31b; *SA — YD*, para. 240, sec. 9). Some sources depict the honor one can pay one's parents after death as being superior to that which can be rendered while they are still alive. These sources maintain that, as long as the parent is alive, there exists a possibility that filial duty may be practiced for less than noble motives, such as the child's desire to inherit the parent's estate; however, after death, honor and homage paid one's parents can flow only from sincere filial devotion and from an authentic desire to serve God (see, e.g., *Sem.*, chap. 9, sec. 19).

Having established a number of specific deeds required of a child regarding his or her parent, talmudic and medieval sources hasten to clarify further the implications of those obligations. For example, after establishing that a child must support his or her parents financially, the Talmud immediately asks whether the funds for support should be drawn from the assets of the parent or of the child. While the sources are unanimous in demanding that a child make a gift of self, of personal services, they are divided about whether a child should give of his or her substance as well. This division of view led to a number of possibilities (see Blidstein 1975, 60–75).

Some maintained that the commandment of honoring parents unequivocally entails the obligation of the child to support his or her parent financially. A number of advocates of this view placed this obligation even upon children who could not afford parental support (see, e.g., *PT. Kid.*, chap. 1, sec. 7). Others claimed that no such obligation exists, especially if the child is devoid of resources (see, e.g., *Kid.*, 32a; *SA — YD*, para. 240). Still others argued that, since "charity begins at home," the child is so obligated, especially if the child is prosperous and the parent is not prosperous (Ahai Gaon 1964, 3:164–65, no. 56; see also Isserles' gloss on *SA — YD*, para. 240, sec. 5). This view claims that a child who is *able* to help his or her parent must do so and indeed may be compelled by the court to do so, whereas a child who is financially unable to render financial support to his or her parent is not obliged to do so. In one version of this view, a child is obliged to donate to the parent at least an amount equal to that which he is obliged to give to charity, that is, a percentage of his wealth, usually between 10 and 20 percent. This approach takes into account both the need of the parent for support and the ability of the child to render that support. The child must give, but despite the child's resources, he is not compelled to give more than he can afford or more than he is obliged to give to the needy in general.

Just as a child is required to perform certain deeds for his or her parent, so is the child obliged to restrain from doing certain things to his or her parent. For example, a child is enjoined from injuring his or her parent either through deeds or through words. Biblical law even required the death penalty for wounding or cursing a parent (e.g., Exod. 21:15, Lev. 20:9; see Deut. 27:16). This punishment, though it appears not to have been enforced in the postbiblical era, is nevertheless reiterated by rabbinic and medieval literature (see, e.g., *San.*, 77a, 84b-85a; *SA — YD*, para. 241). The underlying principle here is that a child is obliged to take pains not to distress his or her parent either physically or emotionally. A child must try to provide his or her parents with happiness and with joy. "A wise man makes his father happy. A fool of a man humiliates his mother" (Prov. 15:20).

According to one commentator, a reason why one should not injure one's parents is because in so doing one injures oneself. Since one's parents are one's own "flesh and blood," since one's soul is "bound up" with that of one's parents, to cause injury to them is to cause injury to oneself. In this view, harming one's parents is a form of masochism (see, e.g., Hafetz 1914, 103a on Lev. 20:9).

The talmudic and medieval sources are keenly aware of the profound psychological strain that may be placed upon a child attempting to fulfill his or her filial responsibilities. Caring for one's parents, for example, may stretch the limits of a child's psychological endurance, especially if the parent becomes senile. In such a case, the child is not freed from filial duty. However, the child is encouraged to arrange for the professional care of the parent (*MT — LR*, chap. 6, sec. 10; *SA — YD*, para. 240, sec. 10). In addition, the behavior of an overbearing parent might psychologically inhibit the child from rendering honor and reverence and might actually encourage the child to reject filial piety altogether. Consequently, the parent is enjoined from becoming too demanding. As the essential issue is the child's moral and religious development and not the imposition of parental authority, a parent may forgo honor due, especially when it contributes to the child's personal development. Maimonides set down the law as follows: "Although children are commanded to go to the above mentioned lengths [in honoring parents], the father is forbidden to impose too heavy a yoke upon them, to be too exacting with them in matters pertaining to his honor, lest he cause them to stumble. He should forgive them and shut his eyes, for a father can forgo the honor due him" (*MT — LR*, chap. 6, sec. 8; see also *Kid.*, 32a).

The *Sefer Hasidim* cautions parents not to be so overbearing as to "enrage the child so that he has no option but to rebel against them" (*SH* 1960, 153, 372, paras. 152, 565). This text also observes that, since even the most attentive child is unable to fulfill the obligations of filial piety completely, the parents would be well advised to relinquish the honor due them, even if the child is not informed that such honor has been waived. The aim of allowing the parent to "waive honor" is to prevent parental inflexibility from engendering the moral degeneration of the child. But, while the parent is encouraged to be flexible when dealing with the child, the parent is simultaneously discouraged from thereby inviting the child's physical or psychological abuse (see Blidstein 1975, 126–27, 155–56).

When to Honor Parents

There are occasions when filial responsibility may temporarily be put aside in the name of a higher duty or for the purpose of fulfilling a more immediate obligation. One such occasion is when filial duty conflicts with the responsibility one owes to one's own wife and children. In this regard, the Talmud quotes a popular contemporary proverb, "A parent's love is for his child; his child's love is for his own children" (*Sota*, 49a).

While marriage does not free an individual from filial duty, it does serve to supplant filial love with the love of a spouse. In his commentary on Genesis (2:24), Nahmanides wrote,

[Scripture] states that the female is the bone of the bone and the flesh of the flesh of the male. . . . His desire is for her to be with him always, as it was implanted in human nature, beginning with Adam for all subsequent generations, for males to cleave to their wives, to leave their parents, and to see themselves as one flesh with their wives. . . . Here [we see that] a man leaves the nearness of his parents and his relatives, and sees that his wife is closer to him than are they.

In certain cases not only could the love of parents be superseded by love for a spouse but the obligation of filial duty could be displaced as well. For example, though men and women are equally obligated to honor their parents, the Talmud makes provision for an exception in instances in which filial duty causes tension in the marriage (*Kid.*, 30b, *MT — HK*, chap. 13, secs. 12–14). In an interesting responsum, the thirteenth-century Spanish scholar Solomon ibn Adret (Rashba) deals with the case of a woman who lives with her husband and her in-laws. There is constant tension between the woman and her mother-in-law, which, in turn, creates marital strife between the woman and her husband. Ibn Adret is asked to give a ruling about whether the woman has a right to demand that she and her husband leave the domicile of her in-laws. He responded, "A woman can certainly tell her husband, 'I refuse to live with people who pain me,' for if her husband may not pain her, she certainly need not live among others who pain her and occasion quarrels between herself and her husband" (1883, 25b, no. 168; see Blidstein 1975, 83–98, 100–109). It is to be hoped that marriage can create a new family without causing tensions with one's parents. However, if the formation of the new family does precipitate conflict, one may limit, but not deny, one's filial responsibilities.

Who Are One's Parents?

In the biblical texts requiring a person to honor and revere his or her parents, it is not clear whether "parents" refers only to an individual's biological parents or to others as well. The postbiblical sources address the issue of who may be included in the category of "parent."

The respect shown by Moses to Jethro, his father-in-law, and the honor shown by David to Saul, his father-in-law, served as the biblical basis for the later requirement of extending filial respect to one's in-laws (see *MRY,* sec. "*Yitro,*" chap. 1, 190; *MP,* chap. 7, sec. 4, 33a; *SA — YD,* para. 240, sec. 24). According to the *Sefer Hareidim,* "The reason why a person must honor one's in-laws is because a husband and a wife are considered as one person, and the parents of one are considered the parents of the other" (Azikiri 1987, chap. 12, 76). Nevertheless, as discussed, a number of authorities restrict the honor due both parents and in-laws when it causes marital tensions between husband and wife.

The honor due parents was also extended to stepparents and even to an older brother (*Ket.*, 103). If a younger brother was distinguished as a scholar, honor was extended to him as well (see *SA — YD*, para. 240, secs. 22–23). A number of sources state that "one's grandchildren are as one's children" and that a parent loves grandchildren more than children (e.g., *Yeb.*, 62b; cf. *BB*, 143b). Nevertheless there is a surprising reluctance to extend the honor due parents to grandparents. In fact, some authorities (e.g., Maimonides) ignore the question, while others reject the existence of an obligation to honor grandparents as one honors parents (see, e.g., *Sota*, 49a). Some maintain that filial responsibility does indeed extend to grandparents, but they say that one should be cautious and not express greater honor toward one's grandparents than toward one's parents (see, e.g., *GR*, chap. 94, sec. 5; Isserles' gloss to *SA — YD*, para. 240, sec. 24; Azikiri 1987, chap. 12, 75–76; note Ibn Asevelli 1959, no. 134 translated and explained in Jacobs 1968, 187–91).

Jewish Parenting

There are few biblical verses that relate to the obligation of a parent toward a child. The Talmud, however, provides the following list of parental obligations: "A father is obliged to circumcise his son, to redeem him [if he is a firstborn; see Num. 18:15], to teach him Torah, to have him wed, and to teach him a craft. Some say, to teach him to swim too. Rabbi Judah said: He who does not teach his son a craft . . . is as though he taught him to steal" (*Kid.*, 29a; see variant readings in *PT.* Kid., chap. 1, sec. 7; *NR*, chap. 17, sec. 1; see also Blidstein 1975, 122–36). According to a variant reading of this text, a father is also obliged to teach his son practical citizenship (*yishuv medinah*) (*MRY*, sec. "*Bo,*" chap. 18, 73).

The parent's obligation to circumcise a son, to redeem him, and to teach him Torah relates to the parent's duty to ensure the perpetuation of tradition and to have the son initiated into the Jewish community. In so doing, the son's history mates with his destiny.

Teaching the child the Torah aims not only at helping to continue tradition, it attempts to produce an intellectually, morally, and spiritually developed person. The parent's obligation to have a child wed, to teach him a craft, and to train him in "practical citizenship" relates to the parent's duty to permit the child to become an independent citizen of society. A crucial step toward a child's independence is his or her becoming independent from the parent. Marriage is considered an important step in a person's independence from his or her parent. With marriage, a new person, a new family, a new sociopolitical unit is established. By obliging a parent to see that his or her child is married, the Talmud prods the parent to recognize and to guarantee the independence of the child.

For a child to be independent, the child must be economically self-sustaining. Teaching a child a way to earn a living is deemed part of a child's moral instruction. As Rabbi Judah candidly observed, "He who does not teach his son a craft may be regarded . . . as if he is teaching him to steal" (*Kid.*, 29a). On this statement Rashi commented, "Because the child has been taught no trade, he will be bereft of sustenance, and will then steal from others." The parent must provide a means to help ensure a child's independent fiscal survival. A parent must also guide a child toward independent physical survival. It is for this reason that one Talmudic opinion requires a parent to teach a child how to swim. "What is the reason [why a parent should teach his child how to swim]?" the Talmud asks. "[Because] his life may depend on it," the text answers (*Kid*, 30b). Finally, the parent is obliged to teach the child "practical citizenship," so that the child may function as an upright and productive member of society. The role of the parent as teacher encompasses not only the intellectual and the religious spheres of existence but also the social and the political dimensions.

The talmudic insistence that a parent is obliged to convey to the child a way of life as well as a way of earning a living may underlie the talmudic view regarding parental obligations to support their children financially. Perhaps because children were apprenticed to a master craftsman or were betrothed early in life, the Talmud — astonishing though it may sound today — had few requirements regarding the obligations of a parent to support a child financially. Financial support was more a social expectation than a legal requirement. Apparently, the central parental duty is deemed by Jewish tradition pedagogic and not financial. The obligation of parents to support their children financially is nowhere explicitly stated in the Bible. That the Talmud records a debate on the question of whether a parent is obliged to provide monetary support demonstrates that "child support" was far from assumed by ancient Jewish law.

Talmudic law and subsequent codes of Jewish law assume no legal obligation upon a mother to support her children, even if she is financially capable of providing such support (see, e.g., Judah Ashkenazi's gloss to *SA — EH*, para. 73, sec. 1). According to one talmudic opinion, neither is a father legally bound to support his own children financially. Though this opinion is ultimately rejected, that it is considered demonstrates a hesitancy on the part of the talmudic rabbis to demand that a father support his children financially.

The final view that emerges from the talmudic debate about whether a father is obliged to support his children financially is that such an obligation exists — but only until the child reaches the age of six! (*Ket.*, 49–50). Maimonides further observed that the obligation of paternal child support must only be consonant with the child's needs and not with the father's wealth. Thus, even if the father is wealthy, his obligation extends only toward meeting the minimal needs of his children. He is under no obligation to support his children at a level corresponding to his resources. From the age of six until the age of puberty, the father's obligation is more moral than legal. He can be socially embarrassed into supporting his children as "charity cases," but he cannot be otherwise compelled by the courts to support them (see also, *SA — EH*, para. 71, sec. 1).

Although Karo finds no legal basis for compelling a father to support his children after the age of six, Karo does posit a legal obligation upon a father who is unable to teach his own son after the age of six, to engage and to pay a suitable teacher (*SA — YD*, para. 245, sec. 4). This requirement demonstrates the centrality of one's child's education within the parental endeavor, according to classical Jewish law and literature. It is presumed that the father will support the child financially during the tenure of the child's schooling.

The Parent as Pedagogue

The course of study that the parent is to teach the child is a course in the art of living as an individual in a society. The goals are to guide the child from ignorance to wisdom, from moral neutrality to virtue, from dependence to independence, from infancy to maturity. The parent must prepare the child to function as a self-sufficient adult in an interdependent society. In the Torah itself, teaching the child the words of the Torah is described as the central parental activity. The passage in Deuteronomy that entered the liturgy as part of the *Shema* requires parents to teach the words of the Torah diligently and constantly to their children (Deut. 6:4–9, 11:13–21). Through Torah study, the parent transmits to his or her child that which has been transmitted to him or her: a tradition, a history, a way of mastering the art of living, an anchor, an identity. Maimonides interpreted the biblical statement — "And you shall teach them to your children" (Deut. 11:19) — as having established a legal requirement upon a father to teach Torah to his children (*MT — TT,* chap. 1, sec. 1; see also *Kid.,* 29a; *SA — YD,* para. 245, sec. 1; Blidstein 1975, 137–57).

Throughout biblical, rabbinic, and apocryphal literature, the duty of a parent to direct his or her child's moral development is stated. For example, the statement in Proverbs (1:8), "My son, heed the instruction (*musar*) of your father; forsake not the teaching (*torat*) of your mother," was later interpreted as a clear obligation of a parent to offer, and of a child to accept, moral guidance. The apocryphal Book of Tobit clearly records a father's moral teachings to his son: "My boy, beware of any immorality," Tobit tells his son (Tob. 4:12). A father is expected to "guide his sons and his daughters in a straight path," counsels the Talmud (*Yeb.,* 62b). Elsewhere, the Talmud warns that "a father should be careful to draw his son away from falsehood" (*Suk.,* 46b).

According to Proverbs (1:8), a child exhibits wisdom when he or she gives joy to a parent by accepting that parent's moral instruction. By practicing the values conveyed by parents, the child thereby honors his or her parents. By internalizing the values of parents, the child guarantees that something of his or her parents will be perpetuated after their deaths, that the traditions conveyed to the child by the parents will survive (*Shab.,* 127a). The quality of "parenting" is demonstrated through the activities of one's child.

A person is obliged to honor a parent even if the parent acts foolishly (e.g., if the parent throws a purse of money into the sea) and even if the parent humiliates the child in public (*Kid.,* 32a; *MT — LR,* chap. 6, sec. 7). However, if the parent is "wicked," if the parent rejects the very moral and religious principles that he or she is supposed to convey to the child, there is a question of whether the child is bound to honor such a parent. On this issue the sources are divided.

According to one view, the obligation upon a child is unrelated to the nature of a parent. As Maimonides stated, "Even if one's parent is an evil person, a habitual transgressor, it is the duty of the child to honor and to revere the parent" (*MT — LR*, chap. 6, sec. 7; see also *SA — YD*, para. 240, sec. 18, para. 241, sec. 4). An alternate view relates that as long as one's parent is "wicked," one is not obliged to honor or to revere that parent. However, if a parent repents of his or her faults, the obligation is immediately reinstated (see e.g., Isserles' gloss to *SA — YD*, para. 240, sec. 18). A comparatively extreme position on this problem is taken by the twelfth-century rabbi Eliezer of Metz, who wrote, "If one's parent is wicked, even by failing to observe a single commandment written in the Torah, one is free from honoring or from revering such a parent" (1837, no. 56, 49b).

Israel ibn al-Nakawa echoed the view of Eliezer of Metz. According to Ibn al-Nakawa, the honor and the reverence of a child for a parent depends upon how well that parent teaches the child, especially in terms of the personal example set. In this view, the obligation upon the child is indeed related to the nature and to the behavior of the parent. It is here, in medieval Jewish ethical literature, that the obligations of the parent to instruct the child in morals become most explicit. As Ibn al-Nakawa wrote, "As the parent is obliged to teach the child ethics, to set the child on the right path, to guide the child in the performance of the commandments and of virtuous deeds, so is the child obliged to heed the parent, to accept the parent's words, and to obey the parent's commands, even regarding secular matters" (1931, 4:18).

According to Ibn al-Nakawa, the focal point of the parent-child relationship is the intellectual, moral, and spiritual development of the child. The parent who guides and who nurtures this development is worthy of honor and of reverence. The parent who neglects or who frustrates this development becomes unworthy of attention, honor, or reverence. He continued, "If the parent is a sinner, and his intention is to mislead the child and to prevent his child from doing the will of the Creator — for example, if the parent teaches the child to rob or to steal or to murder, or something similar, or even to transgress a single religious precept — then the child is obliged to reject the commands of his parent, to rebel against the parent's dicta and to refuse [to obey] the parent's words" (1931, 4:18).

This text points to a number of fundamental concepts related to Jewish views of the nature of parenting and to the duties of a parent toward a child. First and foremost is the claim that pedagogy is the essence of parenting. The primary task of the parent is to teach the child. The primary duty of the child is to learn. Second is the claim that both parent and child are bound by certain identical obligations to God, to tradition, to morality, to law, and to society. The task of the parent is to make the child aware of these obligations through instruction as well as through personal example. As the parent who fails in his or her own moral or religious obligations thereby denies the basis upon which the obligation to honor parents rests, he or she thereby forfeits the right to demand filial devotion on the part of his or her children. If the parent rejects the commandments, the parent cannot then reasonably expect the child to obey the commandments in general, or the commandment to honor parents in particular.

Underlying Ibn al-Nakawa's position are two assumptions. The first is that the obligation of a child toward a parent is contingent upon whether the parent fulfills the central parental obligation toward the child: moral and religious instruction. The second is that filial duty is not an absolute duty. It is subordinate to the duty to the divine, incumbent both upon the child and upon the parent. When there is a clash between one's duties to one's parent and one's obligations to God, the obligation to fulfill the divine will take precedent. For example, a midrash states, "You shall each revere his father and mother, and keep My Sabbaths: I the Lord am your God (Lev. 19:3). . . . One might think that one is obliged to obey one's parents even if they asked one to transgress a commandment of the Torah. Therefore, Scripture says 'and keep My Sabbaths,' i.e., all of you [parents and children] are obliged to honor Me" (*Sifra* 1947, sec. "*Kedoshim*," 87a; see also *Yeb.*, 5b).

The child is obliged to ignore the parent when the parent asks the child to transgress God's commandments; the child is also obliged to set aside the honor of the parent if another commandment must be performed. After the child has performed the competing obligation, the child must attend to the parent (*Kid.*, 32a; *MT—LR*, chap. 6, sec. 13). However, when it is the commandment of studying the Torah that competes with the obligation to honor one's parents, study takes precedence (*Meg.,* 16b; *SA — YD,* paras. 240, sec. 13; 242, sec. 1).

From a psychological perspective, a number of sources indicate that the parent who neglects the moral instruction of the child will eventually resent his or her own child if the child who is devoid of moral instruction becomes a scoundrel. Similarly, the child deprived of parental guidance will inevitably come to resent the parent for the parent's neglect of his or her moral and intellectual development. According to Rashi (on Prov. 13:25), such a child may — with justification — be unable to honor or to revere a parent who has failed to convey moral instruction either pedagogically or by personal example. It thus emerges that proper parental pedagogy is in the best interests of the child, is a fundamental parental obligation, and is also in the self-interest of the parent and in the best interest of a mutually beneficial parent-child relationship.

Part of the art of parenting is knowing when to be tender and when to be firm, when to be insistent and when to be flexible. It was precisely for this reason that the talmudic and medieval sources offered parents the option of "*mehilah,*" (forgoing their honor and their parental authority) (see Blidstein 1975, 126–27, 155–56). Since the essential issue in honoring parents and in rearing children is the moral and spiritual development of the child and not the imposition of parental authority over the child, the parent is cautioned not to spark the child's rebellion by being overbearing or unnecessarily authoritarian.

On the one hand, parental inflexibility must not be permitted to become a catalyst for the moral degeneration of the child. A further concern is that an oppressively dictatorial parent might cause such anguish in the child that the child will become unduly distraught, even to the point of committing suicide (Hahn 1928, 279). On the other hand, the parent is warned not to become so flexible as to induce moral anarchy from the child. While the parent is occasionally encouraged to temper authority over the child, the parent is also cautioned against inviting the child's physical or psychological abuse. The parent is encouraged to find a middle ground — determined by the particular disposition of the child — between being apathetic and being unduly domineering in his or her relationship with the child.

The goal of parental instruction is the development of the child within the framework of a moral and religious tradition. The child thereby becomes a link between the past and the future. Nevertheless, the child's moral instruction is also crucial to the child's ability to function as an informed moral agent in society. As Gersonides observed, when the parent-child relationship functions properly, when the family serves as a conduit for moral values, society as a whole is enriched and improved. In this view, the moral instruction conveyed by parents to their children has implications not only for the individual child, not only for the perpetuation of tradition, but also for the stability of the society of which he or she is a part.

6

Cloning and Reproductive
Biotechnology

PLATO DESCRIBED the human body as a "living tomb," as a
prison (*Phaedrus*, 250). Jewish sources compare the body to the
Temple (see, e.g., Ben Asher 1892, sec. *"zenut,"* 80). As God's presence (*Shekhinah*) resides in the Temple, the soul dwells in the human body, animating it. When God's presence withdraws from the
Temple, the Temple becomes a hollow shell, a ruin. Similarly, when
the soul exits the body, the body is ruined.

To compare the body to the Temple assumes a prior vision of
the Temple. At the center of the Temple was the Holy of Holies.
There the cherubs were located. What were the cherubs doing
there? "Rabbi Kattina said: Whenever Israel came up to [the Temple for] the festival, the curtain would be removed for them [i.e., for
the people] and the cherubs were shown to them. Their [i.e., the
cherubs'] bodies were intertwined with one another and they were
thus addressed — Look! You are beloved before God as the love
between man and woman" (*Yoma*, 54a). On this text, Rashi commented, "They [i.e., the cherubs] cleaved to one another, holding
and embracing each other as the male embraces the female." The
Holy of Holies is thus depicted as a bedroom where the cherubs
engage in the procreative act. Where does God dwell? Between the
cherubs (see, e.g., Numb. 7:89). (On the relationship between the
function of the Temple and procreation, see, e.g., *NR*, chap. 11, sec.
3; *Tan.*, sec. *"Naso,"* 2:17a).

Referring to this talmudic text, the medieval Hebrew treatise,

110

The Holy Letter (*Iggeret ha-Kodesh*) states: "If you comprehend the mystery of the cherubim, you will understand what the sages meant in saying that when a man cleaves to his wife in holiness, the divine presence is manifested. In the mystery of man and woman, there is God" (1976, 51).[1]

The Talmud not only portrays God as "a partner in the work of creation" (*Shab.*, 10a), but also as a partner in the work of procreation (see, e.g., *Nid.*, 31a). As such, God is considered to be both the ultimate parent of humankind as well as the spiritual parent of each child. The human parents provide the child with his or her body through a sexual act. This act, according to the cabalists, stimulates an intercourse between the male (*Tiferet*) and female (*Shekhinah*) divine potencies (*sefirot*) to engender the soul of that child. Engaging in procreation enhances the divine image, while refusing to engage in procreation diminishes the divine image (see, e.g., Tishbi 1961, 2:615).

The ancient and medieval rabbis extended the biblical commandment to honor parents to include the honoring of God qua parent (see above, chap. 5). As was discussed above, others not involved in the conception of the child, such as parents-in-law, teachers, stepparents, and even older siblings, also have been placed under the scope of the commandment to honor one's parents.

Though the question of how far to expand the parameters of the obligation to honor parents has been discussed throughout the centuries, the identity of who are a child's legal parents required little clarification. Parents were those individuals who conceived a child through an act of sexual intercourse. The mother gestated the child

---

1. As Jewish tradition posits both positive and negative attitudes toward the human body (see notes above to chap. 2), it also posits both positive and negative attitudes to human sexuality. For positive attitudes, see, for example, Feldman 1968, 81–105 and sources noted there. (For a variety of attitudes, see, e.g., Idel 1989, 197–225). For negative attitudes, see, for example, Maimonides *GP,* bk. 2, chap. 36, 371 and bk. 3, 533, where Maimonides stated, "One of the intentions of the Torah is purity and sanctification. I mean by this renouncing and avoiding sexual intercourse and causing it to be as infrequent as possible. Consequently, he [i.e., Moses] states clearly that sanctity consists of renouncing sexual intercourse." Also see, for example, the views of Abulafia, "Intercourse is a matter of disgust and one ought to be ashamed of the act" (quoted from a manuscript of *Ozar Eden Ganuz* in Idel 1988b, 204). For antisexual views in Hasidism, see, for example, Elimelekh of Lizensk 1787, sec. "*Bereshit*"; on Nahman of Bratslav, see Green 1979; on Mendel of Kotsk, see Heschel 1973, 216–225.)

in her womb and subsequently birthed the child. The father and mother then raised the child.

New Conceptions

In our times, because of the proliferation of alternative types of family structures, and because of developments in reproductive bio-technology, the issue of parental identity is sometimes not clear-cut. For example, the question of maternal identity in the following case is unambiguous: A woman has sexual intercourse with a man. Conception takes place as a result. The women successfully carries the fetus through pregnancy. She gives birth to the child. Subsequently, she raises the child. In the following case, however, maternal identity is not so obvious: An ovum is donated by a certain woman. The ovum is fertilized in vitro by the sperm of an anonymous donor who is someone other than the ovum donor's husband. The fertilized ovum is then implanted in the uterus of a second woman for four months (i.e., second trimester). Complications develop, and it is then implanted in a third woman who births the child. However, because the fetus carries certain genetic defects, the defective gene is removed and a new gene is inserted from a gene donor. This takes place through the application of genetic splicing to human gametes (thus making the gene donor a prospective "parent" as well).[2] Subsequently, the child is raised by a fourth woman and her husband.

Unlike American law, Jewish law does not recognize adoption

---

2. In gene therapy, specific genes are altered, subtracted, or added to remove predispositions to certain diseases (e.g., hemophilia, Tay-Sachs) or to enhance genetic traits. On the propriety of gene therapy in Jewish law, see, for example, Rosenfeld 1972. Genetic engineering already has brought considerable therapeutic benefits. For example, methods of injecting human insulin into bacteria have led to the mass production of almost unlimited amounts of human insulin whereas previously limited amounts of insulin were available only from the pancreases of dead animals. This has made insulin more readily and cheaply available to millions of diabetics. The infusion of certain human genes into milk-producing animals now allows them to produce milk with easily extractable substances that can treat a myriad of human diseases. Otherwise rare and valuable medicines are being produced through genetic engineering to treat diseases like hepatitis, kidney cancer, whooping cough, and various diseases of the blood. Coupled with present and future techniques in cloning, many other diseases promise to be treated or even cured (see, for example, Kaku 1997, 222–29; Silver 1997, 227–33).

as establishing legal parenthood. In Jewish law an adopted child becomes the responsibility of a "guardian," while the child remains the child of his or her legal parents, with relevant inheritance claims on their estate, remaining obliged to honor them according to the requirements of the biblical commandment, and retaining their name (X son or daughter of Y) (see, e.g., Schachter 1982; Broyde 1988). Consequently, the adoptive parents could never be considered the child's legal parents according to Jewish law, even if they raise the child from birth. They are rather considered by Jewish law to be the agents of the legal parents.

In the past, the genetic mother, the birthing mother, and the "social" mother (i.e., the maternal parent who raised the child) was usually the same individual. Currently, however, a single child may have a multitude of different individual "parents," for example: a genetic father (for instance, through donor insemination), a genetic mother (through ovum donation), a birthing mother (for instance, a "surrogate" mother), a "social" father and a "social" mother (who raise the child) (see, e.g., Silver 1997, 133–37). According to Jewish law, a number of these might qualify as being considered the child's legal parents, and the child might be obliged for various reasons to fulfill the biblical commandment to honor parents with regard to these "parents."[3]

The employment of various methods of reproductive biotechnology raises a plethora of questions not only about parental identity, but also about the identity of the child. For instance, Jewish identity derives from the maternal parent according to Jewish law. If the birthing mother as well as the genetic mother have claims upon maternity, then is the child of a non-Jewish ovum donor (i.e., the genetic mother) and a Jewish birthing mother, a Jew? Is the child of a Jewish ovum donor and a non-Jewish birthing mother, a Jew?

There is a vast and rapidly expanding literature on the legal,

---

3. The complex issue of parental identity in Jewish law has been treated in a number of articles. With regard to maternal identity, discussion focuses around the questions of whether maternal identity derives from the genetic mother or the birthing mother. This is especially poignant with regard to the Jewish identity of the child when either "mother" is not Jewish. Some halakhic authorities have suggested that a child can have more than one "mother," for example, the genetic mother (the ovum donor) and the birthing mother (see, e.g., Bleich 1997, 53–58). Here, too, the Jewish identity of the child would come into question if one of them is not Jewish (see,e.g., Bleich 1997, 58–61, 67–68).

ethical and psychological implications of the use of various techniques of reproductive biotechnology, of which the issue of defining
the identity of both the parents and the child is but one area of
concern.[4]

The use of various methods of reproductive biotechnology has
progressively distanced the conception of a child from heterosexual
intercourse. For example, donor insemination aims at bringing
about conception through the instrumental deposit of semen into
the female genital tract without an act of sexual intercourse. Unlike
artificial insemination, in vitro fertilization distances conception further from intercourse, by having conception occur outside of the
body altogether. Whereas in artificial insemination, the child's birthing mother is also the child's genetic mother, in ovum donation the
child's birthing mother is usually not also the child's genetic mother.
Furthermore, with developments in cryonics, it is now possible to
preserve sperm, eggs, and fertilized embryos indefinitely (see, e.g.,
Silver 1997, 78–88). It is therefore possible, for instance, to have
embryos later born as children whose fertilization occurred generations before the birth of their birthing mother. Hence, these techniques in reproductive biotechnology not only distance conception
and birth from sexual intercourse, thereby obscuring the clarity of
parental definition, but they also disrupt the assumptions of chro-
nology between the conception of parents and their children. It is
now possible, for instance, for a child to have genetic parents sepa-

4. Since, in Jewish law, religious identity follows the identity of the mother,
the issue of maternal identity is more crucial than that of paternal identity. Yet,
paternal identity is also an issue. For example, is donor insemination adultery,
which would mean that the child is a *mamzer* (illegitimate) according to Jewish
law? Some halakhic authorities — most noteworthy, Moshe Feinstein — argued that
donor insemination is not adultery because no act of coitus occurs. Others reject
this view. According to Jewish law, a child fathered by a Gentile has no legally
recognized father; donor insemination by non-Jews is often preferred as it would
obviate a potential for incest (i.e., that the child might marry a relative of its Jewish father). This approach obviates the issue of paternal identity by maintaining
according to Jewish law that the child has no legally recognized father. According
to Eliezer Waldenberg, a child born through in vitro has neither a father nor a
mother, according to Jewish law (see Bleich 1997, 47). To be noted here also is the
question of parental identity in the speculative but not impossible cases of a human
child gestated in and delivered from an animal womb, and that of a child gestated
from conception to birth within an artificial incubator. On parental identity, see, for
example, Bleich 1981, 359–60; Rosenfeld 1997, 36–45; Bick 1997; Oz 1995, and
the definitive article by Broyde (1988).

rated by many generations, for instance, in the case of an ovum from a long-deceased woman fertilized by a currently young man, and birthed by another older woman.

Cloning

To this point, all forms of conception referred to require both male and female genetic material derived from a sperm and an ovum. However, parthenogenesis and cloning further distance conception from sexual intercourse by eliminating the need for sperm in the creation of the embryo.[5] Indeed, in cloning one cannot accurately speak of conception or fertilization of the ovum since none occurs. Since there is no conception, the argument that destroying an embryo brought into being by cloning is murder because ensoulment occurs at the time of conception, becomes a moot point (see, e.g., Silver 1997, 37–40, 43–44. On conception in Jewish law, see, e.g., Feldman 1968, 133–43; Reichman 1997).

In the current state of cloning technology, genetic material is taken from the cell of an individual. The cell's nucleus, containing its genetic material, is then introduced into the nucleus of an ovum whose own nucleic genetic material had been previously destroyed. The new cell now contains a full set of the genetic material of the person from whom the nucleic genetic material had been taken. Unlike other methods of reproductive biotechnology, for example, in vitro, a child resulting from this procedure would be genetically identical to the donor of the genetic material. In other methods (ex-

5. In parthenogenesis an ovum develops into an embryo, usually by electronic stimulation. The resulting child is always female and her heredity comes entirely from her mother. A "virgin birth" could then occur. It is unknown, but speculated that such births have occurred. Here, there is gestation of an embryo without the presence of sperm. The male is eliminated from the reproductive process. It may be noted that Rashi, quoting a midrash, already discusses parthenogenesis in animals. Regarding Jacob's sheep, Rashi observes that Jacob utilized prenatal influences upon his sheep to ensure certain genetic traits. As the midrash puts it, "The water became seed inside them, so that they had no need of a male" (see Rashi to Gen. 30:37, *GR*, chap. 73, sec. 10). Physicist Kaku writes that "parthenogenesis . . . could become the dominant mode of human reproduction" (1997, 254). On parthenogenesis in Jewish tradition, see, e.g., Rosenfeld 1997, 68. Rosenfeld maintains that parthenogenesis would obviate the halakhic problems related to donor insemination by eliminating it as being unnecessary. A child born through parthenogenesis, unlike a clone, would not be genetically identical to its mother.

cept parthenogenesis), each parent provides half of the child's chromosomes, whereas in cloning the donor of the genetic material provides all the chromosomes. What is not yet known is whether genetic materials in the "white" of the egg, that is, the part of the ovum other than the nucleus, would affect the genetic disposition of a child born through cloning techniques. This element, the mitochondrial DNA found in the cytoplasm of the ovum, creates proteins needed to function, and interprets genetic information flowing from the nucleus and responds to it by building up all the structures that make up the cell. Certain diseases might be passed down to a child through mitochondrial DNA. Furthermore, because of the mitochondrial DNA, it might be that the clone is actually not completely genetically identical to the donor of the nucleic genetic material.

In cloning, the issue of parental identity differs from other methods of reproductive biotechnology. For example, since the child would be genetically identical to the donor of the nucleic materials, the donor would genetically be the child's identical twin. Therefore, the genetic parent would not be the donor, but the parents of the donor. If, however, one considers the donor of the nucleic materials to be the legal parent, would the donor be the father or the mother? If one considers the birthing mother as the maternal parent (notwithstanding the fact that the ovum donor contributed mitochondrial DNA to the process), could we then consider the donor of nucleic materials to be the paternal parent by analogizing the donation of nucleic materials to a sperm donor? If so, what if the donor of nucleic material were a woman? Could a woman then be considered a father? In other words, are we bound to gender-specific definitions when defining paternal and maternal parenting roles either in the "conception" or in the raising of a child (see, e.g., Broyde 1997, 40–41)? To complicate the matter of parental identity further, what if men carried embryos through gestation and consequently gave birth to them? Would a man then be a mother? Suggested by the 1995 film *Junior*, this is not beyond the realm of possibility (see, e.g., Silver 1997, 191–96).

As is already apparent, the use of new methods of reproductive biotechnology raises many seemingly unprecedented questions that at present may be posed, but that are not easily resolved. However, perhaps less complicated than questions related to the ethical implications of the use of various methods of reproductive biotechnology, such as parental identity, are questions about the propriety of the use of such methods, for example: artificial insemination, in vitro fertilization ("test tube babies"), ovum donation, GIFT (gamete intrafallopian transfer), ZIFT (zygote intrafallopian transfer), ICSI (Intra-Cytoplasmic Sperm Injection), use of surrogate mothers, and more.[6] Furthermore, though most of these techniques were originally devised and utilized to treat infertile married couples, they are currently also being employed to engender children for single parents, homosexual "marriages," and for women who are past the usual age of childbearing, thereby raising new public policy issues on the nature of family structure and parenthood.

As with regard to a myriad of other issues in reproductive biotechnology, the propriety of cloning according to Jewish ethics and law may be examined by determining whether cloning is legally required (*hovah*), forbidden (*assur*), or permitted (*reshut*).

The vast majority of religious ethicists, the current public policy of the U.S. government, and the majority of American citizens oppose the cloning of human beings.[7] Indeed, the first week after the story of the cloning of the sheep "Dolly" was announced in 1997, 90

---

6. On in vitro, see, for example, Bleich 1978, 86–90. On surrogate mothers, see, for example, Bleich 1998. On artificial insemination, see Jakobovits 1959, 244–50; Rosner 1970. There is estimated to be over one million children alive today who were born through donor insemination (see, e.g., Silver 1997, 155). On various forms of reproductive biotechnology and on issues of parental identity in Jewish law, see, for example, Dorff 1996, Feldman and Wolowelsky 1997. Dorff advocates the maternal identity of the birthing mother (1996, 46; see also Bleich 1997, 49–50); and Rosner (1991, 101–93). Already in 1972 Rosenfeld discussed this issue. Referring to a number of responsa published by Rabbi Yosef Schwartz of Banyad, Hungary, on the question of the maternal identity of a child born to a woman who received a transplant of another woman's sexual organs (i.e., ovaries), he ruled that the birthing mother rather than the genetic mother (i.e., the donor of the ovaries)is to be considered the mother (see Rosenfeld 1972, 75–78).

7. A flurry of discussion about the propriety of cloning took place in the 1970s. After a long hiatus, a flood of discussion and public policy debate occurred after the 1997 cloning of a sheep in Scotland named "Dolly." Furthermore, novels about cloning human beings such as the frightening *The Boys from Brazil*, later made into a film (Levin 1976) and the more optimistic 1973 novel *Joshua Son of None*, about the fictional cloning of President Kennedy, helped to shape popular attitudes about cloning (Freedman 1973). Also, Woody Allen's 1973 movie *Sleeper* satirized cloning. Further, David Rorvik's 1978 *In His Image: The Cloning of a Man* claimed that a human being already had been cloned under private auspices (on Rorvik's book and reaction to it, see, e.g., Kolata 1998, 93–119).

percent of Americans polled stated that the cloning of human beings should be banned. Two out of three Americans considered the cloning of animals to be morally unacceptable, while 56 percent said they would not eat meat from cloned animals (see, e.g., Silver 1997, 92). Translated into Jewish legal parlance, there seems to be a broad American consensus that the cloning of human beings ought to be forbidden (*assur*). But, do Jewish law and ethics affirm this view?

Many religious ethicists oppose cloning on the grounds that it is "playing God." However, as we have already seen, the Talmud and later authorities sanction the human creation of life, including human life; albeit, with certain caveats and restrictions, particularly ethical ones. Such activity is not understood to be a usurpation of a divine prerogative by Jewish religious literature, but as an expression of human creativity in the image of God (see chap. 4).

Many religious ethicists, particularly Catholics, have prohibited human cloning on the grounds that it is unnatural, and therefore immoral. However, just as cloning may be imitative of divine creativity, so may it be considered to be imitative of nature. Since cloning occurs in nature, as in the case of identical twins, cloning cannot be considered unnatural. Furthermore, unlike other forms of bioengineering that have the potential of bringing new, potentially harmful and dangerous organisms into existence, cloning only duplicates already existent and known natural entities. The unforeseen, dangerous implications of various other forms of bioengineering do not seem present in the application of cloning techniques. Even scientists who oppose the cloning of human beings on moral grounds are compelled to admit that cloning is a natural phenomenon, and that biologically, each of us began life as a clone (just as according to midrashic sources noted above in chap. 4, each of us began life as a Golem; see, e.g., Hudock 1973, 549–56; Idel 1990, 34–38).[8]

8. In May 1971, James Watson, one of the scientists who discovered DNA, published an article in *Atlantic Monthly* in strong opposition to cloning human beings. This was followed in March 1972 by a provocative article on cloning in *The New York Times Magazine* by Willard Gaylin. These popular articles stimulated public debate on the issue, though the actual cloning of a human being seemed decades away. However, already in the 1970s, ethicists voiced their strong opposition to the cloning of human beings, foremost among them: Paul Ramsey (1970, 60–103); Leon Kass (1972; 1985, 64–79); Hans Jonas (1974, 155–67). Few then advocated

In ancient and medieval times, witchcraft and sorcery were prohibited as being scripturally forbidden, and were considered to be
demonic activities outside of the order of nature. For example, legend tells that Albertus Magnus created an anthropoid who acted as
his servant. St. Thomas Aquinas denounced and destroyed the anthropoid as the work of the Devil. Yet, Jewish religious literature,
as we have seen, did not consider such creative activities to be
either unnatural or demonic, but expressions of *imitatio Dei* (see
chap. 4).

In reflecting upon Rabbi Hanina's and Rabbi Oshaia's weekly
creation of a calf, and presumably also on Rava's creation of a
"man," the Talmud specifically excludes such activities from the categories of sorcery and witchcraft, deeming such activities "entirely
permitted" (*San.*, 67b). Discussing this text, the medieval talmudic
commentator Menahem Meiri wrote that since "all natural actions
cannot be considered witchcraft, even the knowledge to create new
beautiful creatures that are not engendered through sexual reproduction, as is noted in books about natural science, cannot be proscribed" (1965, 248). Cloning, which is an example of asexual
reproduction, seems to have been anticipated by this observation.

Judah Loew considered creativity to be the crucial component
of human nature by means of which the human being can transcend
nature by manifesting an attribute humans share with God. For
Loew, in augmenting God's original creation, human creativity becomes a natural way of transcending nature, and of allowing nature
to expand beyond its original limitations. In Loew's words:

> Human creativity transcends nature. When God created the laws
> of nature in the six days of creation, the simple and the complex,

cloning of human beings, most noteworthy, the biologist Joshua Lederberg and the
theologian Joseph Fletcher (1974, 71–116, 154–60; Lederberg's foreword, vi–xii).
For a detailed description of the development of cloning and the public policy
debate surrounding it, see, for example, Kolata 1998. On Ramsey and Kass's 1967
reaction to Lederberg's advocacy of cloning humans, see Kolata 1998, 90. After the
cloning of "Dolly," President Clinton publicly announced that he found cloning of
humans "morally reprehensible" (see Kolata 1998, 229). Subsequently, Clinton pro-
posed a legislative ban on human cloning (see, e.g., Fiore 1997, 32). At Clinton's
directive, the National Bioethics Advisory Commission issued a report on cloning
that advocated a three to five year ban on human cloning. This ban did not include
human embryos or animals, nor did it state that cloning of human beings is morally
wrong (see, e.g., Kolata 1997, 18).

and finished creating the world, there remained additional power to create anew, just like people create new animal species through inter-species breeding. . . . Human beings bring to fruition things that were not previously found in nature; nonetheless, since these are activities that occur through nature, it is as if it entered the world to be created (*BG,* chap. 2, 38)

According to Loew, such forms of human creativity are imitative of nature, and cannot therefore be considered outside of the natural order, and hence, unnatural (*BG,* chap. 2, 27–28; see also President's Commission 1982, 31–32). In this view, activities such as cloning are not instances of "playing God," but rather are ways in which human beings fulfill the divine mandate to imitate God, to serve as God's "partners in the work of creation" (*Shab.,* 10a). From this perspective, human beings are not only part of nature, but they can be agents for creating nature as well.

The unprecedented nature of human beings cloning other human beings cannot be considered presumptively forbidden by Jewish law. Indeed, a principle of Jewish jurisprudence set down by Solomon ibn Adret, would establish an initial presumption in favor of cloning. In a responsum, Ibn Adret states clearly that "whatever has not been specifically forbidden is presumed to be permitted" (1883, no. 364).

It has often been observed that the introduction of new medical techniques, especially in bioengineering, transplant surgery, and reproductive biotechnology, are often popularly opposed at the outset, only to become accepted as normal medical procedures later on. When, for example, donor insemination, heart transplants, and in vitro fertilization were initially introduced, they were denounced as immoral by many religious ethicists and rejected as offensive to public morality. Currently, these are standard and widely used medical procedures. In vitro, for instance, is routinely practiced in U.S. fertility clinics, free from state regulations that govern many other forms of medical treatment (see Silver 1997, 77; Andrews 1999, 31–49, 207–47). The first reported in vitro fertilization occurred in England in 1978. By the end of 1994, the total number of children born as a result of this method was estimated at 150,000. By 2005, there could be more than 500,000 such children born *annually* in the United States alone if such services expand at their current rate (see Silver 1997, 69).

Already in 1966, physicians Kleegman and Kaufman wrote, "Any change in custom or practice in this emotionally charged area [of assisted reproduction] has always elicited a response from established custom and law of horrified negation at first; then negation without horror; then slow and gradual curiosity, study, evaluation, and finally a very slow steady acceptance" (quoted in Silver 1997, 75).

People who intuitively tend initially to oppose new developments in biotechnology often tend to change their minds when confronted with the possible benefits of the use of such techniques to themselves and their loved ones. For example, parents with children with debilitating genetic diseases, spouses of patients with irreversible spinal injuries, children of parents with various forms of cancer, married couples with certain types of infertility or sterility, often change their attitudes regarding the use of fetal tissue from cloned embryos when they become aware of the possible therapeutic or curative potentialities of such procedures. For instance, a Princeton professor asked a class whether they would approve of the use of genetic engineering on their children for any reason. More than 90 percent said, "no." But, when confronted with the hypothetical scenario in which genetic engineering might be used to provide absolute protection against AIDS, half changed their minds (see Silver 1997, 96).

Jewish law and ethics would not consider the cloning of human beings to be forbidden. As Elliot Dorff has put it, "human cloning should be regulated, not banned" (1997, 6; 1999, 322). Indeed, whereas most non-Jewish religious ethicists have consistently opposed the ethical propriety of cloning human beings, Jewish ethicists, particularly those from the more traditional camps, have consistently maintained that there is no a priori prohibition in Jewish law against cloning humans, and that with certain controls, cloning of human beings is permissible according to Jewish law (see, e.g., Broyde 1997; Dorff 1997; Rosenfeld 1977; Sherwin 1997, and others cited in these articles).

While the cloning of human beings does not appear to be prohibited by Jewish law, neither is it obligatory (*hovah*) in most cases. Even an individual who would have no other way of engendering a child but through cloning is not obliged to do so. Like any other commandment, the commandment to "be fruitful and multiply" (Gen. 1:28) (obligatory according to Jewish law only upon men), can only be expected to be fulfilled if one has the normal capacity to do so. A person is not obliged to fulfill a commandment that exceeds his or her biological abilities. As J. D. Bleich has written summarizing Jewish law's attitude toward the use of reproductive biotechnological methods: "Although Halakhah may demand employment of extraordinary and heroic measures in prolonging life, with regard to the generation of life it requires only that which is ordinary, normal and natural. However, so long as the methods employed in assisted procreation do not entail transgression of halakhic structures such methods are discretionary and permissible" (1998, 147).

Certain types of cloning might be considered both obligatory and desirable. For example, saving a human life (*pikuah nefesh*) is obligatory, and bioengineering, including certain forms of cloning, has produced lifesaving pharmaceutical substances. Developments in cloning have and will continue to produce lifesaving and life-extending opportunities. Though not all of these developments relate to the obligation of saving human life, many of those that do not—for example, those related to agriculture and animal husbandry, relate to another biblical commandment, that is, "guarding one's self" (*shmor et nafshotekha*) (Deut. 4:9), which ancient and medieval Jewish commentators read as an obligation to preserve, sustain, and improve human health. For example, cloning plants has replicated species (some "designed" through genetic engineering) that resist certain types of blight and disease that otherwise might make such plants unavailable (causing hunger) or dangerous for human or animal consumption. Use of cloned bioengineered cows can produce healthier meat and milk. Cloned bio-organisms massively reproduced through genetic engineering provide pharmaceuticals that can cheaply and effectively treat diseases such as diabetes, various infectious diseases, and other diseases such as Parkinson's, cystic fibrosis, hemophilia, and so forth. Cloning of animals, especially primates such as monkeys, promises to accelerate scientific research in finding cures for a wide variety of diseases that afflict human beings, including heart disease and cancer. Thus, in certain circumstances, where there is an opportunity to fulfill certain religious commandments, such as saving life and preserving health, the cloning of plants and animals can be considered both desirable and obligatory.

The cloning of human embryos also holds forth great promise

for the treatment of many diseases and physical afflictions. Since cells, organs, and limbs of a cloned embryo would have the identical genetic structure as that of the nucleic DNA donor, the use of such fetal materials to treat the medical problems of such donors would not be subject to the problem of "rejection" as when such materials are derived from other organ donors. Cloned "organ-differentiated" embryonic cells might be used to generate new organs such as hearts or livers for lifesaving organ transplants. When scientists figure out how embryonic cells differentiate into particular tissues, for example, heart or liver tissue, they will be able to force a cloned embryo to generate that particular tissue. That tissue, for example, bone marrow, spinal tissue, heart tissue, would then be transplanted into the donor body, potentially bringing about a regenerative cure for a host of degenerative diseases without the possibility of rejection. For example, spinal regeneration for spines irreparably damaged as the result of traumatic accidents could permit paralyzed and immobile people to move and to walk again. Use of cloned fetal tissue also holds forth curative promise for stroke victims.

Combined with gene therapy, cloning may be utilized to "set back" the "time clock" of differentiated tissue to then regenerate as a specific type of tissue, and be used to treat and even to cure a wide variety of diseases. Because of the promise that the use of fetal tissue from cloned embryos holds forth for treating and even curing diseases and physical afflictions, even many of those who virulently oppose the cloning of human beings find themselves in favor of the use of fetal tissue from cloned embryos that could help them or their loved ones. (On the use of fetal tissue, see, e.g., Bleich 1989, 69–96.)

Objections to the cloning of embryos, to treat organic disease, physical disabilities, or infertility, raises similar questions as does abortion with regard to the status of embryos. Cloned embryos can either be allowed to be delivered at term or they may be destroyed, preferably in early stages of development. Those who consider the destruction of embryos to be a form of homicide strongly oppose the cloning of human embryos. For some, the destruction of embryos after a certain stage of gestation is ethically problematic, whether this stage is limited to forty days after formation (see, e.g., *Yeb.*, 69b), or to "quickening," or to viability outside the womb. However, for those who consider an embryo before birth not to be a legal person but a limb of its mother (*Git.*, 23b), the cloning of human embryos would be less problematic. Nonetheless, without a clear therapeutic purpose for cloning embryos, even advocates of cloning embryos would be hard pressed to justify its implementation. Once born, however, the cloned human embryo, like any other born human being, would be completely protected by the law as he or she would have the full legal status of a human person.

As was stated above (chap. 4), an embryo brought into being through "artificial" means such as a clone might qualify for the status of "Golem" (cf. Broyde 1997, 45–48). While biologically indistinguishable from an embryo conceived through heterosexual intercourse, a cloned embryo, precisely because of the manner in which it came to be, could be considered a "Golem," especially since no act of conception takes place (see, e.g., Bleich 1997, 72–73; Bick 1997, 93; see also Breitowitz 1997). As we have seen in the preceding discussion of Zvi Ashkenazi's responsum about the question of whether to include a Golem in a quorum for prayer, there is no presumption of homicide or feticide with regard to the destruction of an entity while in the golemic state (see chap. 4). At most, as in the case of abortion, such an action would be a tort rather than a crime. As in cases of abortion, even if the embryo is considered a potential legal person, its sacrifice to preserve an already existing human life would be justifiable according to Jewish law (see *M. Ohalot*, chap. 7, sec. 6).[9]

From the preceding discussion, it emerges that cloning of hu-

9. There has been a tendency in recent decades by halakhic authorities to view the destruction of embryos either through abortion or other means as feticide, "akin to homicide," or even as homicide. This view is remarkably close to that of Pope John Paul II and various Catholic bioethicists. John Paul II consistently links abortion to the modern "culture of death" that he sees epitomized by the Holocaust (see, e.g., Bernstein and Politi 1996, 518). Recent similar condemnations of abortion in Orthodox Jewish circles may similarly have been formulated as a response to the Holocaust and as a reaction to the strong "pro-choice" advocacy by secular Jewish organizations and by Jewish feminists in the United States. Nonetheless, there is no precedent in classical Jewish literature for equating abortion with murder. In Jewish law, abortion has always been considered a tort rather than a crime, and certainly not as murder. For this reason, traditional halakhic decisors have historically taken a rather lenient view on abortion, though there is a vast literature regarding Jewish views of abortion on the specific issue of the diversion of contemporary halakhists from the comparatively "liberal" views of their predecessors (see Sinclair 1980).

man beings is neither forbidden nor can it be considered obligatory. Rather, it remains in the category of that which is permitted (*reshut*) under certain circumstances. As Moshe Tendler has put it, reflecting on the talmudic metaphor of the honey and the sting of a bee: Are we really prepared to ban cloning, that is, to give up the bee's honey, because we are so afraid of its sting (see Kolata 1998, 18)?

A potential ethical problem with regard to cloning human beings would be a case in which genetic material is taken from an individual against his or her will and is subsequently used to produce a clone of that individual. However, the problem here does not substantially differ from the unauthorized use of extracorporeal body parts, for example, the use of a patient's hospital-administered blood tests for unauthorized experimental use; or, the unauthorized use in treating infertility of donor sperm or a donor ovum.

More important with regard to human cloning is the question of the identity of the clone. As was stated, the clone, once born, would have full human status with all the protections of law and morality afforded to other human beings. While the clone would have the same genetic composition as that of the donor of the genetic nucleic material, the clone would be a unique and discrete human person with his or her own personal history and experiences. Born into a different historical environment and shaped by different experiences than the nucleic donor, the clone would live a very different life from that of the donor. Fears such as those generated by novels like *The Boys from Brazil*, that cloning Hitler would inevitably produce a "new" Hitler, are unfounded. As physicist Michio Kaku has written, "Cloning Hitler may do no more than produce a second-rate artist. Similarly, cloning an Einstein does not guarantee that a great physicist will be born, since Einstein lived in a time when physics was in deep crisis. . . . Great individuals are probably as much the product of great turmoil and opportunity as the product of favorable genes" (1997, 254).

A clone would be a "product" not only of his or her genetic inheritance, but also of his or her times, specific influences, upbringing, and experiences. These would necessarily differ from those of the nucleic donor. Furthermore, to assume that a clone would be a photostat of the nucleic donor would be to affirm a form of genetic determinism, claiming that genes determine everything about a person's future, including moral character. Such a position is in opposition to the fundamental Jewish presupposition of moral volition and free will. If, as the Talmud presumes, even God cannot determine an individual's moral character, then how can we assume that genes can do more (see, e.g., *Nid.*, 16b; *MT—HT*, chap. 5, secs. 3, 4)?

7

Zedakah as Social Welfare

RABBINIC LEGEND RECOUNTS that with Abraham's discernment that there is one God who created the world, Judaism begins. The talmudic rabbis asked: How did Abraham make this discovery? Their answer is in the form of a parable: "Abraham may be compared to a man who was traveling from place to place when suddenly he saw a palace aflame. 'Is it possible that there is no master who cares for this palace?' the man wondered. Then the master of the palace appeared and said, 'I am the master of this palace.'" (*GR*, chap. 39, sec. 1, see especially commentaries of David Luria and Zev Einhorn, who translate the Hebrew term *doleket* as "aflame" rather than "illuminated").

One interpretation of this parable is that Abraham is every person. The palace is the world. From the existence of the palace, we can infer that the palace has a master. That master is God. Though the world is aflame with conflict, God remains the master of the world. Other interpretations amplify the meaning of the parable. The world is aflame. God's Presence in the world — called *Shekhinah* by the talmudic rabbis and the Jewish mystics, is trapped in the palace. What is the task of the person who sees the palace on fire? What is our task in the world? To enter the flaming palace, to save the master of the palace, to prevent the palace from being destroyed, and to labor to restore it. A crucial aspect of the human mission, according to the Jewish mystics, is the maintenance and repair of God's world (see, e.g., Idel 1988a, 170–72).

That the world is aflame with strife has been a perennial observation of Jewish tradition, beginning with the Scriptures. The words of Job (9:24) echo throughout Jewish history and tradition: "The earth is given unto the hands of the wicked." It is a premise of Jewish theology, confirmed by the experience of the Jewish people in history, that ours is an unredeemed world. Shortly after the Holocaust, Martin Buber wrote, "we [Jews] demonstrate with the bloody body of our people the unredeemedness of the world" (quoted in Simon 1948, 26).

Ethics in a Premessianic World

According to a rabbinic tradition, the revelation at Sinai was supposed to initiate the redemption of the world. But, as Moses received the Torah at Sinai, the people built the Golden Calf, and God's plan for redemption was thereby frustrated. Moses saw the people worshipping the idol and he smashed the tablets.

The tablets Moses carried as he descended the mountain are described by Scripture as having been written with "the finger of God" (Exod. 31:18). According to a rabbinic tradition, the entire Torah was written on that first set of tablets (see, e.g., Heschel 1965, 2:348–50). After he smashed the first set of tablets, Moses wrote a second set. We read (Exod. 34:4): "Moses carved two stone tablets, like the first." On this verse, a midrash comments: "God said to Moses: It was I who wrote the first tablets, as it says — written with the finger of God. But now *you* write the second tablets and I will assist you" (*Exod. R.,* chap. 47, sec. 2). The medieval commentators asked: Why was the first set of tablets written by God while the second set was written by Moses? Are the two sets different? Why did Moses break the first set? The following is one line of interpretation offered to answer these questions.

The first set of tablets was written by God. It was completely spiritual. It represented a perfect Torah for a perfect and redeemed world. It represented the essential Torah — the Torah as it really is; the Torah whose abode is in heaven, the spiritual realm. In this view, Moses did not break the tablets out of anger, but he broke them from his awareness, after seeing the people worshipping the Golden Calf, that the world remained corrupt and unredeemed. God realized that the perfect Torah, the spiritual Torah, the Torah written by "the hand of God" for a redeemed world, had no place in an unredeemed world. God, therefore, revised the divine plan for the world — the Torah, to allow it to speak to an imperfect world.

The form of the Torah that we have in this world, does not address a redeemed world, but the unredeemed world in which we live. The form the Torah now takes is adjusted to the realities of our world. The "second" set of tablets written by Moses deals with violence, war, murder, crime, deception, and sin, which are features of human experience in our world. Gershom Scholem summarized this cabalistic teaching as follows:

> The first tablets contained a revelation in keeping with the original state of man (before Adam sinned). . . . This was the truly spiritual Torah, bestowed upon a world in which Revelation and Redemption coincided, in which everything was holy and there was no need to hold the powers . . . [of evil] in check. . . . But the utopian moment soon vanished. When the first tablets were broken, 'the letters engraved on them flew away,' that is, the purely spiritual element receded. . . . On the second tablets the Torah appears in a historical garment. . . . A hard shell is placed around the spiritual Torah, indispensable in a world governed by the powers of evil. (1965, 69–70)

The Jewish mystics taught that the Torah is in exile in our world, alienated from its completely spiritual nature (see, e.g., Heschel 1955, 270–71). Indeed, for the Jewish mystics, everything in our world is in a state of exile, of alienation. This includes not only the Torah and the human condition, but also the *Shekhinah* — God's Presence in the world. For the Jewish mystics, the moral quest, the path toward redemption, begins with the realization of the unredeemed state of the world. It begins with the awareness that human history is a divine disappointment, that God's hopes for a redeemed world have been sabotaged by undesirable human deeds. The moral quest begins with the awareness that existence in history means existence in exile, that the world is yet to be redeemed.

Though God's Presence (*Shekhinah*) in our world is in exile, God both transcends the world and is present in the world. From God's transcendent attributes, divine grace flows into the world. God's grace can move the world, its inhabitants and the *Shekhinah* closer to redemption. For the Jewish mystics, the necessary catalyst for stimulating the flow of transcendent divine grace is the human performance of sacred and moral deeds. In this regard, commenting on the verse in Psalms (121:5), "The Lord is your shadow," Levi

Yitzhak of Berditchev said, "Just as a person's shadow does whatever a person does, so does God, as it were, do whatever a person does. Consequently, a person should perform sacred and good deeds such as showing compassion to those in need, so that God will likewise bestow goodness upon God's creatures" (1996, sec. "*Naso*," 70b; see also Idel 1988a, 173–81).

This idea, central to Jewish mysticism, is that human deeds not only influence God, but they also influence God's relationship to us. There is a flow upward of our activities that affects the divine realm (i.e., the *sefirot*). However, there is also a perpetual downward flow of divine blessing and grace from God to the world. When the flow upward is characterized by human acts of virtue, it affects the downward flow in a good and positive way. But, when the flow upward of human deeds is characterized by sinful and undesirable acts, it affects the downward flow in a negative way. In this view, the nature and quality of divine grace is, in a very direct way, related to the spiritual and moral quality of human deeds.

Though unredeemed, the world is yet redeemable. There is a partnership between God and human beings with its foundations in a divine-human covenant. God and human beings are interdependent. Both divine grace and human deeds are necessary in order to achieve the goal God and humans both desire — the redemption of the world.

Our actions affect the divine and God requires our assistance to help realize the divine purpose for the world. The theological boldness of this idea is already expressed by the talmudic rabbis. Commenting on the verse in Isaiah (43:12) "You are My witnesses says God," a second-century rabbi said, "When you are My witnesses, I am God. But, when you are not My witnesses, it is as if I am not God" (*Sifre on Deut.* 1939, sec. 346, 403–4). Commenting on the verse in Psalms "To God we give strength" (60:14), a rabbinic text says, "When the people of Israel perform God's will, they add strength to God. But, when they do not perform God's will, they — as it were, weaken the great power of God" (*PRK*, chap. 26, 166b).

Though human beings can work to make the world worthy of redemption, they cannot redeem the world; only God can. A verse in Isaiah (5:16) states that "The Lord of Hosts is exalted through justice." A midrash interprets this to mean that God is exalted through our doing justice, that moral deeds are prerequisites for divinely initiated redemption. The text reads, "Because you exalt me through justice, I will act with righteousness and cause My holiness to dwell among you. And if you practice justice and righteousness, I will redeem you with a complete redemption" (*DR*, chap. 5, sec. 7). As Abraham Heschel wrote, "In messianic times evil will be conquered by God who is one, but in historical times, evils must be conquered one by one" (1955, 377).

Whereas for Christianity messianic redemption is a fact, for Judaism it is a hope. Christianity assumes that the Messiah has come; Judaism assumes that the Messianic Age is yet to dawn. For Christian ethics, the Kingdom of Heaven has been inaugurated with the advent of the Messiah in the person of Jesus Christ. For Jewish ethics, the Kingdom of Heaven is yet to be realized. Consequently, Christian ethics tends to view the world in "messianic" terms while Jewish ethics tends to view the world in "messy" terms. For example, when discussing economic justice, many contemporary Christian ethicists call for the imminent realization of full employment and an end to poverty. Jewish ethicists perceive this view as a messianic hope rather than a realistic confrontation with the problems presently besetting us in our "messy" world. An example of the messianic approach characteristic of a great deal of Christian ethics is the "U.S. Catholic Bishops' Pastoral Letter on the Economy" ("Economic Justice for All" 1986; see also Strain 1989). In that document, the eradication of poverty and the attainment of full employment are considered realizable goals, rather than desirable hopes. Nowhere does this document quote the biblical assumption that "there will never cease to be needy ones in your land" (Deut. 15:11) (see, e.g., Sherwin 1989, 81–93).

With regard to social welfare, Jewish ethics assumes that there are infinite needs but finite resources that can be used to address those needs. Jewish ethics considers poverty and hardship to be perennial features of life in a premessianic world. Consequently, Jewish ethics insists that though the social and economic needs of the disadvantaged must be addressed and that they must be assuaged, it would nonetheless be unrealistic to assume that they could be completely eliminated. Consequently, Jewish ethical teachings regarding social and economic welfare relate more to treating the dis-ease of the individual in need rather than trying to completely cure the economic or social afflictions of society as a whole.

Jewish social welfare is individual-centered, "client" centered. Jewish ethics deals with the problems of the individual poor, rather

than with trying to solve the problem of poverty. Jewish ethics focuses on the individual in need and upon the specific needs of that
individual rather than being overly preoccupied with remedying all
the ills of society at large. Trying to solve the problem of poverty as
a whole may lead to evasion of the present needs of the poor. Trying
to bring about the messianic world in premessianic times inevitably
leads to frustration, which in turn can lead to despair and inaction.
Millennial thinking cannot effectively address current social situations.

From what has been said, one may suggest that the often-evoked
term "Judeo-Christian ethics" is a misnomer. There is Jewish
ethics, and, there is Christian ethics. There is no Judeo-Christian
ethics (see, e.g., A. Cohen 1971). The theological assumptions and
categories, the native language of moral discourse, and the textual
resources and methodologies that characterize Jewish and Christian
ethics differ so substantially that to perpetuate the claim that a
Judeo-Christian ethics exists would be a misunderstanding of both
Judaism and of Christianity. Furthermore, the often made claim
that there is a confluence of Jewish and Christian ethics because
both traditions affirm the sanctity and the moral authority of the
Hebrew Scriptures does not hold up under analysis. While the text
may be the same for both traditions, interpretations of the text differ radically. Because how the text is taken to mean so often differs,
it cannot functionally be considered the same text, especially in
terms of its application to ethical issues. Judaism and Christianity
are characterized by how each tradition has interpreted scriptural
texts that it considers sacred and significant. Judaism is not the
Hebrew Scriptures, but rather how subsequent Jewish tradition
has taken them to mean, and what Jewish tradition has taken
Scripture to mean is not usually what Christian tradition has taken
these same texts to mean. Hence, Judaism and Christianity differ
theologically, hermeneutically, and ethically. Jewish and Christian
ethics are not the same.

One of the many ethical issues that can be utilized as a means of
demonstrating some of the vital differences between Jewish ethics
and Christian ethics is aid to the indigent (see, e.g., Urbach 1951,
18–27). Christian ethics considers helping those in need as acts of
"charity" and "philanthropy." Both terms derive from etymological
roots in Latin and Greek that refer to love (*caritas*), specifically to
the love of other people (*philanthropia*). In this view, we should help
those in need because of our love for them. But, the poor, the indi-

gent, the insane, and the critically ill do not usually evoke our benevolence, our love, unless we are those rare saints that populate
the world from time to time. Help for the needy based upon love is
too unreliable to help ensure their welfare, their aid. Consequently,
Jewish ethics bases help for the needy upon social obligation,
rather than upon spontaneous love. Although such spontaneity may
be desirable, in the final analysis it is undependable. The needs of
the indigent are too constant and numerous, and their conditions
often too precarious to rely upon the spontaneous altruism of the
potential donor. For Jewish ethics, *zedakah* rather than "charity" is
required. *Zedakah* is etymologically related to the Hebrew word for
"righteousness," "*zedek.*" In this view, one regularly helps the needy
because it is right. *Zedakah* is a regular and continuous social obligation, and not the result of a passing passion (see, e.g., *OZ*, 303).[1]

Biblical Roots

Biblical law could not leave the care of the needy to impulsive,
though altruistic giving, to "charity" or "philanthropy." Nor could it
leave too general or too vague the admonition to "open your hand
to the poor and the needy" (Deut. 15:14). Beginning with biblical
law, abstract categories of justice and righteousness were translated
into specific legal requirements for providing financial assistance to
those in economic need.

The biblical laws of *zedakah* assume and address an agricultural
society. These laws establish a number of specific ways of aiding the
needy. According to one biblical injunction, the products of the cor-
ners of each field should not be collected by the harvesters of the
field but should be left for the needy to take. Neither the products
of a field nor of a vineyard should be completely collected; something should be left for the poor (Lev. 19:9–10, 23:22). On each
seventh year, the land is to be left fallow. Whatever the land pro-
duces during that year may be claimed by the needy (Exod. 23:10–

1. There is an extensive secondary literature on *zedakah* (see, e.g., Frisch
1924; Bergman 1944; Kohler 1916, 229–53; Chipkin 1949, 1043–73), including:
specialized studies on *zedakah* in the rabbinic period (see, e.g., Brooks 1983; Urbach 1951), the medieval period (see, e.g., Abrahams 1958; Baron 1942, 2: 319–
33), the implications of *zedakah* for modern society (see, e.g., Twersky 1963; Tamari
1987, 25–61, 248–69), and, on Jewish philanthropic activity in the United States
(see, e.g., Raphael 1979; Lurie 1961; Bernstein 1983).

11). According to the Talmud, this institution of a sabbatical year is to remind us that the earth ultimately belongs to God, that God owns what we possess (see, e.g., *San.*, 39a).

That which was not reaped when a field was harvested went to the needy (Deut. 24:19). A tithe of all one's net yield was to be given to the needy (Deut. 26:12). On festivals special contributions were to be made so that the needy could also rejoice at those times (Deut. 16:9–14). Each fiftieth year, on the Jubilee, all real estate holdings were to be returned to their original owners (Lev. 25:9–15). In this way, the impoverished could be restored economically. Furthermore, interest could not be charged of one in need (Lev. 25:35–37, Exod. 22:24). Discussing this prohibition against charging interest, the commentaries observe that the Hebrew word *neshekh* (interest) is related to the word *neshikhah* (a bite). As Rashi put it (commenting on *Suk.*, 49b), "*Neshekh* means interest since it is like the bite (*neshikhah*) of a snake which bites making a small wound on one's foot which he does not feel, but suddenly it blows up as far as his head. So with interest — one does not feel it and it is not at first noticeable until the interest increases and causes one to lose much money."

The biblical characterization of a just society was one where the needy were cared for, where the vulnerable were protected. The unjust society, the society deserving of destruction, such as Sodom and Gomorrah, is one that neglects the indigent. For example, the prophet Ezekiel observed, "Only this was the sin of your sister Sodom: arrogance! She and her daughters had plenty of bread and untroubled tranquillity; yet she did not support the poor and the needy" (Ezek. 16:49).

The legal obligation of *zedakah*, established by the Bible, was developed by the talmudic rabbis and was codified in the medieval legal codes. Through this process of development, an attempt was made to relate the laws of *zedakah* to a society that was primarily commercial rather than primarily agricultural, to an urban as well as to an agrarian society. Despite these adaptations of biblical agricultural statutes to later socioeconomic situations, the understanding of *zedakah* as a legal duty and as a religious imperative remained constant. According to Maimonides, one who gave *zedakah* fulfilled a positive commandment. One who did not give *zedakah* violated a negative commandment (*MT—MA*, chap. 7, secs. 1–2). Furthermore, Maimonides insisted, "It is our duty to be more careful in the performance of the commandment of almsgiving than in that of any other positive commandment" (*MT—MA*, chap. 10, sec. 1).

Justice and Benevolence

Despite the emphasis upon *zedakah* as an unequivocal religious, social, and legal obligation, it would be a mistake to conclude that the idea of altruism and benevolence is absent from Judaism. Though some authors claim that the Jewish conception of *zedakah* is deficient in that it emphasizes law to the neglect of love, such a claim can hardly be substantiated by the Jewish sources themselves. Rather, Jewish religious literature seeks instead to strike a balance between law and love, between obligation and generosity.

Zedakah represents the minimal requirement, but more is hoped for, more is expected. *Zedakah* is a necessary but insufficient expression of concern for the well-being of others. *Zedakah* is complemented by *gemilut hasadim*, acts of loving-kindness.

Zedakah is what is required by law. *Gemilut hasadim* is an expression of love and of profound concern for others. According to Rashi (in his commentary on *Suk.*, 49b), *zedakah* denotes the act of giving, whereas *gemilut hasadim* refers to the noble intentions infused within the act. According to Judah Loew, the difference between the obligation of giving *zedakah* and the virtue of doing *gemilut hasadim* is that *zedakah* is determined by the needs of the recipient, whereas *gemilut hasadim* flows from the goodness of the benefactor. In *zedakah*, the recipient benefits only from the benefactor's money whereas in *gemilut hasadim*, the recipient enjoys the good nature of the benefactor (*NO*, sec. "Netiv Gemilut Hasadim," chap. 2, 1:154). Judah Loew offered this distinction as a commentary to the following talmudic statement: "In three respects is *gemilut hasadim* superior to *zedakah*. *Zedakah* can be done only with one's money, but *gemilut hasadim* can be done with one's person and with one's money. *Zedakah* can be given to the poor alone, but *gemilut hasadim* can be given to the rich as well as to the poor. *Zedakah* can be given only to the living while *gemilut hasadim* can be done both to the living and to the dead" (*Suk.*, 49b).

Zedakah is justice in action. *Gemilut hasadim* is mercy and love in action. "What is *gemilut hasadim*?" *Sefer Ma'alot ha-Middot* asks. "That one will be merciful to all creatures, as the Creator, may He be blessed, is merciful and full of compassion." By practicing *zedakah*, one fulfills social obligations. By practicing *gemilut hasadim,* one expresses *imitatio Dei,* that which we have in common with God. Through *gemilut hasadim* one articulates one's having been created in the image of the divine (*MM,* 84).

Giving *zedakah* fulfills legal requirements; *gemilut hasadim* transcends legal demands. In *The Guide of the Perplexed,* Maimonides discussed this distinction between *zedakah* and *hesed* (the root of *hasadim*). According to Maimonides, *zedakah* refers to giving one one's just due, while *hesed* refers to absolute beneficence. *Zedakah* means granting something to someone who has a right of entitlement. *Hesed* is the practice of benevolence toward one who has no claim upon what he or she receives (*GP,* bk. 3, chap. 53, 630–32).

Among the actions identified as acts of loving-kindness, as expressions of *gemilut hasadim,* are visiting the sick, burying the dead, comforting the mourner, caring for animals, hospitality to strangers, and giving *zedakah* without ulterior motives. Whereas the Talmud put restrictions upon how much *zedakah* one might give, acts of loving-kindness were assigned no such limitations (*M. Pe'ah,* chap. 1, sec. 1).

Acts characterized as *gemilut hasadim* are considered expressions of loving-kindness because they may be done selflessly, without thoughts of recompense from the recipient. For example, when Jacob is dying, he asks Joseph to treat him with "kindness (*hesed*) and with truth (*emet*)" (Gen. 47:29). On this verse, Rashi commented, "The kindness that is shown to the dead is a true kindness (*hesed shel emet*), for [in such a case] one does not expect the payment of recompense [from the recipient]."

Isaac Aboab wrote that "*zedakah* given selflessly for the sake of Heaven, graciously and compassionately, is called *gemilut hasadim*" (1961, 420). Thus Aboab identified *gemilut hasadim* as an exalted variety of *zedakah.* Aboab refused to assign *zedakah* to one realm and *gemilut hasadim* to another. Instead, Aboab perceived a certain fluidity between dutiful actions and benevolent actions. For Aboab, as well as for others, actions that may benefit others embrace a wide spectrum from self-serving or reluctant giving of *zedakah* to perfectly selfless acts of loving-kindness (see, e.g., *Tos. AZ,* 17b).

Motivations of Donors

According to a well-established tradition, giving *zedakah* offers the promise of reward as well as protection from sickness, death, and harm. Despite their attempt to encourage benevolence and generosity, the sources felt obliged to appeal to more base human motives to stimulate the giving of *zedakah*. In their view, selflessness was a goal to which few could or would aspire. Therefore, given the predilections of human nature, it became popular to appeal for *zedakah* by invoking the promise of reward, the assurance of protection, and the fear of punishment for failing to contribute to *zedakah*. Thus, especially in talmudic and in medieval sources, giving *zedakah* was portrayed as bestowing prophylactic if not magical protection upon the donor. For example, the following talmudic statements portray giving charity as a way of fending off calamity, as a way of bringing redemption, as a way of guaranteeing well-being:

> Rabbi Isaac also said, he who gives a small coin to a poor man obtains six blessings. . . . Rabbi Joshua ben Levi said, he who does charity habitually will have sons wise, wealthy and versed in *aggadah*. . . . Rabbi Judah says: Great is charity in that it brings the redemption nearer. . . . Death is stronger than all [strong things in the world], but charity saves from death. . . . Why this double mention of *zedakah* [in Prov. 10:2, 11:4]? One [mention refers to] delivery from an unnatural death, and one [mention refers to] delivery from the punishments of purgatory (*gehinom*). (*BB*, 9b)

Similarly, the High Holiday liturgy continuously reminds the penitent that *zedakah* is one way to "avert the evil decree." According to some sources, giving charity has the power to prevent harm in this world and in the next, to ensure well-being in this world and in the next, and even to guarantee the resurrection of the dead. An entire chapter of the midrash *Pirke d'Rabbi Eliezer* offers examples of how giving charity made possible (and therefore will continue to make possible) the resurrection of the dead (*PRE* 1946, chap. 33).

The Talmud compares a poor person, a blind person, a diseased person, and a childless person to a dead person (*Ned.*, 64b). Post-talmudic sources, such as the *Me'il Zedakah*, concluded that *zedakah* can not only deliver one from death but also from situations that are comparable with death, such as those noted by the Talmud.[2] In a

2. The *Me'il Zedakah* is the only work in classical Jewish literature totally devoted to the explication of the meaning and requirements of giving *zedakah*. A lengthy but diffuse work, *Me'il Zedakah* was published only twice, that is, in 1731 in

similar vein, the *Midrash on Psalms* understands the verse "Blessed is he that considers the poor; the Lord will deliver him in time of trouble" (Ps. 41:1) to mean that God will deliver one who "is considerate and gives money to the poor" (*MP,* chap. 41, sec. 2, 130a).

The tension between the always present requirements of the needy and the desired virtue of the donor pervades the literature regarding *zedakah.* According to some traditions, on the one hand, the act of *zedakah* is essential; the motivation of the donor is secondary. The donor whose primary intention is the expectation of reward, protection from harm, social approval, or personal aggrandizement is still adjudged as having fulfilled the *mitzvah* of *zedakah,* even though helping the needy might not have been the central motivation behind his or her gift (see, e.g., Devorkes 1974, 49–54). Even a stingy, recalcitrant, resentful donor was considered by most legal authorities as having fulfilled the mitzvah of giving *zedakah.* What is paramount is that the indigent be served. On the other hand, some refused to consider recalcitrant or self-serving giving as fulfilling the *mitzvah* of giving *zedakah.* For these sources, *zedakah* given with improper intentions perverts the very aim of the entire institution of *zedakah* — the establishment of a just society; such actions are examples of good deeds badly done (see, e.g., Rashi to *Hag.,* 5a).

Texts such as the *Me'il Zedakah* railed against those who gave *zedakah* to attain divinely conferred or socially bestowed rewards. This treatise warned that those who used *zedakah* as a tool to attain social approval or social status will ultimately become destitute, that giving *zedakah* for self-glorification is a religious abomination rather than a religious virtue. *Orhot Zaddikim* even claimed that "he who gives *zedakah* to the poor grudgingly loses the merit of the deed,

Smyrna and in 1859 in Lwow (Lemberg). An abridged edition, *Zedakah le-Hayyim,* was published in 1873 by the Turkish rabbi Hayyim Palaggi. Only one significant study was written on *Me'il Zedakah* (Cronbach 1936, 1937–38, 1939). Elijah ha-Kohen of Smyrna, the author of *Me'il Zedakah,* was a prolific writer, a popular preacher, an erudite scholar and cabalist, and an important Jewish communal leader in eighteenth-century Turkey. Some of his works were published, whereas others survive only in manuscript form or were altogether lost. There is evidence that he was a Sabbatean, a follower of the seventeenth-century Jewish pseudo-messiah, Shabbatai Zevi. Either his Sabbatean leanings or the thoroughly diffuse and disorganized nature of the *Me'il Zedakah* have prevented it from achieving the wide circulation and popularity one might otherwise expect of the only exhaustive study of *zedakah* in Jewish literature.

even though he gives much; it is better that he give only one coin with a pleasing countenance" (*OZ*, 305). This text echoes an earlier rabbinic statement, "If one gives his fellow all the good gifts in the world with a downcast face, Scripture accounts it to him as though he had given him naught" (*ARN*, chap. 3, 9a).

Besides the tension between the actions and the intentions of the donor, the literature regarding *zedakah* articulates a further tension between the obligation of the donor to give and the ability of the donor to give. On the one hand, *zedakah* was viewed as an obligatory tax with defined minimal and maximal amounts. On the other hand, *zedakah* was perceived as a gift, an expression of generosity, limited only by the beneficence of the donor.

Biblical law established and rabbinic law developed the view that everyone was obliged to donate, even the poor (*Git.*, 7a). The codes set 10 percent as the average expected donation. Less brands one an evil person. One-third of a shekel is defined as the minimal donation. One-fifth of one's income is established by the Talmud as the ceiling on donations to *zedakah* (*MT — MA*, chap. 7, sec. 5; *SA — YD*, para. 249, secs. 1–2; see also *Ket.*, 50a). This ceiling was instituted because the rabbis apparently felt that individuals might otherwise impoverish themselves, thereby becoming clients of social welfare through overexuberant or impulsive giving. This quantification circumscribes the limits of *zedakah*. Unlike *gemilut hasadim*, *zedakah* is defined within precise parameters. However, those who saw no clear distinction between *zedakah* and *gemilut hasadim*, those who considered a gift surpassing 20 percent to be well within the grasp of the extremely wealthy, and those who perceived the condition of the indigent to be too precarious to be dependent upon strictures on giving, refused to be bound by these limitations.

The endeavor of Maimonides and others to identify levels of *zedakah* may be an attempt to diffuse these tensions presented by the literature on *zedakah*.[3] Rather than present opposing views as con-

---

3. Although Maimonides' "eight levels" are the best known, others also depicted levels of benevolence in a series of gradations. Whereas Maimonides' are offered in descending order, others are presented in ascending order in order to describe the ascent on the rungs of the ladder of benevolent action. Legal codes, such as *Arba'ah Turim* (*AT — YD*, para. 249) and *Shulhan Arukh* (*SA — YD*, para. 249) follow Maimonides' approach. However, Moses of Coucy's *Sefer Mitzvot Gadol* and Ibn al-Nakawa's *Menorat ha-Ma'or* present the levels in an ascending order (see Cronbach's 1941 study of the whole matter of the gradations of benevolence).

tradictions, Maimonides placed these often conflicting opinions as points on a spectrum. On one side is the altruistic donor who preserves the individuality and the dignity of the person in need. On the other side is the self-serving or reluctant donor who must be cajoled into giving. A spectrum of attitudes and motivations links these two extremes. The mitzvah of *zedakah* covers a wide field, from selflessness to niggardliness, from minimal legal obligation to extreme selfless generosity, from self-serving intention to the saintly service of others.

Theological Assumptions

The obligation to help the needy rests upon the theological assumption that all wealth ultimately belongs to God, and correlatively, that human beings must properly fulfill their roles as stewards of God's possessions by aiding those in need (see, e.g., Schechter 1924, 238–77).

Scriptural verses, such as the following, attest to the biblical view that God is the owner and the proprietor of the world and of everything contained therein: "The earth is the Lord's and the fullness thereof" (Ps. 24:1). "Mine is the gold and the silver, says the Lord of hosts" (Hag. 2:8). "Riches and honor are Yours to dispense; You have dominion over all. . . . All is from You, and it is Your gift that we have given to You" (1 Chron. 29:12, 14).

Verses such as these are cited in the talmudic and medieval sources to reinforce and to expand the notion that *what we own, we owe*. For example, the *Ethics of the Fathers* (PA, chap. 3, sec. 8) observes, "Give God of God's own, for both you and whatever is yours are God's, as David said (1 Chron. 29:14): 'All is from You, and it is Your gift that we have given You.'" Along similar lines, the medieval ethical treatise *Sefer Ma'alot ha-Middot* says, "Come and see how beloved of God are those who give *zedakah*. For, even though they give nothing of their own but of that which is God's, as it is written, 'Mine is the gold and the silver, says the Lord' (Hag. 2:8), and it is also said, 'all is from You, and it is Your gift that we have given You' (1 Chron. 29:14), nevertheless, the Holy One, blessed be He, accounts it to you as if you have given of your own [property]" (*MM*, 94).

The notion of human stewardship is also affirmed in rabbinic literature and amplified in medieval ethical literature. For example, a midrash quotes God as saying, "Honor the Lord from whatever substance God has bestowed upon you. You are only My steward" (*PR*, chap. 25, 126b). According to the *Sefer Hasidim*, a wealthy individual who does not help support the poor is to be considered a thief. "God says to him [the wealthy person]: I have supplied you with abundant wealth so that you may give to the needy to the extent of your means. Yet, you did not give. I [God] shall punish you as if you have robbed those people and as if you have denied having in your possession something that I entrusted to you. The wealth I put into your hand for distribution to the poor, you appropriated for yourself" (*SH* 1924, para. 1345, 331; *SH* 1960, para. 415, 297; see also Cronbach 1949).

A final example of a classical Jewish text that describes charity as the fulfillment of human stewardship and trusteeship for God's possessions is from *Torat Moshe*, a commentary to the Pentateuch by the sixteenth-century cabalist Moses Alsheikh. A verse in Exodus (22:24) reads, "If you lend money to my people, to the poor who is in your power, do not act toward him as a creditor: exact no interest from him." Commenting on this verse, Alsheikh used the word *epitropos* to characterize the loaner. This talmudic term, which derives from the Greek, denotes a court-appointed guardian or trustee (see Jastrow 1950, 102). According to Alsheikh, by giving *zedakah* in the form of an interest-free loan to the poor, one is simply administering funds for social welfare entrusted into one's hands by the owner of the funds, namely, God (1879, 1:80b). This idea, that giving *zedakah* is actually the administration of funds deposited in our trust by God, is known as the doctrine of "deposit" (*pikadon*) and is found throughout medieval Hebrew literature (see, e.g., Ibn Pakuda 1973, 222, 227; Matt 1876, 100a; see also Ben Sasson 1954, 142–66; 1959, 73–74).

If divine ownership of all property and human stewardship of that property is the first premise of *zedakah*, then the divine commandment to respond to the pressing and omnipresent neediness of the poor is the second premise upon which *zedakah* rests. The requirement to give *zedakah* is based upon the biblical assumption that in premessianic times there will always be those in need. Unlike certain Christian (particularly Calvinist) traditions that consider poverty to be a divine punishment for sin, Judaism considers poverty to be a human tragedy. Jewish sources condemn the view of the uncharitable that disparages the poor in their attempt to surrender social responsibility toward the poor. Indeed, without the presence of the poor, the rich would be unable to fulfill the mitzvah of *zedakah;* in other words, the rich need the poor as much as the poor need the rich.

In advocating the cause of the needy, the *Me'il Zedakah* defends the perpetual requirements of the poor against the endless disparagements of the uncharitable. For example, the *Me'il Zedakah* rejects the view that poverty is a state that people bring upon themselves either by their own indolence or as a divine punishment for sin. Abraham Lincoln's view that God must have loved the poor since he made so many of them is similar to views found in the *Me'il Zedakah* and in earlier Jewish literature. Abraham Cronbach thus summarized the view of the *Me'il Zedakah:* "To the contention that the poor are devoid of decency, the answer is that the poor are devoid of iniquity" (1937–38, 637).

That poverty is a virtue is not a dominant motif in Jewish literature; however, neither is it a theme unknown to Jewish literature. Two of the most important works in Jewish mystical-ethical literature, the *Sefer Hasidim* and the *Zohar,* exalt poverty as a religious virtue.

According to the *Zohar,* the poor are not alienated from God because of their sins. Instead, they are endeared to God because of their impoverished state. The *Zohar* teaches:

> The prayers of the poor are received by God ahead of all other prayers. "Happy is he who is considerate of the poor" (Ps. 41:2). . . . How great is the reward that the poor merit of the Lord . . . for they are closest to God. . . . The poor man is closer to God than anyone else . . . for God abides in these broken vessels, as it is written, "I dwell on high, amid holiness, but also with the contrite and humble in spirit" (Isa. 57:15). . . . Therefore we have been taught that he who reviles the indigent scoffs at the Divinity. . . . Happy is he who encounters a poor man, for this poor man is a gift sent to him by God. (cited in Baer 1966, 1:265)

Furthermore, according to the *Zohar,* *zedakah* brings about the union between the "male" and "female" potencies within the divine (see, e.g., Tishbi 1961, 2:441).

Were poverty a divine punishment, then *zedakah* would not be the fulfillment of a religious imperative but a presumptive human intervention upon God's execution of justice (see, e.g., *BB,* 10a).

Though the poor are cherished as individuals, for most Jewish sources, poverty is nonetheless depicted neither as a virtue nor as a punishment, but as a personal calamity. According to one talmudic text, poverty deprives a person of one's senses; poverty can make one mad (*Erub.*, 41b). Another talmudic source compares poverty with death (*Ned.*, 64b), and a third source observes that "poverty in one's home is worse than fifty plagues" (*BB*, 116a). A midrashic text summarizes this apprehension of poverty as a calamity: "There is nothing in the world more grievous than poverty — the most terrible of all sufferings. . . . Our teachers have said: If all troubles were assembled on one side and poverty on the other, poverty would outweigh them all" (*Exod. R.*, chap. 31, secs. 12, 14).

The catastrophe of poverty was understood not only as posing a physical and a psychological danger as far as the poor were concerned, but as a moral danger as well. Driven by destitution, the indigent person might become prone to immoral acts.

Treating the Welfare Recipient

Already in the talmudic period, our sources were aware that needs varied both in kind and in degree. The various levels of giving *zedakah* outlined by Maimonides, as well as by others, paralleled a recognition that needs also existed on a series of levels. Just as there were levels and degrees of aid, so were there levels and degrees of need. It is noteworthy, and perhaps not coincidental, that Maimonides identified eight levels of *zedakah*, while a midrash notes that biblical Hebrew has eight words to denote the poor (*LR*, chap. 34, sec. 6).

The literature on *zedakah* relentlessly observes that need cannot be quantified only on the basis of objective criteria. An individual's needs cannot be determined through calculating the objective minimum that any person might require to be sustained. The sources refuse to objectify another person's need. Rather, each person is perceived as an individual with subjective, individualistic, and even idiosyncratic needs. The demands of his or her personality, past experience, self-respect, and personal dignity are never overlooked. The goal in Jewish social welfare — not always attainable, though never forgotten — is to provide the individual that which is "sufficient for *his* need" (Deut. 15:8). That the individual need of the client is of paramount concern is expressed in the following talmudic text. Commenting on the verse, "Rather, you must open your hand and lend him sufficient for whatever he needs" (Deut. 15:8), the Talmud says, "'For whatever he needs' (Deut. 15:8) [includes] even a horse to ride and a slave to run before him. It is related about Hillel the Elder that he bought for a certain poor man who was of a good family a horse to ride upon and a slave to run before him. On one occasion he could not find a slave to run before him, so he himself ran before him for three miles" (*Ket.*, 67b). Maimonides interpreted this text to mean that the poor man mentioned in the text was not simply of a good family but was once rich (*MT— MA*, chap. 7, sec. 3).

Since poverty is more psychologically debilitating for a person who has lost his or her wealth than it is for a person who has never had wealth, the needs of the formerly wealthy are greater. To ensure the dignity of this person, more than the gift of a dole is required. Maimonides' demand that the personal experience and economic history of the individual must be considered when giving him *zedakah* is talmudic in origin:

> It has been taught that if a person [who was rich] has become poor and requires public assistance, if he had been used to vessels of gold, they give him vessels of silver; if of silver, they give him vessels of copper; if copper, they give him vessels of glass. Rabbi Mena said: They give him vessels of silver or glass only for his personal use. How about that teaching which said that if a man had been used to wear clothes of fine wool, they give him clothes of fine wool? Again, these are only for his personal use. (*PT. Pe'ah*, chap. 8, sec. 8; in Maimonides, see *MT—MA*, chap. 7, sec. 3)

The attitude articulated by this text reveals the talmudic rabbis' intense awareness of the fragility of economic life and the vulnerability of the wealthy to its fluctuations. Consequently, rabbinic views on *zedakah* incorporate this awareness. In the words of a midrash, "There is an ever rotating wheel in this world, and he who is rich today may not be so tomorrow" (*Exod. R.*, chap. 34, sec. 6).

Zedakah is both person centered and need centered. The gift must be appropriate to the person and to that person's particular present need. On the verse, "Open your hand to your brother" (Deut. 15:11), a rabbinic midrash comments, "To one for whom bread is suitable, give bread; for one who needs dough, give dough;

for one who requires money, give money; for one who needs to be fed, feed him" (*Sifre Deut.* 1939, sec. "*Re'eh,*" para. 118, 177). This approach of the talmudic rabbis, later codified in medieval legal codes, is that *zedakah* is a response to a specific individual situation and need; it is not a solution to an abstract social problem (see, e.g., *MT—MA,* chap. 7, sec. 3; *AT—YD,* para. 250).

To help ensure the dignity of the poor, efforts were made to guarantee the anonymity both of the donor and of the recipient of *zedakah.* In cases in which the rich had lost their possessions, joining the ranks of the poor, anonymity was especially desired. For example, "Just as there was a 'vestry of secret givers' in the Temple, so there was one in every city, for the sake of noble people, who had come down in life, so that they may be helped in secret" (*PT. Shek.,* chap. 2, sec. 16; see also *Ket.* 67b; *BB,* 9b).

According to Maimonides' eight levels of charity, giving anonymously to a poor person who does not know the identity of his benefactor is the next to highest kind of *zedakah.* It protects the dignity of the recipient and expresses the altruism of the benefactor. However, according to Maimonides and many other sources, the highest form of *zedakah* is not a gift but a loan. By giving a loan or by entering into partnership with the needy person his or her dignity is preserved by allowing him or her to maintain at least a facade of self-sufficiency. In such cases, to be sure, there is no requirement or even an expectation that the loan be repaid. Nor is any interest attached to the loan. The goal of this form of *zedakah* is to preserve the dignity of the needy and to help extricate him or her from being needy, to allow him or her to attain economic self-sufficiency.

Once again, in the case of giving *zedakah* as a loan, one finds a special sensitivity toward the needs of the previously wealthy. For example, a talmudic text recounts that Rabbi Jonah examined how to fulfill the mitzvah of *zedakah.* "What did Rabbi Jonah do? When he saw a previously wealthy poor person he would say: I have heard that you have inherited some wealth. Take this loan now and you will repay me. After he took it, he [Rabbi Jonah] would say: It is a gift for you" (*PT. Shek.,* chap. 5, sec. 4; see also *MP,* chap. 41, sec. 3, 130b).

The view that a loan is better than a gift has firm talmudic precedent: "He who lends [money to the poor] is greater than he who gives a charitable gift; and he who forms a partnership [with the poor] is greater than all" (*Shab.,* 63a). On this text, Rashi commented that a loan is better than a gift because a poor person, who might be ashamed to accept a gift, would readily agree to a loan. Also, a donor might be willing to make a loan of a greater sum than he might be willing to make a gift. A second text succinctly states, "One who gives *zedakah,* many blessings come upon him; superior to him is one who lends his funds [to the poor]; superior to all is one [who forms a partnership with the poor] on terms of half the profits [for each] or on terms of sharing what remains" (*ARN,* chap. 41, 66a). According to a number of sources, lending is superior to giving because loans are common between the rich as well as the poor, whereas *zedakah* is for the poor alone. A dole demeans by the very fact that the recipient is on a level subordinate to that of the donor, but in the case of a loan, both parties are deemed equal. Such loans were, of course, free of interest.

The aim of giving loans to the poor was to help them to exchange dependency for self-sufficiency. Just as rabbinic sources were concerned about the need to rescue the poor from indigency, so are they preoccupied with the need to prevent one from sliding into poverty. *Zedakah* was not only to be therapeutic but preventive as well. Commenting on the phrase in Leviticus (25:35), "then you shall uphold him," Rashi warned, "Do not let him come down until he falls [completely] for then it will be difficult to raise him. Rather, uphold him at the time that his means [begin to] fail. To what is this comparable? To a burden that rests on a donkey. While it is still on the donkey one [person can] hold it and set it back in place, but if it fell to the ground even five people cannot set it back in its place."

To make sure that communal funds were distributed to the truly needy, means to investigate the authenticity of need were developed and employed. Funds were always too sparse to expend on "deceivers." In addition, as the *Me'il Zedakah* observes, the presence of "cheats" was often used as an excuse not to contribute by recalcitrant potential donors. According to Maimonides, if a person asks for food, that is, for the fulfillment of an immediate need, such a person's need is not to be investigated. The need may be too pressing to endure an inquiry. However, if a person asks for other types of aid, such as clothing, the need is not immediate and life threatening; therefore, an investigation into the grounds for the request is warranted (*MT—MA,* chap. 7, sec. 6). Regarding imposters, the Mishnah teaches, "He that does not need to take yet takes shall not depart from this world before he falls in need of his fellows. . . . And if a man is not lame or dumb or blind or halting, yet he makes himself like unto one of them, he shall not die in old age until he becomes like one of them, as it is written, 'He that searches after mischief, it shall come upon him' (Prov. 11:27)" (*M. Peah*, chap. 8, sec. 9; cf. *Ket.*, 68a; *ARN*, chap. 3). Furthermore, as Maimonides noted, community officials would investigate the claims of potential clients seeking communal welfare to remove imposters from community welfare roles.

Besides admonishing and seeking to unmask imposters, Maimonides dealt with the case of the truly needy person who hesitates or refuses to accept aid. In such a case, Maimonides counseled that aid should be given as a gift or as a loan. Maimonides' source seems to be this talmudic statement: "Our rabbis taught: If a person has no means and does not wish to be maintained [out of the poor funds] he should be granted [the sum he requires as] a loan and it can be presented to him as a gift; so [says] Rabbi Meir. The sages however said that it is given to him as a gift and then it is granted to him as a loan" (*Ket.*, 67b; *MT—MA*, chap. 7, sec. 9).

According to Maimonides, who relied on talmudic sources, the deceiver is accursed. The indigent individual who is too proud to accept help needed for survival is self-destructive. The truly needy, however, is entitled to receive what is needed. Nevertheless, every effort must be made before one begins to receive public aid. "One should always restrain oneself and submit to privation rather than be dependent upon other people or cast himself upon public charity" (*MT—MA*, chap. 10, sec. 18).

Infinite Needs, Finite Resources

The constant disparity between available funds and ever present need required setting priorities in the dispensing of aid. For Maimonides, charity begins at home. The first priority is the support of one's own family. While one is required to help the indigent, one is forbidden to join them in the process. Maimonides writes, "A poor person who is one's relative has priority over all others, the poor of one's own household have priority over the other poor of his city, and the poor of his city have priority over the poor of another city" (*MT—MA*, chap. 7, sec. 13). Similarly, Isaac Aboab insists that a person's first obligation is self-support, then support of one's parents, support of one's children, and only then is one obliged to render support for the needy (1961, 411. Cf. *AT — YD*, para. 251).

In meeting the needs of others, priorities were established. As already noted, one is obliged to care for one's own family before one is required to take care of another's family. Immediate needs, such as hunger, were to supersede other, less pressing needs. A woman's needs were to take precedent over those of a man because she was considered more vulnerable than a man to harm or to abuse. The needs of orphans were given priority because they had no family; no one else but the community could care for them (*MT — MA*, chap. 6, sec. 12).

Communal funds aided the indigent and others. Brides were provided with dowries, newlyweds with furnishings. The dead were buried, the sick cared for and attended. Interest-free loans were made. Newly arrived immigrants were cared for until they could plant roots of their own. In the rabbinic period and throughout the Middle Ages, Jews were held for ransom by kings, pirates, and other extortionists. Therefore, ransoming of captives — especially, women and children — became a priority of communal *zedakah* funds (e.g., *BB*, 8b; *MT — MA*, chap. 8, secs. 10–12). All of the needs for which communal funds were expended would have been left unattended if observance of the mitzvah of *zedakah* had been neglected.

The Moral Dangers of Wealth

Zedakah is a way not only of physically and fiscally helping the needy but a way of aiding him or her morally as well. But, wealth, like poverty, also has its moral temptations.

In the prayer announcing the new moon, the liturgy asks God for "a life of riches and honor" (see *Ber.*, 16b). Similarly in the Grace After Meals, one entreats God to "feed us, sustain us, support us, deliver us, release us from our afflictions . . . and to spare us from shame and embarrassment." These prayers recognize that fiscal security is literally the lifeblood that sustains our physical and spiritual well-being. In this regard, Hayyim ben Betzalel of Friedberg pointed out that one Hebrew term for "money" is *damim*, which also means "blood." "Money is called '*damim*,'" he writes, "because just as blood sustains a person's life, so is money essential for life, and one who has no money is like one who is thought of as being dead" (1965, pt. 3, chap. 5, 58). Similarly, the Talmud notes, "All the members of the body depend on the heart, and the heart depends upon the purse" (*PT. Ter.,* chap. 8, sec. 4 end).

A minimal modicum of wealth is a necessary but not sufficient feature of life. Whether wealth is good or bad depends upon how it is used. According to Ephraim Lunshitz, wealth may be compared to fire, because like fire, we cannot live without it, but like fire, if left out of control, it can destroy us (see Bettan 1939, 291).

In his commentary to the Talmud (on *Shab.,* 125b), Samuel Edels said that there are three common motivations for the acquisition of wealth. The first is that wealth brings honors. The wealthy are honored by others. The second is the financial support of one's family. One must acquire wealth to ensure that the members of one's family are provided with what they need. The third is independence. One does not want to be dependent upon the benevolence of others for one's basic sustenance. This expression of the desirability of not being reliant upon others for our daily sustenance is expressed in the Grace After Meals: "May we never be dependent upon the gifts of others nor upon their favors." In this regard, Judah Loew taught that wealth can liberate from dependence upon others for one's sustenance or a person can become enslaved by his or her own wealth. Wealth can both liberate and fetter; it all depends upon our attitude toward what we have (see, e.g., Weiss 1969, 315–21). Wealth can have a person as much as a person can have wealth.

The passion for the limitless acquisition of wealth was recognized as a peculiar and morally dangerous propensity of the wealthy. For example, as Saadya Gaon observed:

I have come to the conclusion that all is well with the acquisition of money so long as it comes to a person spontaneously and with ease. However, once one passionately engages in the quest for wealth, one realizes that it entails immense efforts of thought and exertion, keeping one awake at night and plagued by hardship by day, so that even when one has acquired what one desires, one is often unable to sleep properly. . . . When a person makes money the object of all his strivings and devotes himself to it with mad ambition and avidity . . . then the love of money becomes for him like a consuming fire, like a wilderness, like death or barrenness that are never sated. (1948, 379)

There are even those, the Talmud observes, who value their money more than their lives (*Ber.*, 61b). According to the eighteenth-century preacher, Jonathan Eibshitz, of all the temptations toward immorality one faces, the greatest is posed by money. As one is admonished not to waste or misuse wealth, one is warned against the temptations of miserliness, avarice, and arrogance that can readily afflict the wealthy (1863, pt. 1, Sermon no. 7, 57b).

In the Gospel of Mark (10:25), Jesus is quoted as saying, "It is easier for a camel to go through the eye of a needle than for a rich man to enter the Kingdom of God." However, the Talmud says, "In accordance with the camel is its burden" (*Ket.*, 67a). For Jewish tradition, the wealthy have an opportunity not granted to others. Heaven can be theirs — not by surrendering their wealth but by using it as faithful stewards for the sake of God, and in fulfillment of the will of God that the indigent be cared for.

It is told that the Hasidic master Naftali of Ropshitz once prayed to God that the wealthy be willing to give and that the needy be willing to receive. After he had so prayed, he was asked if his prayer had been answered. The master responded that it had been half answered.

"Does this mean," asked the questioner, "that the wealthy will give and the needy will receive half of what is required?"

The master thought for a moment and said, "I asked God for two things: that the wealthy should give what is required and that the needy should accept it. My prayer was half answered because I was assured that the needy are ready to accept what may be given. Whether the wealthy are willing to give what is needed, I still do not know" (see, e.g., Wiesel 1978, 97–98).

8

Repentance as Moral
Rehabilitation

SCRIPTURE DESCRIBES the human being as created in the image
of God (Gen. 1:26), but also as "dust" (see, e.g., Gen. 3:9, 18:27;
Job 42:6; Ps. 103:14). On the one hand, "each person is obliged to
say: The world was created for my sake" (*San.*, 37a), and, on the
other hand, "if a person becomes too proud, he should be reminded
that the gnats preceded him in the order of creation" (*San.*, 38a).
The human being is God's partner in the work of creation (*Shab.*,
10a) as well as a creature derived from a fetid drop of semen who
ends up in a place of worms and maggots (*PA*, chap. 3, sec. 1).
Human beings share qualities both with angels and animals (*Hag.*,
16a; see also *GR*, chap. 8, sec. 11; *GR*, chap. 14, sec. 3). The Jewish
view of human nature hovers between such sets of polar opposites:
dust and divinity, animal and angel, creature and creator.

Jewish thought perceives not only human existence, but all of
creation as being characterized by polarity. In Judah Loew's words,
"Everything that exists in the world is either of a certain essence or
its opposite" (*HA*, 2:89). Only the one God who creates the universe
is beyond dichotomies, whereas everything created by God exists in
pairs of polar opposites. According to a midrash, "God said to Israel, 'My children, everything that I created, I have created in pairs:
heaven and earth, sun and moon, Adam and Eve, this world and the
world to come. However, My Glory is One and unique in the
world.' As it is written, 'Hear O Israel, the Lord our God, the Lord
is One' (Deut. 6:4)" (*DR*, chap. 2, sec. 31).

Each entity depends upon and derives meaning from its polar counterpart. Without down, there cannot be up. Without evil, there could not be good. As one medieval text puts it, "God made each thing and its opposite. . . . All things cleave to one another, the pure and the impure. There is no purity except through impurity" (*Midrash Temurah* in *Agadat Bereshit* 1876, 49). According to the late-nineteenth-century Hasidic master Zadok of Lublin, even a specific halakhic decision implies the validity of its opposite (1903, 9b).

The presence of such interdependent yet polar opposites also characterizes the realm of the human heart. As the *Zohar* states, "Good issues from evil, and compassion issues from justice, and all are intertwined, the good inclination and the evil inclination, right and left . . . all depends upon one another . . . otherwise, the world could not exist for even an instant" (1883, 3:79b). In the human heart, described by the talmudic rabbis as the source of reason and emotion, God implants both the good inclination (*yetzer ha-tov*) and the evil inclination (*yetzer ha-ra*) (see, e.g., Schechter 1909, 255). How a person utilizes these inclinations determines the moral quality of his or her behavior.

Not only the good inclination, but the evil inclination as well is candidly described by the talmudic rabbis as having been created by God (see, e.g., *Ber.*, 61a; *GR*, chap. 14, sec. 4). In itself, the evil inclination (*yetzer ha-ra*) is not necessarily evil. However, it becomes evil when it is misused (see, e.g., Schechter 1909, 267). Otherwise, paradoxically, the evil inclination is considered good. For example, commenting on the verse, "And God saw everything God had made and behold it was very good" (Gen. 1:31), a midrash observes that while the good inclination is good, the evil inclination can be considered very good, because without it human beings would neither build a house, nor marry, nor beget children, nor engage in commerce (see *GR*, chap. 9, sec. 7). In other words, without the basic human drives and ambitions engendered by the evil inclination, the perpetuation of human civilization would become endangered (see, e.g., Rashi to *San.*, 107b). The stronger a person's evil inclination, the greater the individual's potential for greatness. As the Talmud says, "The greater the person, the greater their evil inclination" (*Suk.*, 52a).

The evil inclination is not only responsible for sustaining human civilization, but according to Judah Loew it is the catalyst for making manifest the divine image in which human beings are created (see, e.g., Jacobson 1987, 102–36). Paradoxically, through sinning, Adam demonstrates that human beings are Godlike in that they are morally independent beings. Yet, by making manifest the quality of moral volition that human beings share with God, human beings simultaneously alienate themselves from God through sin. The human task then becomes reconciliation with God through the performance of the commandments, the cultivation of the moral virtues, and repentance (see, e.g., Weiss 1969, 213–20, 347–50; c.f., *GP*, bk. 1, chap. 2, 24–25).

The evil inclination can engender good, but it can also bring about evil. Channeled in the right direction, it enhances life. Allowed to its own vices and devices, "the evil inclination grows stronger every day within a person and seeks to kill him" (*Suk.*, 52b). Left untempered, undisciplined, the evil inclination can become evil. Left unrestrained, it can take control, divesting the individual of self-control and moral choice: "At first he [i.e., the evil inclination] is like a lodger, then a guest, and finally a host" (*GR*, chap. 22, sec. 6). Left to its own devices, the evil inclination can become the antithesis of the good inclination, with the human heart being a battleground where two competing forces wage war. Whichever side wins the battle determines the moral disposition of the individual. Left unchecked, the evil inclination can bring about the moral disintegration of the human personality. Only God, in the messianic era, can decisively defeat and destroy the evil inclination, while in the meantime the evil inclination can wreak its havoc (*Suk.*, 52; see Schechter 1909, 278, 290). Fortunately, however, there are God-given weapons to combat its influence, such as: study of the Torah, good deeds, and especially repentance (see, e.g., Schechter 1909, 273–79; on repentance, see, e.g., *Tan.*, sec. "*Noah*," para. 13, 19a).

Because free will is given, sin is inevitable, and repentance is available. "There is no person who does not sin" (1 Kings 8:46; 2 Chron. 6:36).[1] However, as God informs Cain, "Sin couches at the

1. Although the idea of "original sin" is not usually identified with Judaism, it does appear in a variety of forms in classical Jewish literature (see, e.g., Cohon 1948; Cohen-Aloro 1987; Schechterman 1988). To be sure, many sources, particularly medieval Jewish texts polemicized against the notion of original sin (see, e.g., Lasker 1988). For example, the *Zohar* states (1883, 1: 57b–58a): "Adam comes before every person at the moment of death in order to declare that the person is dying not because of Adam's sin, but on account of his or her own sins." See also

door . . . yet you can be its master" (Gen. 4:7). According to a rabbinic legend, "When Cain went forth [after killing Abel], Adam met him and asked: What happened at your trial [for killing Abel]? Cain answered: I repented and was pardoned. When Adam heard this, he slapped himself on the face, and said to Cain: So great is the power of repentance, and I did not know it!" (*LR*, chap. 10, sec. 5).

As Maimonides writes, were an individual to believe that there were no remedy for sin, "he would persist in his error and sometimes perhaps disobey even more because of the fact that no stratagem remains at his disposal. If, however, he believes in repentance, he can correct himself and return to a better and more perfect state than the one he was in before he sinned" (*GP*, bk. 3, ch. 36, 540).

The Nature of Sin

Though biblical Hebrew uses about twenty words to denote "sin," three of these terms are prominent: *heit, pesha, avon. Heit* denotes missing the mark, failing in one's duty, committing an offensive action. *Pesha* denotes a breach, in the sense of a breach of a covenant, or of a breach of a relationship. *Pesha* also can refer to an act of rebellion, particularly against God. *Avon* denotes crookedness, a figurative way of referring to transgression and the guilt incurred by it. Though postbiblical Jewish literature does not always sustain the distinctions among these varieties of sin, it does perpetuate the various meanings that these different terms denote. Furthermore, various views regarding the nature of repentance are predicated upon these different views of the nature of sin. For example, once sin is understood as an act causing a breach in a relationship, repentance is perceived as a process that aims at healing that breach. Once sin is viewed as an act of alienation, repentance is perceived as an act of reconciliation. If sin means departure, *teshuvah* — repentance — means return. Whereas sin causes a breach, a wound, repentance effects a cure, a healing.

Before the destruction of the Temple, the sacrificial cult served as the primary vehicle for repentance. In this regard, it is significant that the Hebrew word for "sacrifice" — *korban* — derives from the root meaning "to bring near," that is, the sacrifices reduce the alien-

---

the fascinating short responsum of Abraham ben David (1965, no. 11, 55) discussed by Jacobs (1975, 49–50).

ation between God and the penitent. After the destruction of the Temple, the rabbis assigned to the process of repentance many of the spiritual goals of the individual previously accomplished by means of the sacrificial cult. As Maimonides succinctly put it, "At the present time, when the Temple no longer exists, and we have no altar for atonement, nothing is left but repentance" (*MT – HT,* chap. 1, sec. 3). Consequently, various parts of the process of repentance were compared to a sacrifice. For example, Eliezer Azkiri (1987, chap. 63, 243–44), described the words of confession and that which is denied the self in ascetic practices related to repentance as a sacrifice.[2] Similarly, the cabalist Elijah di Vidas in *Reshit Hokhmah,* described the contrition of a broken heart as a penitential sacrifice (sec. *"Sha'ar Teshuvah,"* chap. 3, 109a). Indeed, the Talmud already compares the fat and blood lost through a penitential fast as a substitute for the atonement sacrifice (see *Ber.,* 17a).

Just as there can be no remedy without there being a malady, so without repentance there could be no sin. A constant motif of Jewish religious literature is the comparison of sin to illness and repentance to its cure. Thus, without the spiritual illness of sin, the healing power of repentance could not become manifest; the world could not be brought closer to healing, reconciliation or redemption. As the Talmud puts it, "Great is repentance for it brings healing to the world. . . . Great is repentance for it brings about redemption" (*Yoma,* 86). Furthermore, as Bahya ben Asher wrote, "Repentance is a cure, as it is written, 'Return and be healed' (Isa. 6:10). It is a cure because sin is the sickness of the soul. Just as the physical body is subject to health and sickness, so is the soul. The health of the body is indicated by its good deeds, and its sickness by its sins. Just as a physical sickness is cured by its antithesis, so is the sick, sinful soul restored to health by its antithesis" (1892, 66a; cf. Ibn

2. Various harsh ascetic practices related to *teshuvah* have been observed by Jews. For historical reasons, these bear mention. Such practices included self-mortification, self-flagellation, voluntary "exile," long fasts, sleep deprivation, and more. Specific mention may be made of *teshuvat mishkal* where the penitent inflicted pain upon himself at least equal to the pleasure experienced during the committing of a particular sin. These were practiced by the *Hasidei Ashkenaz,* and were incorporated into later treatises of Jewish ethics. The observance of these practices demonstrates that the popular notion that asceticism and Judaism are incompatible is a fiction that cannot be substantiated on the basis of historical fact or textual evidence (see, e.g., *OZ,* 510–53; Elbaum 1992; Marcus 1981).

Pakuda 1973, 330, 333; Aboab 1961, 593; Azikiri 1987, chap. 62, 240; *OZ*, 460–61).

For Bahya ben Asher and other thinkers, sin is a moral malady that afflicts the soul, robbing one of spiritual health in the same way that a physical ailment deprives one of physical health. However, whereas some bodily illnesses are incurable, the restoration of spiritual health is perpetually possible and is readily available through repentance. In this regard, Joseph Albo wrote, "It is like the case of a person who is suffering from a serious illness which is regarded as incurable. Then a physician comes and says to the patient: I will tell you of a drug which will cure you of your illness. The patient thinks that since it can cure what is regarded as an incurable disease, the drug must be very costly, and extremely difficult to obtain. But the physician says: Do not think there is any difficulty in obtaining this drug" (1930, 3: chap. 25, 224).

According to Albo, a substantial impediment to the restoration of spiritual health through repentance is the individual's failure to recognize the existence of his or her malady. Awareness of illness is the first step toward a cure. Without such an awareness, the malady can only worsen. "If a person does not recognize or know that he has sinned, he will never regret doing the thing he does, nor repent, as a sick person cannot be cured as long as he does not know or feel that he is sick, for he will never seek a cure. So if one does not know he has sinned, he never will repent" (1930, 4: chap. 26, 237).

Once an individual is aware of his or her malady, it can only be expected that a cure will be sought. For sin, there is but one cure — repentance. As Bahya ibn Pakuda stated, one "must have firm knowledge that repentance is the only cure for his malady, the path to recovery from his bad deed and evil act, through which he may correct his error and rectify his misdeed" (1973, 333).

In Ibn Pakuda's work, as in much of the literature regarding sin and repentance, considerable discussion is devoted to factors that inhibit repentance and thereby prevent spiritual well-being.[3] One,

---

3. In most of medieval literature on *Teshuvah*, twenty-four obstacles to repentance are listed (see, e.g., *MT—HT*, chap. 4, secs. 1–6; Gerondi 1971, 69–71; Meiri 1950, 72–112; *OZ*, 480–89). Isaac al-Fasi is the first scholar to list these twenty-four obstacles, in his commentary to the end of the Talmudic tractate *Yoma*. For example, (Rabbenu) Nissim, in his super-commentary to al-Fasi on the Talmud,

already noted, is a lack of awareness of spiritual illness. A second is habit. As Ibn Pakuda related, "Another thing which makes repentance difficult is that habit makes wrongdoing almost necessary to a person, like the natural actions from which it is almost impossible for one to abstain" (1973, 346). Habit undercuts the process of repentance because it deprives the individual of moral volition, which is the underlying premise that makes both moral behavior as well as moral rehabilitation possible. Regarding habit, Moses Hayyim Luzzatto observed, "He who has thus become a slave to habit is no longer his own master, and cannot act differently, even should he want to. His will is held in bondage by certain habits which have become second nature with him" (1966, 122).

Just as harmful physical habits must be broken before bodily health can be attained, so deleterious moral habits must be eliminated before spiritual well-being can be achieved. Intellectual resolve to liberate oneself from improper actions is a necessary but not a sufficient step in the process of repentance. Subsequent actions must prove to be correlative with intellectual resolutions.

The Process of Moral Rehabilitation

For much of medieval Jewish literature, intellectual resolve is the first step of a three-step process of repentance. According to Albo, "the elements of repentance by which a person may be cleansed of his iniquities and purified of his or her sin before God are correction of *thought, speech* and *action*" (1930, 4: chap. 26, 235). In his mystical-ethical treatise *Shnei Luhot ha-Brit*, Isaiah Horowitz observed that, since sins are committed by thought, by speech, and by action, repentance must also embrace these three elements (1960, 3:173b). Albo defined intellectual resolve or "correction of thought" as feeling regret on account of one's sins. "Correction of speech" signifies that one should confess one's sins. "Correction of action" means that one must not repeat one's sinful actions.

Regret, remorse, and intellectual recognition of one's sins constitutes the first necessary step on the road to moral rehabilitation.

---

observed, "I do not know where this has been [previously] taught." Similarly, in a responsum, Maimonides stated that an earlier source than al-Fasi is also unknown to him (1948, no. 121, 1: 216–17).

According to the sixteenth-century sage Moses di Trani, this intellectual factor in repentance is the most important of the three elements: "The essence of repentance is regret over the past and departure from sin in the future. Without both of these elements, repentance cannot be complete. . . . Therefore, the essence of repentance is intellectual in two ways: that one have thoughts of remorse and that one intellectually resolve to depart from the sin one has committed" (1852, 29b, cf. Ibn Zaddik 1903, 71). For di Trani the essentials of repentance are remorse and resolve: remorse over what happened and resolve not to repeat it. Remorse without resolve is invalid because it indicates that the remorse is insincere. Resolve without remorse is invalid because a motivation other than contrition might underlie that resolve. It may be that the opportunity to recommit a specific act does not become available, or it may be that the sinner no longer finds the specific sin attractive.

Without the intellectual awareness that one has acted incorrectly, the process of repentance is thwarted at the outset. According to Albo, a major obstacle to such awareness is the human tendency to blame others for their own mistakes. Albo calls this tendency "self-excuse." As an example, Albo refers to Adam, who tried to excuse himself for his sin by blaming Eve for his own transgression. But for Albo, "self-excuse" provides no alibi, "for man was given reason so that he should always watch his conduct and not sin" (1930, 4: chap. 26, 237–38).

While self-excuse is one of many motives that may inhibit repentance, there is a variety of motives that may initiate repentance: fear of divine punishment, fear of alienation from one's better nature, or alienation either from one's fellow or from God. Another motive, already discussed, may be the desire for moral well-being.

Awareness of the reality of one's own mortality can also serve as a powerful stimulant for self-examination and for repentance (see, e.g., Schechter 1909, 276). The talmudic rabbis perceived the recognition of human finitude not as a cause for fatalistic morbidity but as an opportunity for self-improvement. Realizing the transient nature of one's own existence can lead to an avoidance of sin and to a desire for repentance.

Because life is so fragile, so precarious, repentance must not be deferred. "Rabbi Eliezer said: Repent one day before your death. His disciples asked him: Master, does a person know the day of his death? To this question, he responded: Even more so then; let a person repent today, for tomorrow he might die, and all his days will have been spent in repentance" (*Shab.*, 153a).

Regarding Hillel's often-quoted phrase, "If not now, when?" (*PA*, chap. 1, sec. 14), Samuel of Uceda wrote, "The text does not say 'If not *today*, when?' in order to inform us that even today itself is in doubt regarding whether one will survive or not, for at every instant one potentially can die. Therefore, since all one has is the present moment, the text reads, 'If not *now*, when?'" (Samuel of Uceda, 16b).

Samuel of Uceda refers back to Jonah Gerondi's work where Gerondi commented, "'If not now, when?' i.e., I cannot afford to delay for one or two days my exertions on behalf of the perfection of my soul. . . . When perfection of the soul is delayed, the evil inclination grows stronger . . . and self-improvement becomes difficult thereafter . . . It may be that one's days will not be prolonged and that one will die before one has rendered his portion of repentance" (1971, 117–19).

Underlying much of the discussion in rabbinic and medieval sources regarding repentance as a response to the fear of death is the assumption of a life after death, where one's deeds will be examined and judged. While the performance of virtuous deeds and doing repentance are understood to be beneficial in their own right, they are also viewed as instruments to accrue reward and to avoid divine punishment in the world to come. From this perspective, fear of death is linked to fear of God, fear of divine punishment, and fear of possible obliteration in the world to come (see, e.g., *PR*, chap. 44, sec. 8, 184a). Along these lines, Bahya ibn Pakuda interpreted the talmudic statement, "Repent one day before your death" (*Shab.*, 153a), as an admonition to prepare for the next life in this life by accumulating good deeds and by repenting of bad deeds in the here and now. In Bahya's words, "Are we not obliged to fear for ourselves . . . and consider the matter of our provisions for the next world before there is need of it, even one day before?" Among the conditions of remorse that Bahya listed is "fear of God's speedy punishment." Among the conditions of one's "undertaking never to repeat one's sins" is "imagining your death while the Lord is angry with you for your former failure to fulfill your obligations toward Him" (1973, 351, 335, 337–38).

While fear is an accepted and an often effective motive for repentance, many sources consider love to be the preferable motivation for repentance (see, e.g., *Yoma,* 86b). According to Isaiah Horowitz, repentance out of fear is always tainted by self-interest, "One should not repent out of fear, namely, out of fear of punishment, for then one repents for one's own sake. Rather, one should repent out of love for the Creator and for sake of God's Name" (1960, 3:175b). Albo taught that repentance motivated by either fear of punishment or fear of death is not repentance at all (1930, 4: chap. 25, 225–26; see also Sherwin 1991, 51–62). For one who truly loves God, the alienation from God caused by sin, like the separation of any lover from his or her beloved, becomes unbearable. Reconciliation becomes not merely desirable but crucial.

Repentance out of love flows from a desire for return, for healing a rupture of relationship rather than from a hope of reward or from a fear of punishment. The more intense the love, the more significant the relationship, the greater the yearning for reconciliation. In this regard, Elijah di Vidas commented, "Sin causes the alienation of the love between an individual and God, as it is written, 'Your sins have separated you from your God' (Isa. 59:2). Therefore, since a lover does not wish his beloved to become estranged from him, the one who is obliged to the other should confess his faults to his beloved, saying to her: Truly, I have sinned against you, but do not leave me because of my offense" (di Vidas, sec. *"Sha'ar Teshuvah,"* chap. 3, 113a).

Similarly, Maimonides described repentance as a means of reconciliation between the individual and God: "Great is repentance for it brings one near to the divine. . . . Last night a certain individual was separated from God, as it says: 'Your sins have separated you from your God' (Isa. 59:2). . . . Today, the same person [having repented] becomes closely attached to the divine" (*MT—HT,* chap. 7, secs. 6, 7).

To effect complete reconciliation, the return must be mutual. Therefore, repentance requires both a human initiative and a divine response. The corollary of human contrition is divine grace (*ḥesed*) (see, e.g., Albo 1930, 4:232 and 464). A midrash observes, "Consider the parable of a prince who was far away from his father—a hundred days journey away. His friends said to him: Return to your father. He replied: I cannot; I have not the strength. Thereupon his father sent word to him saying: Come back as far as you are able, and I will go the rest of the way to meet you. So the Holy One says to Israel: 'Return to Me, and I shall return to you' (Mal. 3:7)" (*PR,* chap. 44, para. 9, 184b-185a).

The medieval Jewish mystics maintained that God has not only a desire for, but a vested interest in, human repentance. According to the cabalists, sin harms the soul of the sinner, and it also injures God. In the words of the *Zohar* (1883, 3:122a): "Whosoever transgresses the laws of the Torah causes damage above, as it were, causes damage below, damages himself, and damages all worlds." In this view, repentance repairs the damage one's sin causes to one's own self, and it restores God from the harm done against God. For the Jewish mystics, therefore, repentance is *for God's sake*, as well as for our own. It fulfills a divine and a human need (see, e.g., Horowitz 1960, 3:180a). "Repentance," says the *Zohar* (1883, 3:122a), "repairs all. It repairs what is above and below. It repairs damage to oneself and to all worlds." Repentance unifies God's Name, fragmented by human sin. Repentance must be done "for the sake of My Name" (Isa. 48:9), "for My Name's sake" (Ezek. 20:44) (see also Tishbi 1961, 2:735–44).

As was already noted, remorse and resolve represent the first of three steps in the process of repentance. The motivations for this first step have been discussed. Confession is the second step. From an intellectual awareness of one's misdeeds and out of a resolve not to repeat them, the penitent moves toward a specification of his or her faults by making a verbal declaration. Confession translates intellectual assent into verbal commitment. To Maimonides (*MT—HT*, chap. 2, sec. 2, p. 82), "It is necessary that one make oral confession and utter the resolutions one has made in one's mind" (literally: "in one's heart") (cf. *AT—OH*, para. 607; Meiri 1950, 194–201).

Confession constitutes a concrete act of renouncing one's misdeeds. It serves as a transition between the intellectually abstract and the concrete changes in behavior that must follow to make repentance complete and to validate the sincerity of the penitent's resolve (see Abramowitz 1961, 65–94). Maimonides identified confession as a religious obligation. Summarizing the vast biblical and rabbinic literature regarding confession that preceded him and adding some embellishments of his own, Maimonides wrote (*MT—HT*, chap. 1, sec. 1):

With regard to all the precepts of the Torah, affirmative or negative, if a person transgressed any one of them, either willfully or in error, and repents and turns away from his sin, he is duty bound to confess before God, blessed be He, as it is written,

"When a man or a woman shall commit any sin people commit, to do a trespass against the Lord, and that person be guilty, then they shall confess their sin which they have done" (Num. 5:6–7); this means confess in words, and this confession is an affirmative commandment. How does one confess? The penitent says: "I beseech you, O Lord, I have sinned, I have acted perversely, I have transgressed before you, and I have done such and such, and I repent and am ashamed of my deeds, and I never shall do this again." This constitutes the essence of the confession. The fuller and more detailed the confession one makes, the more praiseworthy he is.

Confession of sin became both a public and a private activity. The prayerbook contains public confessionals, recited during communal prayer (such as those recited on the Day of Atonement), and private confessionals (such as the deathbed confessional).[4] Regarding private confession, Isaiah Horowitz recorded that his father would make private confession of his sins three times daily. "And every night before he would retire he would list the deeds he performed that day. Then, he would sit alone and contemplate them. He would scrutinize the actions he performed not only that day but all the days of his life up until that point" (1960, 3:171b). Horowitz further noted the custom of a particular sage to pray that he not be allowed to become angry because "the sin in which all other sins are subsumed is the sin of anger," for anger "is the cause of all sins."

One of the texts upon which Maimonides and others based standard formulae for confession was the talmudic citation, "Our rabbis taught: How does one make confession? [One says:] I have done wrong (*aviti*), I have transgressed (*pashati*), I have sinned (*hatati*)" (*Yoma*, 36b; see also *Sifra*, sec. "*Aharei*," chap. 2, sec. 9, 80b-81a). The talmudic discussion that follows this citation refers to

4. A form of private confession not usually identified with Judaism is confession to another person. Although not pervasive in Judaism, this form of confession was practiced by the medieval *Hasidei Ashkenaz* as well as by adherents to various schools of nineteenth-century eastern European Hasidism, especially the Brazlaver Hasidim. In both these movements, confession was made to a spiritual mentor who would then assign the penitent tasks to perform (i.e., penances) to affect the realization of repentance. For this practice among the *Hasidei Ashkenaz*, see Marcus 1981, 77–78, 131, 141–65. In later Hasidism see Wertheim 1960, 22–23. On confession to a friend in Hasidism, see Joseph Weiss 1985, 160–67. On confession in Brazlaver Hasidism, see, for example, Arthur Green 1979, 45–46; Rappoport-Albert 1973, 65–75.

the distinction among the three previously mentioned varieties of sin: *heit, avon, pesha.* Confession therefore must be made for each of these types of sin. This is why the three varieties of sin are mentioned in the confessional: *Aviti* refers to *avon, pashati* refers to *pesha,* and *hatati* refers to *heit.* The Talmud distinguishes among these three by defining *heit* as an unwitting offense, *avon* as a deliberate misdeed, and *pesha* as an act of rebellion.

Pesha denotes an act of human rebellion against divine sovereignty. In this view, sin represents an act of treason against the Kingdom of Heaven and against the authority of God as sovereign of the universe. From this perspective, repentance entails a reacceptance of God's kingship, a reaffirmation of the laws of God's kingdom, a reinstatement of the individual as a citizen of the kingdom of God (see Schechter 1909, 219–63, 293–343).

Sin as rebellion means that the individual recognizes neither God nor God's law as providing viable standards for human behavior. *Pesha* infers an individual's refusal to be accountable to any standards of morality other than those that he or she arbitrarily establishes. Actions become self-serving rather than being aimed at serving God or at helping others. Repentance means a restoration of one's relationship with a source beyond the self, a reaffirmation of the binding quality of God's law upon human affairs.

The third and final step in the process of repentance is what Albo termed "correction of action." Unless one's intellectual remorse and resolve are translated into concrete action, one's repentance is incomplete and ineffectual. Unless one's verbal confessions result in enacted commitment, one's confession becomes a lie; it is not an expression of sincere remorse. "Correction of action" requires the avoidance of past sins and the performance of deeds of virtue. In this regard, Maimonides summed up talmudic teachings. "What is complete repentance? When an opportunity presents itself for repeating an offense once committed, and the offender, while able to commit the offense, nevertheless refrains from doing so, not out of fear or failure of vigor, but because he is truly repentant" (*MT— HT,* chap. 2, sec. 1. See also *M. Yoma,* chap. 6, sec. 2, chap. 8, sec. 9; *Yoma,* 86b; *Ta'anit,* 16b).

Jonah Gerondi, who compared sin to an illness from which one ought to be cured, commented, "His soul is sick because of those [sinful] deeds, and one who begins to recover from an illness must guard against a relapse" (1971, 50–51). Other sources observe that, like the process of healing physical illness, the process of recovering from a moral malady is not immediate but requires time and effort.

The two steps that constitute "correction of action" are "depart from evil, and do good" (Ps. 34:15). *Orhot Zaddikim* lists abandonment of sin and reversing one's deeds as being among the essentials of repentance. When discussing "reversing one's deeds," this text cites a midrash, "If you have committed bundles of transgressions, counteract them by performing corresponding bundles of sacred deeds" (*LR*, chap. 21, sec. 5; *OZ*, 473). Similarly, the twelfth-century philosopher Abraham bar Hiyya said, "The definition of repentance is the regret of a man for his evil deeds and sins, the implication being that after he has committed the transgression, he repents and firmly observes the commandment he has transgressed" (1969, 87–88).

If performed out of fear of punishment, such deeds may not bring about atonement, as they may be intended as a means of bribing God by offering good deeds in exchange for divine forgiveness. Only if performed out of love and out of a sincere desire for moral rehabilitation do virtuous deeds surely expiate past misdeeds (see, e.g., *OZ*, 478–79). To effect complete repentance, sincerity of deed, thought, and speech are all required. Repentance absolves the misdeeds of the past and initiates the virtues of the future.

Teshuvah is a process of return, rehabilitation, and renewal. A sin is an action that alienates an individual from himself or herself and from God. *Teshuvah* denotes return to one's own self and to God. But, because a sin against God may also be an offense against one's fellow, repentance was not deemed truly complete unless reconciliation also was made with the injured party (see, e.g., *RH*, 17b; *MT—HT*, chap. 2, sec. 9). Furthermore, in seeking God's forgiveness, one is obliged to forgive those who have trespassed against him or her (see, e.g., *Yoma*, 85b, 87a; *BK*, 110a). In so doing, the individual practices *imitatio Dei* by granting forgiveness and practicing mercy. Like God, the individual desires and achieves reconciliation. Thereby, theology and ethics become intertwined. What characterizes God's dealings with us becomes a feature of our relationship with one another.

According to a midrash, after David sinned, he entreated God, "Master of the World, You are a great God and my sins are also great. It is only becoming for a great God that such a God should forgive great sins" (*LR*, chap. 5, sec. 8). By forgiving those who have sinned against him or her, the human person can share in that divine greatness. By seeking the forgiveness of God and of others, the divine image each person bears, though disfigured by sin, may be restored.

Without sin, repentance would not be possible, but without repentance true virtue would not be attainable. It is precisely for this reason that the repentant sinner is exalted even above the purest saint (*Ber.*, 34b; *Zohar* 1883, 1:106b; see also Ibn Pakudah 1973, 345).

According to the Talmud, ethical development is vouchsafed in the hands of each individual. Even God, especially God, does not determine how an individual exercises his or her moral choice. In this regard, a talmudic passage observes that there is an angel called "Night" who oversees the conception of each child. At the moment of conception, the angel inquires of God whether the child just conceived will grow to be weak or strong, poor or rich, and God announces its fate. But, when the angel asks whether the child will become wicked or virtuous, God remains silent, for only the individual person may determine his or her own moral character (*Nid.*, 16b).

Ethical living offers each individual the opportunity of creating his or her life as a work of art, of molding oneself in the image of God. Sin disrupts the creative process, while repentance offers a path to repairing the damage done to the portrait of the image of God. Repentance, according to the talmudic rabbis, is a form of re-creation. To the penitent, God says, "I account it to you as though you were re-created" (*PT. RH*, chap. 4, sec. 8; see also *LR*, chap. 29, sec. 12; *PR*, 169a).[5]

5. A valuable anthology of references in classical Jewish literature on *Teshuvah* is Abramowitz 1961. On sin and repentance in rabbinic theology, see, for example, Petuchowski 1968, Moore 1966, 1: 460–545, Schechter 1909, 219–41, 293–343, Urbach 1987, 462–71, and Buchler 1967. Most of the significant medieval sources regarding repentance are referred to in this chapter. On sin and repentance in modern Jewish theology, see, for example, Kohler 1968, 238–56, Cohon 1962, 273–314, Jacobs 1973, 243–68, Metzger 1968 on Rabbi Kook, and Peli 1984 on Soloveichik.

Glossary
Works Cited
Index

Glossary

Adam Ilaya: Supernal Man; see also *sefirot*
Adam Kadmon: Primordial Man; see also *sefirot*
agada: Nonlegal talmudic literature; see also *Haggada*
assur: forbidden, according to Jewish law
avon: sin
ba'al tashhit: refers to the biblical prohibition against unwarranted destruction of natural resources
bat kol: a heavenly voice serving as an instrument of revelation
ben: son of
Deus Absconditus: the concealed aspect of the divine; see also *En Sof*
emes: see *emet*
emet: truth
En Sof: the concealed aspect of the divine, God as God actually and essentially is, the source of the *sefirot*
Festschrift: a volume of scholarly essays published in someone's honor
gehinom: purgatory or hell
gemilut hasadim: acts of loving-kindness
Golem: literally "formless"; an anthropoid
goses: a terminally ill person, usually with less than three days to live
haggadah: see *agada*
halakhah: Jewish religious law
hesed: mercy, divine grace
hashlamah: completion
hasid: a pious person, a follower of the Hasidic movement
hovah: a legal obligation
ibn: son of
imago Dei: the image of God
imitatio Dei: virtuous acts that imitate God's actions

169

in vitro: conception outside the womb

in vivo: conception and gestation in the womb

Jüdische Wissenschaft: a modern approach to Jewish scholarship, The Scientific Study of Judaism

kal va-homer: "from the light to the weighty"; a form of talmudic logic, a fortiori

Kaddish: a prayer in the Jewish liturgy requiring a quorum to be recited

Kedushah: a prayer in the Jewish liturgy requiring a quorum to be recited

Korban: a sacrifice to God given at the Holy Temple

mamzer: an illegitimate child, a child of an adulterous or incestuous union

mehilah: the waiver or renunciation of a legal claim or entitlement

meit: dead

me'od: very much, also used for emphasis

middot: literally "weighty"; refers in medieval Hebrew to moral virtues

midrash: singular of *midrashim*

midrashim: collections of rabbinic sayings

minyan: a quorum for prayer, traditionally consisting of a minimum of ten men over the age of religious majority, that is, thirteen years

mitah yafa: a good death

mitzvah: a religious commandment, a religious obligation

musar: moral instruction, ethics

neshekh: a bite, also a loan on interest

neshikhah: a bite

Nezikin: a section of the Talmud, generally dealing with tort law and judicial procedure

non sequitur: a logical fallacy where the conclusion does not follow from the premises

pesha: sin

pikadon: a pledge, a bailment

pikuah nefesh: the legal obligation to save a human life

reshut: a legally permissible act

sefirah: singular of *sefirot*

sefirot: the ten divine attributes, powers, potencies. Usually presented in the form of a tree, a series of circles, or a human body. Configured as a body, they represent the Primordial Man also called the Supernal Man. See *Adam Ilaya, Adam Kadmon*

Shekhinah: God's presence in the world; the lowest of the ten *sefirot,* usually described as having female characteristics

Shema: a prayer in the Jewish liturgy

shiur komah: literally "the measurement of the height"; refers to the structure of the *sefirot*

sitra ahara: Aramaic for "the other side"; the demonic

tefillin: phylacteries used in various Jewish prayer services

tereifah: literally "torn"; usually refers to food that does not conform to Jewish dietary laws; also refers to an animal or a human being with irreparable organ damage

teshuvah: literally "return"; repentance

Tiferet: one of the *sefirot;* the "male" counterpart of *Shekhinah*

tikkun: literally a "correction"; an act of repair or improvement

tzaddik: a righteous person; a Hasidic leader

tzayyar: an artist

tzur: a rock

yetzer ha-ra: the human inclination to do evil

yetzer ha-tov: the human inclination to do good

yishuv medinah: good citizenship

Zedakah: social welfare, almsgiving

Zedek: righteousness, justice

zeirufei ha-otiot: the use of number or letter combinations in the practice of magic

Works Cited

Aboab, Isaac. [1514] 1961. *Menorat ha-Ma'or.* Jerusalem: Mosad ha-Rav Kook.

Abrahams, Israel, ed. 1926. *Hebrew Ethical Wills.* Philadelphia: Jewish Publication Society.

———. 1958. *Jewish Life in the Middle Ages.* New York: Meridian.

Abramowitz, Hayyim. 1961. *Heikhal ha-Teshuvah.* Bnei Brak: Nezah.

———. 1971. *Ha-Dibrah ha-Hamishit.* Jerusalem: Reuven Mass.

Abrams, Elliott. 1997. *Faith or Fear.* New York: Free Press.

Abravanel, Don Isaac. [1579] 1964. *Peirush La-Tanah.* 6 vols. Jerusalem: Bnei Abarbanel.

Agadat Bereshit. 1876. Warsaw: Lebensohn.

Ahai Gaon. [1546] 1964. *She'iltot.* 6 vols. Edited by S. K. Mirsky. Jerusalem: Mosad ha-Rav Kook.

Albo, Joseph. [1485] 1930. *Sefer ha-Ikkarim* (The *book of principles*). 6 vols. Translated by Isaac Husik. Philadelphia: Jewish Publication Society of America.

Alsheikh, Moses. 1879. *Torat Moshe.* 2 vols. Warsaw: Munk.

Altmann, Alexander. 1968. "*Homo Imago Dei* in Jewish and Christian Theology." *Journal of Religion* 48: 235–59.

———. 1969. *Studies in Religious Philosophy and Mysticism.* Ithaca, N.Y.: Cornell Univ. Press.

Andrews, Lori. 1986. "My Body — My Property." *Hastings Center Report* 16, no. 5: 28–39.

———. 1999. *The Clone Age.* New York: Henry Holt.

Annas, George. 1989. "A French Homunculus in a Tennessee Court." *Hastings Center Report* 19, no. 6: 20–22.

Arama, Isaac. 1522. *Akedat Yitzhak.* Salonika: N.p.

Ashkenazi, Judah. *Be'er Heiteiv.* In Karo, *Shulhan Arukh* [with commentaries].

Ashkenazi, Zevi. [1767] 1970. *Sheilut u-Teshuvot.* Jerusalem: N.p.

Avot d'Rabbi Natan. 1887. Edited by Solomon Schechter. Vienna: N.p. Translated by Judah Goldin under the title *The Fathers according to Rabbi Nathan* (New Haven: Yale Univ. Press, 1955). Also in *Talmud.*

Ayash, Judah. 1683. *Shevet Yehudah.* Livorno, N.p.

Azikiri, Eliezer. [1601] 1987. *Sefer Hareidim.* Jerusalem: N.p.

Azulai, Hayyim Joseph David. 1843. *Birkhei Yoseif.* Vienna: N.p.

Baer, Yitzhak. 1966. *A History of the Jews in Christian Spain.* 2 vols. Philadelphia: Jewish Publication Society of America.

Bamberger, Bernard. 1961. "*Qetana, Na'arah, Bogereth.*" *Hebrew Union College Annual* 32: 281–94.

Bar Hiyya, Abraham. [1860] 1969. *The Meditation of the Sad Soul (Sefer Hegyon ha-Nefesh).* Translated by Geoffrey Wigoder. London: Routledge and Kegan Paul.

Baron, Salo W. 1942. *The Jewish Community.* 3 vols. Philadelphia: Jewish Publication Society of America.

———. 1958. *A Social and Religious History of the Jews.* Vol. 8. New York: Columbia Univ. Press.

Barrett, William. 1978. *The Illusion of Technique.* New York: Doubleday.

———. 1986. *Death of the Soul: From Descartes to the Computer.* Garden City, N.Y.: Anchor Press.

"Bat Mitzvah." 1971. *Encyclopedia Judaica,* vol. 4, 246. Edited by Cecil Roth. Jerusalem: Keter.

Beauchamp, Tom L., and James F. Childress. 1979. *Principles of Biomedical Ethics.* New York: Oxford Univ. Press.

Bekhor Shor, Joseph. 1956. *Peirush al-ha-Torah.* 3 vols. Jerusalem: Tehiya.

Ben Asher, Bahya. 1892. *Kad ha-Kemah.* Lwow: N.p. *The Encyclopedia of Torah Thoughts.* 1980. Translated by Charles Chavel. New York: Shilo Publishing House.

Ben Asher, Jacob. [1550]. Reprint, N.d. *Arba'ah Turim* [with commentaries]. 7 vols. New York: Grossman.

Ben Azriel of Vilna, Zevi. 1733. *Beit Lehem Yehudah.* Zulka: N.p.

Ben Betzalel, Hayyim. [1593] 1965. *Sefer ha-Hayyim.* Jerusalem: Weinfeld.

Ben David, Abraham. 1964. *Teshuvot u-Fesakim.* Jerusalem: Hosad ha-Rav Kook.

Ben Gershon, Levi (Gersonides). 1547. *Peirush ha-Ralbag al-ha-Torah.* 2 vols. Venice: Bomberg.

Ben Matityahu, Benjamin Ze'ev. 1539. *Binyamin Ze'ev.* Venice: N.p.

Ben Meir, Shabbatai. *Siftei Kohein.* In Karo, *Shulhan Arukh* [with commentaries].

Ben Samuel Ha-Levi, David. *Turei Zahav.* In Karo, *Shulhan Arukh* [with commentaries].

Ben Samuel, Jacob. 1696. *Beit Ya'akov.* Dyrenfuerth: N.p.

Ben Sasson, Hayyim Hillel. 1954. "Wealth and Poverty in the Teachings of the Preacher Rabbi Ephraim of Lunschitz" [in Hebrew]. *Zion* 19: 142–66.

———. 1959. *Hagut ve-Hanhagah.* Jerusalem: Mosad Bialik.

Ben Yekutiel, Yehiel. 1968. *Sefer Ma'alot ha-Middot.* Jerusalem: Eshkol.

Bergman, Yehudah. 1944. *Ha-Zedakah be-Yisrael.* Jerusalem: Tarshish.

Berlin, Saul. 1793. *Besomin Rosh.* Berlin, N.p.

Bernstein, Carl, and Marco Politi. 1996. *His Holiness.* New York: Doubleday.

Bernstein, Philip. 1983. *To Dwell in Unity.* Philadelphia: Jewish Publication Society of America.

Bettan, Israel. 1939. *Studies in Jewish Preaching.* Cincinnati: Hebrew Union College Press.

Bick, Ezra. 1997. "Ovum Donations: A Rabbinic Conceptual Model of Maternity." In *Jewish Law and the New Reproductive Technologies,* Edited by Emmanuel Feldman and Joel B. Wolowelsky, 83–105. Hoboken, N.J.: Ktav.

Bin Gorion, Emmanuel, ed. 1976. *Mimekor Yisrael: Classical Jewish Folktales.* Translated by I. M. Lusk. Philadelphia: Jewish Publication Society of America.

Blackstone, William. 1765. *Commentaries on the Laws of England, of the Rights of Persons.* Oxford: Clarendon Press.

Bleich, J. David. 1977. *Contemporary Halakhic Problems.* New York: Yeshiva Univ. Press.

———. 1978. "Test-Tube Babies." *Tradition* 17, no. 3: 86–90.

———. 1981. "Maternal Identity." *Tradition* 19, no. 4: 359–60.

———. 1989. "Fetal Tissue Research." *Tradition* 24, no. 4: 69–90.

———. 1991. "In Vitro Fertilization: Questions of Maternal Identity and Conversion." *Tradition* 25, no. 4: 82–102.

———. 1997. "In Vitro Fertilization: Questions of Maternal Identity and Conversion." In *Jewish Law and the New Reproductive Technologies,* edited by Emmanuel Feldman and Joel B. Wolowelsky, 46–82. Hoboken, N.J.: Ktav.

———. 1998. "Surrogate Motherhood." *Tradition* 32, no. 2: 146–67.

Blidstein, Gerald. 1975. *Honor Thy Father and Mother.* New York: Ktav.

Bloch, Hayyim. 1925. *The Golem.* Translated by Harry Schneiderman. Vienna: Vernay.

Boaz, Joshua. *Shiltei ha-Gibborim.* In *Talmud* [with commentaries].

Borowitz, Eugene B. 1990. *Exploring Jewish Ethics.* Detroit: Wayne State Univ. Press.

Breitowitz, Yitzchok A. 1997. "Halakhic Approaches to the Resolution of

Disputes Concerning the Disposition of Preembryos." In *Jewish Law and The New Reproductive Technologies,* edited by Emmanuel Feldman and Joel B. Wolowelsky, 155–186. Hoboken, N.J.: Ktav.

Brooks, Roger. 1983. *Support for the Poor in the Mishnaic Law of Agriculture.* Chico, Calif.: Scholars Press.

Broyde, Michael J. 1988. "The Establishment of Maternity and Paternity in Jewish and America Law." *National Jewish Law Review* 3: 117–58.

———. 1997. "Cloning People and Jewish Law: A Preliminary Analysis." *Journal of Halacha and Contemporary Society* 24: 27–65.

Buber, Martin. 1948. *Tales of the Hasidim.* 2 vols. Translated by Olga Marx. New York: Schocken.

Buchler, Adolph. [1928] 1967. *Studies in Sin and Atonement.* New York: Ktav.

Caidin, Martin. 1972. *Cyborg.* New York: Warner.

Capek, Joseph, and Karel Capek. *R.U.R.* 1961. Translated by P. Selver. London: Oxford Univ. Press.

Catechism of the Catholic Church. 1994. Mahwah, N.J.: Paulist Press.

Chipkin, Israel. 1949. "Judaism and Social Welfare." In *The Jews,* edited by Louis Finkelstein, 1043–73. Philadelphia: Jewish Publication Society of America.

Chodos, Israel. 1938. "A Critical Edition of Shem Tov Ben Joseph Falaquera's *Bate Hanhagat Guf ha-Bari.*" *Ha-Rofe ha-Ivri* 10, no. 1: 113–25.

Cohen, Arthur A. 1971. *The Myth of the Judeo-Christian Tradition.* New York: Schocken.

Cohen, Boaz. 1966. *Studies in Jewish and Roman Law.* 2 vols. New York: Jewish Theological Seminary of America.

Cohen, Steven. 1983. *American Modernity and Jewish Identity.* New York: Tavistock Publications.

Cohen-Aloro, Dorith. 1987. "The Zohar's View of Magic as a Consequence of the Original Sin" [in Hebrew]. *Da'at* 19:31–65.

Cohn, Hayyim. 1971. "Homicide." In *Encyclopedia Judaica,* edited by Cecil Roth, 8:944–46. Jerusalem: Keter.

Cohn-Sherbok, Dan, ed. 1991. *A Traditional Quest: Essays in Honour of Louis Jacobs.* Sheffield, England: Sheffield Academic Press.

Cohon, Samuel S. 1948. "Original Sin." *Hebrew Union College Annual* 21:275–331.

———. 1962. *Judaism.* New York: Schocken.

Cordovero, Moses. [1588] 1965. *Tomer Devorah.* Tel Aviv: Friedman. Translated by Louis Jacobs under the title *The Palm Tree of Deborah.* (London: Vallentine, Mitchell, 1960.)

Crichton, Michael. 1969. *The Andromeda Strain.* New York: Knopf.

Cronbach, Abraham. 1936. "The *Me'il Zedakah*." *Hebrew Union College Annual* 11:503–67.

———. 1937–38. "The *Me'il Zedakah*." *Hebrew Union College Annual* 12–13:635–96.

———. 1939. "The *Me'il Zedakah*." *Hebrew Union College Annual* 14:479–557.

———. 1941. "The Gradations of Benevolence." *Hebrew Union College Annual* 16:163–86.

———. 1949. "Social Thinking in the Sefer Hasidim." *Hebrew Union College Annual* 22:1–147.

Dann, Jack, ed. 1974. *Wandering Stars*. New York: Harper and Row.

Davidson, Avram. 1974. "The Golem." In *Wandering Stars*, edited by Jack Dann, 41–48. New York: Harper and Row.

David, Yonah, ed. 1975. *Shirei Amitai*. Jerusalem: Achshav.

Davis v Davis v King. 5th Jud. Ct., Tennessee E-14496, September 21, 1989.

Del Zio v Manhattan's Columbia Presbyterian Medical Center No. 74–3558 S. District of N.Y., Nov. 14, 1978.

de La Mettrie, Offray. 1912. *Man, A Machine*. LaSalle, Ill.: Open Court.

Deuteronomy Rabbah. In *Midrash Rabbah*.

Devlin, Patrick. 1965. *The Enforcement of Morals*. London: Oxford Univ. Press.

Devorkes, Eliakum. 1974. *Ispaklarit ha-Zedakah*. Jerusalem: N.p.

Di Trani, Moses. 1852. *Beit Elohim*. Warsaw: Goldman.

Di Vidas, Elijah. [1579] N.d. *Reshit Hokhmah*. Tel Aviv: Esther Press.

Dorff, Elliot N. 1991. "A Jewish Approach to End-Stage Medical Care." *Conservative Judaism* 43, no. 3: 3–52.

———. 1996. "Artificial Insemination, Egg Donation and Adoption." *Conservative Judaism* 49, no. 1: 3–60.

———. 1997. "Human Cloning: A Jewish Perspective." Presentation to The National Bioethics Advisory Commission, Mar. 14.

———. 1999. *Matters of Life and Death*. Philadelphia: Jewish Publication Society.

Dorff, Elliot, and Louis E. Newman, eds. 1995. *Contemporary Jewish Ethics and Morality*. New York: Oxford Univ. Press.

"Economic Justice for All: Catholic Social Teaching and the U.S. Economy." 1986. *Origins* 16, no. 24: 409–55.

Edels, Samuel. *Hiddushei Halakhot ve-Aggadot*. In *Talmud* [with commentaries].

Edelstein, Ludwig. 1943. *The Hippocratic Oath: Text, Translation and Interpretation*. Baltimore: Johns Hopkins Press.

Edwards, Paul. 1972. "My Death." In *Encyclopedia of Philosophy*, edited by Paul Edwards, 5:416–19. New York: Macmillan.

Eibshitz, Jonathan. 1863. *Ya'arot Devash*. Lwow: N.p.

Eiger, Akiva. *Gilyonei Maharshah.* In Karo, *Shulhan Arukh* [with commentaries].

Einhorn, Ze'ev. *Maharzu.* In *Midrash Rabbah* [with commentaries].

Eisenstadt, Abraham Zvi. *Pithei Teshuvah.* In Karo, *Shulhan Arukh* [with commentaries].

Eisenstein, Judah, ed. 1915. *Otzar Midrashim.* 2 vols. New York: Grossman.

Elbaum, Jacob. 1992. *Teshuvat ha-Leiv ve-Kabbalat Yesurim.* Jerusalem: Magnes Press.

Eliezer of Metz. [1566] 1837. *Sefer Yere'im.* Livorno: Rokeah.

Elijah ha-Kohen of Smyrna. 1731. *Me'il Zedakah.* Smyrna: N.p.

Elimelekh of Lizensk. 1787. *Noam Elimelekh.* Lwow: N.p.

Emden, Jacob. 1884. *Sheilat Ya'avetz.* Lwow, N.p.

———. *Commentary on the Talmud* [in Hebrew]. In *Talmud* [with commentaries].

Encyclopedia ha-Talmudit. 1947–. Jerusalem: Makhon ha-Encyclopedia ha-Talmudit.

Engel, George L. 1977. "The Need for a New Medical Model: A Challenge for Biomedicine." *Science* 196: 129–35.

Even-Shushan, Abraham. 1969. *Ha-Milon Heh-Hadash.* 3 vols. Jerusalem: Kiryat Sefer.

Exodus Rabbah. In *Midrash Rabbah.*

Al-Fasi, Isaac. *Hilkhot Rav Alfas.* In *Talmud* [with commentaries].

Faur, José. 1986. *Golden Doves with Silver Dots.* Bloomington, Ind.: Indiana Univ. Press.

Federbush, Simon. 1952. "The Problem of Euthanasia in Jewish Tradition." *Judaism* 1, no. 1: 64–68.

Fein, Leonard. 1988. *Where Are We?* New York: Harper and Row.

Feinstein, Moshe. 1963. *Iggerot Moshe — Yoreh Deah.* 2 vols. New York: Balshon.

———. 1996. *Responsa of Rav Moshe Feinstein: Care of the Critically Ill.* Translated by Moshe David Tendler. Hoboken, N.J.: Ktav.

Feldman, David M. 1968. *Birth Control in Jewish Law.* New York: New York Univ. Press.

Feldman, Emmanuel, and Joel B. Wolowelsky, eds. 1997. *Jewish Law and the New Reproductive Technologies.* Hoboken, N.J.: Ktav.

Finkelstein, Louis, ed. 1949. *The Jews.* Philadelphia: Jewish Publication Society of America.

Fiore, Mark. 1997. "Clinton Proposes Legislation to Ban Research on Cloning of Humans." *Chronicle of Higher Education,* June 20, 32.

Fletcher, Joseph F. 1974. *The Ethics of Genetic Control.* Garden City, N.Y.: Anchor.

Freedman, Nancy. 1973. *Joshua Son of None.* New York: Delacorte Press.

Freehof, Solomon B. 1960. *Reform Responsa.* Cincinnati: Hebrew Union College Press.

Friedenwald, Harry. 1944. *The Jews and Medicine.* 2 vols. Baltimore: Johns Hopkins Univ. Press.

Frisch, Ephraim. 1924. *An Historical Survey of Jewish Philanthropy.* New York: Cooper Square Publishers.

Ganzfried, Solomon. 1860. *Kitzur Shulhan Arukh.* Lwow: N.p.

Gaylin, Willard. 1972. "We Have the Awful Knowledge to Make Exact Copies of Human Beings." *New York Times Magazine,* Mar. 6, 10–11, 41–44, 48–49.

Geduld, Harry, and Ronald Gottesman. 1978. *Robots.* Boston: Little, Brown.

Genesis Rabbah. In *Midrash Rabbah.*

Gerondi, Jonah. [1500] 1971. *Gates of Repentance (Sha'arei Teshuvah).* Translated by Shraga Silverstein. Jerusalem: Feldheim.

Gershuni, Judah. 1978. "The First Test Tube Baby in the Light of Jewish Law [in Hebrew]." *Or ha-Mizrah* 27, no. 1: 15–20.

Ginzberg, Louis. 1955. *Legends of the Jews.* 7 vols. Philadelphia: Jewish Publication Society of America.

Givurtchav, Simon, ed. 1962. *Sefer ha-Besht.* 2 vols. Jerusalem: Horeb.

Goldsmith, Arnold L. 1981. *The Golem Remembered.* Detroit: Wayne State Univ. Press.

Goodfield, June. 1977. *Playing God.* New York: Random House.

Green, Arthur. 1979. *Tormented Master: A Life of Rabbi Nahman of Bratslav.* University, Ala.: Univ. of Alabama Press.

Greenwald, Leopold. 1947. *Kol Bo Al Avelut.* New York: Moriah Printing Co.

Gruber, Mayer I., ed. 1993. *The Solomon Goldman Lectures.* Vol. 6. Chicago: Spertus College of Judaica Press.

Haas, Peter. 1985. "Toward a Semiotic Study of Jewish Moral Discourse: The Case of Responsa." *Semeia* 34: 59–85.

Hafetz, Moses. 1914. *Malekhet Mahshevet.* Warsaw: Cahana.

Halevi, C. D. 1987. "Disconnecting a Terminal Patient from an Artificial Respirator." In *Crossroads,* 147–55. Jerusalem: Zomet.

Ha-Levi, David. *Turei Zahav.* In Karo, *Shulhan Arukh* [with commentaries].

Ha-Levi, Judah. 1924. *The Kuzari.* Translated by H. Slonimsky. New York: Schocken.

Hahn, Joseph Yuspa. 1928. *Yosif Ometz.* Frankfurt: Hermon.

Haliburd, G. B. 1978. "Euthanasia." *Jewish Law Annual* 1: 196–99.

Halkin, Abraham S. 1944. "Classical and Arabic Material in Ibn Aknin's 'Hygiene of the Soul.'" *Proceedings of the American Academy for Jewish Research.* 14: 25–147.

Heller, Aryeh Leib. 1888. *Ketzot ha-Hoshen.* Lwow: N.p.

Heschel, Abraham Joshua. 1955. *God in Search of Man.* New York: Harper and Row.

———. 1965. 2 vols. *Torah min ha-Shamayim B'Ispaklariah shel ha-Dorot.* London: Soncino.

———. 1966. *The Insecurity of Freedom.* New York: Farrar, Straus and Giroux.

———. 1973. *A Passion for Truth.* New York: Farrar, Straus and Giroux.

———. 1996a. *Moral Grandeur and Spiritual Audacity.* New York: Farrar, Straus and Giroux.

———. 1996b. *Prophetic Inspiration After the Prophets: Maimonides and Other Medieval Authorities.* Hoboken, N.J.: Ktav.

The Holy Letter (Iggeret ha-Kodesh). [1546] 1976. Translated by Seymour J. Cohen. New York: Ktav.

Horowitz, Isaiah. [1649] 1960. *Shnei Luhot ha-Brit.* 3 vols. Jerusalem: Edison.

Hudock, George A. 1973. "Gene Therapy and Genetic Engineering." *Indiana Law Journal* 48: 533–58.

Ibn Adret, Solomon. 1883. *She'eilot u-Teshuvot.* Pietrikov: Belkhatavsky.

Ibn al-Nakawa, Israel. 1931. *Menorat ha-Ma'or.* 4 vols. New York: Bloch.

Ibn Asevelli, Yom Tov. 1959. *She'eilot u-Teshuvot.* Edited by J. Kapah. Jerusalem: N.p.

Ibn Attar, Hayyim. *Or ha-Hayyim.* In *Mikraot Gedolot.*

Ibn Daud, Abraham. 1852. *Emunah Ramah.* Frankfurt: N.p.

Ibn Ezra, Abraham. *Commentary on the Torah* [in Hebrew]. In *Mikraot Gedolot.*

Ibn Falaquera, Shem Tov ben Joseph. [1846] 1976. *The Book of the Seeker (Sefer ha-Mevakesh).* Translated by M. H. Levine. New York: Yeshiva Univ. Press.

Ibn Gabirol, Solomon. 1901. *The Improvement of the Moral Qualities.* Translated by Stephen S. Wise. New York: Columbia Univ. Press.

Ibn Pakuda, Bahya. [1490] 1973. *Duties of the Heart (Hovavot ha-Levavot).* Translated by Menahem Mansoor. London: Routledge and Kegan Paul.

Ibn Verga, Solomon. [1683] 1955. *Shevet Yehudah.* Jerusalem: N.p.

Ibn Zaddik, Joseph. 1903. *Olam ha-Katan.* Edited by S. Horovitz. Breslau: Schatzky.

Ibn Zimra, David. 1781. *Teshuvot ha-Radbaz.* 3 vols. Furth: N.p.

Idel, Moshe. 1988a. *Kabbalah: New Perspectives.* New Haven: Yale Univ. Press.

———. 1988b. *Mystical Experience in Abraham Abulafia.* Albany: SUNY Press.

———. 1989. "Sexual Metaphors and Praxis in Kabbalah." In *The Jewish Family,* edited by David Kraemer, 197–225. New York: Oxford Univ. Press.

————. 1990. *Golem.* Albany: SUNY Press.

Isserles, Moses. *Darkhei Moshe.* In Ben Asher, *Arba'ah Turim.*

————. *Mapah.* In Karo, *Shulhan Arukh.*

Jacob, Walter, and Moshe Zemer, eds. 1995. *Death and Euthanasia in Jewish Law.* Pittsburgh: Freehof Institute of Progressive Halakhah.

Jacobs, Louis. 1964. *Principles of the Jewish Faith.* New York: Basic Books.

————. 1966. "The Doctrine of the Divine Spark in Man in Jewish Sources." *Studies in Rationalism, Judaism and Universalism,* edited by R. Loewe, 87–114. New York: Humanities Press.

————. 1968. *Jewish Law.* New York: Behrman House.

————. 1973. *A Jewish Theology.* New York: Behrman House.

————. 1975. *Theology in the Responsa.* London: Routledge and Kegan Paul.

————. 1979. "Eating as an Act of Worship in Hasidic Thought." *Studies in Jewish Religious and Intellectual History,* edited by Sigfried Stein and Raphael Loewe, 157–66. University, Ala.: Univ. of Alabama Press.

————. 1981. "Rabbi Aryeih Laib Heller's Theological Introduction to His *Shev Shema Tata.*" *Modern Judaism* 1: 184–217.

Jacobson, Yoram. 1987. "The Image of God and Its Status as the Source of Human Evil According to Judah Loew of Prague" [in Hebrew]. *Da'at* 19: 103–36.

Jakobovits, Immanuel. 1959. *Jewish Medical Ethics.* New York: Bloch.

Jastrow, Marcus. 1950. *A Dictionary of the Targumim, the Talmud Babli and Yerusalmi.* 2nd ed. 2 vols. New York: Pardes.

Jonas, Hans. 1974. *Philosophical Essays.* Englewood Cliffs, N.J.: Prentice-Hall.

Kaku, Michio. 1997. *Visions.* New York: Anchor Books.

Karo, Joseph. *Beit Yoseif.* In Ben Asher, *Arba'ah Turim* [with commentaries].

————. *Maggid Mishnah.* In Moses Maimonides, *Mishneh Torah* [with commentaries].

————. [1564] 1911. *Shulhan Arukh.* 4 vols. Vilna: Romm.

Kasimow, Harold, and, Byron L. Sherwin, eds. 1992. *No Religion Is an Island: Abraham Joshua Heschel and Interreligious Dialogue.* Maryknoll, N.Y.: Orbis Books.

Kass, Leon R. 1972. "New Beginnings in Life." In *The New Genetics and the Future of Man,* edited by Michael P. Hamilton, 15–63. Grand Rapids, Mich.: William B. Eerdmans.

————. 1985. *Toward a More Natural Science.* New York: Free Press.

Kaufmann, Yehezkel. 1960. *The Religion of Israel.* Translated and abridged by Moshe Greenberg. Chicago: Univ. of Chicago Press.

Kimhi, David. *Commentary to the Bible* [Hebrew]. In *Mikraot Gedolot.*

Kirshenbaum, Aaron. 1976. *The "Good Samaritan" and Jewish Law.* Tel Aviv: Tel Aviv Univ. Press.

Knobel, Peter. 1995. "Suicide, Assisted Suicide, Active Euthanasia." In *Death and Euthanasia in Jewish Law,* edited by Walter Jacob and Moshe Zemer, 27–59. Pittsburgh: Freehof Institute of Progressive Halakhah.

Kochan, Lionel. 1990. *Jews, Idols and Messiahs.* Oxford: Basil Blackwell.

Kohler, Kaufmann. 1916. *Hebrew Union College and Other Addresses.* Cincinnati: Ark.

Kohler, Kaufmann. 1968. *Jewish Theology.* New York: Ktav.

Kolata, Gina. 1997. "Ethics Panel Recommends Ban on Human Cloning." *New York Times,* June 8, 18.

———. 1998. *Clone.* New York: William Morrow.

Kraemer, David. 1989. "Images of Childhood and Adolescence in Talmudic Literature." In *The Jewish Family,* edited by David Kraemer, 65–80. New York: Oxford Univ. Press.

Kurzweil, Ray. 1999. *The Age of Spiritual Machines.* New York: Viking.

Lainer, Gershon Hanokh. 1903. *Sidrei Taharot — Ohalot.* Pyotrkow: N.p.

Lasker, Daniel. 1988. "Original Sin and Its Refutation According to Hasdai Crescas" [in Hebrew]. *Da'at* 20: 127–35.

Lebinger, Israel. 1915–16. "The Minor in Jewish Law." *Jewish Quarterly Review* 6: 459–93.

———. 1916–17. "The Minor in Jewish Law." *Jewish Quarterly Review* 7: 89–111, 145–74.

Leivick, Hapler. 1927. *Der Golem.* Vilna: Kletzkin. *The Golem.* 1972. In *Great Jewish Plays,* 217–356. Translated by Joseph C. Landis. New York: Avon.

Levi Yitzhak of Berditchev. [1798] 1996. *Sefer Kedushat Levi ha-Shalem.* New York: Mahon Kedushat Levi.

Levin, Ira. 1976. *The Boys from Brazil.* New York: Dell.

Lieberman, Saul. 1965. *Greek in Jewish Palestine.* New York: Feldheim.

Liebman, Charles S. 1973. *The Ambivalent American Jew.* Philadelphia: Jewish Publication Society of America.

Lipschutz, Israel. 1830. *Tiferet Yisrael.* Hanover, Germany: N.p.

Loew, Judah. [1589] 1969. *Derekh Hayyim.* New York: Judaica Press.

———. 1969. *Hiddushei Aggadot.* 4 vols. New York: Judaica Press.

———. [1595] 1969. *Netivot Olom.* 2 vols. New York: Judaica Press.

———. [1599] 1969. *Tiferet Yisrael.* New York: Judaica Press.

———. [1578] 1972. *Gur Aryeh.* 5 vols. Jerusalem: Yahadut.

Lunshitz, Ephraim. *Kelei Yakar.* In *Mikraot Gedolot.*

Luria, David. *Hiddushei ha-Radal.* In *Midrash Rabbah* [with commentaries].

Lurie, Harry. 1961. *A Heritage Affirmed.* Philadelphia: Jewish Publication Society of America.

Luzzatto, Moses Hayyim. [1740] 1966. *Mesilat Yesharim — The Path of the Upright.* Translated by Mordecai M. Kaplan. Philadelphia: Jewish Publication Society of America.

Maimonides, Moses. [1560] 1912. *The Eight Chapters of Maimonides on Ethics* [*Shemoneh Perakim*]. Translated and edited by Joseph Gorfinkle. New York: Columbia Univ. Press.

———. 1948. *Teshuvot ha-Rambam.* 3 vols. Edited by J. Blau. Jerusalem: Mekitzei Nirdamim.

———. [1885] 1957. *Hanhagat ha-Beruit.* Translated (into Hebrew) by Moses ibn Tibbon. Edited by S. Muntner. Jerusalem: Mosad ha-Rav Kook.

———. [1480] 1963. *Guide of the Perplexed* (*Moreh Nevuhim*). [Abbrev. in text as *GP*]. Translated by Shlomo Pines. Chicago: Univ. of Chicago Press.

———. [1509] 1963. *Mishneh Torah* [with commentaries]. [Abbrev. in text as *MT*]. New York: Friedman.

———. 1963. *Peirush la-Mishnah* (*Commentary to the Mishnah*). [Abbrev. in text as *CM*]. 3 vols. Edited by Joseph Kapah. Jerusalem: Mosad ha-Rav Kook. Also in *Talmud* [with commentaries].

———. 1963. *Treatise on Asthma.* Translated by S. Muntner. Philadelphia: Lippincott.

———. 1971a. *The Medical Aphorisms of Moses Maimonides.* 2 vols. Translated by Fred Rosner and S. Muntner. New York: Yeshiva Univ. Press.

———. [1510] 1971b. *Sefer ha-Mitzvot.* Edited by Joseph Kapah. Jerusalem: Mosad ha-Rav Kook.

Marcus, Ivan. 1981. *Piety and Society.* Leiden: E. J. Brill.

Matt, Moses. 1876. *Mateh Moshe.* Warsaw: N.p.

Meiri, Menahem. 1950. *Hibbur al-ha-Teshuvah.* Edited by Alexander Schrieber. New York: Schulzinger.

———. 1964. *Beit ha-Behirah — Avodah Zarah.* Jerusalem: Tehiya.

———. 1965. *Beit ha-Behirah — Sanhedrin.* Jerusalem: Tehiya.

Mekhilta d'Rabbi Yishmael. [1515] 1960. Edited by Hayyim Horovitz and Israel Rabin. Jerusalem: Wahrmann. Translated by Jacob Lauterbach. 1933. 3 vols. Philadelphia: Jewish Publication Society of America.

Metzger, Alter. 1968. *Rabbi Kook's Philosophy of Repentance.* New York: Yeshiva Univ. Press.

Meyrink, Gustav. 1964. *The Golem.* Translated by Madge Pemberton. New York: Ungar.

Midrash Rabbah. [1545] 1921. [with commentaries]. 2 vols. Vilna: Romm. English translation by H. Freedman and Maurice Simon, eds. 1939. 10 vols. London: Soncino.

Midrash Samuel. 1893. Edited by Solomon Buber. Cracow: Fisher.

Midrash Tanhuma. [1520] 1885. Edited by Solomon Buber. 2 vols. Vilna: N.p.

Midrash Tehillim. [1512] 1891. Edited by Solomon Buber. Vilna: Romm. Translated by William G. Braude, under the title *Midrash on Psalms.* (New Haven: Yale Univ. Press, 1959).

Midrash Temurah. In Eisenstein 1915, and, in *Agadat Bereshit* 1876.

Mikraot Gedolot (Hebrew Scriptures with commentaries). [1517] 1959. 5 vols. New York: Tanach.

The Minor Tractates of the Talmud. 1965. 2 vols. Edited by A. Cohen. London: Soncino.

Moore, George Foot. 1966. *Judaism in the First Centuries of the Christian Era.* 3 vols. Cambridge, Mass.: Harvard Univ. Press.

Moses Hayyim Ephraim of Sudlykow. [1808] 1963. *Degel Mahaneh Efraim.* Jerusalem: Hadar.

Nahmanides, Moses. 1960. *Peirush ha-Ramban al-ha-Torah.* Edited by Charles Chavel. 2 vols. Jerusalem: Mosad ha-Rav Kook. Also in *Mikraot Gedolot.*

———. 1964. *Kitve Rabbenu Moshe ben Nahman.* Edited by Charles Chavel. 2 vols. Jerusalem: Mosad ha-Rav Kook.

Nahman of Bratslav. [1806] 1966. *Likkutei Moharan.* 2 vols. New York: Braslaver.

Newman, Louis E. 1995. "Woodchoppers and Respirators: The Problem of Interpretation in Contemporary Jewish Ethics." In *Contemporary Jewish Ethics and Morality,* edited by Elliot N. Dorff and Louis E. Newman, 140–160. New York: Oxford Univ. Press.

———. 1997. "Covenantal Responsibility in a Modern Context: Recent Work in Jewish Ethics." *Journal of Religious Ethics* 25, no. 1: 185–210.

Nissim (Rabbenu Nissim). *Ran.* In *Talmud* [with commentaries].

Orhot Zaddikim. 1969. Translated by Seymour J. Cohen. New York: Feldheim.

Oz, Sholomit Joy. 1995. "Genetic Mother vs. Surrogate Mother." *Touro International Law Review* 6: 437–60.

Ozick, Cynthia. 1982. *Levitation.* New York: Knopf.

Palaggi, Hayyim. 1840. *Hikkeke Lev.* 2 vols. Salonika: N.p.

Palestinian Talmud [*Talmud Yerushalmi*] [with commentaries]. 6 vols. 1886. Krotoschin: N.p.

Peli, Pinhas, ed. 1984. *Soloveichik on Repentance.* Ramsey, N.J.: Paulist Press.

Pesikta d'Rav Kahana. 1868. Edited by Solomon Buber. Lyck: Mekitzei Nirdamim. Translated by William G. Braude and Israel J. Kapstein. 1975. Philadelphia: Jewish Publication Society of America.

Pesikta Rabbati. 1880. Edited by Meir Friedman. Vienna: Herausgebers. Translated by William G. Braude. 1968. 2 vols. New Haven: Yale Univ. Press.

Petuchowski, Jacob. 1968. "The Concept of *Teshuvah* in the Bible and Talmud." *Judaism* 17, no. 3: 175–86.

Phillips, Michael J. 1992. "Corporate Moral Personhood and Three Conceptions of the Corporation." *Business Ethics Quarterly* 2, no. 4: 435–59.

Piller, Charles, and Keith Yamamoto. 1988. *Gene Wars*. New York: Morrow.

Pirke d'Rabbi Eliezer [1852] 1946. New York: Ohm. Translated by Gerald Friedlander. 1916. London: N.p.

Plato. [1892] 1937. *The Dialogues of Plato*. Translated by B. Jowett. 2 vols. New York: Random House.

———. *Charmides*. In *Dialogues of Plato*.

———. *Laws*. In *Dialogues of Plato*.

———. *Phaedrus*. In *Dialogues of Plato*.

President's Commission for the Study of Ethical Problems in Medicine and Biomedical and Behavioral Research. 1982. *Splicing Life*. Washington, D.C.: U.S. Government Printing Office.

Ramsey, Paul. 1970. *Fabricated Man*. New Haven: Yale Univ. Press.

Raphael, Marc Lee, ed. 1979. *Understanding Jewish Philanthropy*. New York: Ktav.

Rappoport-Albert, Ada. 1973. "Confession in the Circle of Rabbi Nahman of Bratslav." *Bulletin of the Institute of Jewish Studies* 1: 65–75.

Rashi (Solomon Yitzhaki). *Commentary to the Bible* [Hebrew]. In *Mikraot Gedolot*.

———. *Commentary to the Talmud* [Hebrew]. In *Talmud* [with commentaries].

Reichman, Edward. 1997. "The Rabbinic Conception of Conception." In *Jewish Law and the New Reproductive Technologies*, edited by Emmanuel Feldman and Joel B. Wolowelsky, 1–35. Hoboken, N.J.: Ktav.

Reines, Charles. 1961. "The Jewish Attitude Toward Suicide." *Judaism* 10, no. 2, 160–70.

Reischer, Jacob. 1860. *Shevut Ya'akov*. Lwow: N.p.

Rorvik, David. 1978. *In His Image: The Cloning of a Man*. Philadelphia: J. B. Lippincott.

Rosenberg, Judah. 1909. *Nifla'ot ha-Maharal*. Pyotrkow: N.p.

Rosenfeld, Azriel. 1966. "Religion and the Robot." *Tradition* 8, no. 3: 15–26.

———. 1967. "Refrigeration, Resuscitation and the Resurrection." *Tradition* 9, no. 3: 82–94.

———. 1972. "Judaism and Gene Therapy." *Tradition* 13, no. 2: 71–80.

———. 1977. "Human Identity: Halakhic Issues." *Tradition* 16, no. 3: 58–74.

———. 1997. "Generation, Gestation, and Judaism." In *Jewish Law and the New Reproductive Technologies*, edited by Emmanuel Feldman and Joel B. Wolowelsky, 36–45. Hoboken, N.J.: Ktav.

Rosenzweig, Franz. 1970. *The Star of Redemption*. Translated by William W. Hallo. New York: Holt, Rinehart and Winston.

Rosner, Fred. 1970. "Artificial Insemination in Jewish Law." *Judaism* 19, no. 4: 452–64.

———. 1991. *Modern Medicine and Jewish Ethics.* Hoboken, N.J.: Ktav.

Rosner, Fred, and J. David Bleich. 1969. *Jewish Bioethics.* New York: Hebrew Publishing.

Roth, Cecil, ed. 1971. *Encyclopedia Judaica.* 20 vols. Jerusalem: Keter.

Rothberg, Abraham. 1970. *The Sword of the Golem.* New York: McCall Publishing.

Saadya Gaon. 1948. *Book of Beliefs and Opinions.* Translated by Samuel Rosenblatt. New Haven: Yale Univ. Press.

Saltzman, Steven. 1982. "The Sanctity of Life in Jewish Law." D.H.L. diss., Jewish Theological Seminary of America.

Samuel of Uceda. [1579] N.d. *Midrash Shmuel.* Jerusalem: Brody-Katz.

Saul, John. 1982. *The God Project.* New York: Bantam.

Schachter, Melech. 1982. "Various Aspects of Adoption." *Journal of Halacha and Contemporary Society* 4: 93–155.

Schechter, Solomon. 1909. *Some Aspects of Rabbinic Theology.* New York: Macmillan.

———. 1924. *Studies in Judaism: Third Series.* Philadelphia: Jewish Publication Society of America.

Schechterman, Deborah. 1988. "Maimonides's View of Original Sin as Reflected in Jewish Thought in the Thirteenth Century and in the Fourteenth Century" [in Hebrew]. *Da'at* 20: 65–135.

Scholem, Gershom. 1965. *On The Kabbalah and Its Symbolism.* Translated by Ralph Manheim. New York: Schocken.

———. 1971. *The Messianic Idea in Judaism.* New York: Schocken.

———. 1991. *The Mystical Shape of the Godhead.* New York: Schocken.

Schreiber, Moses. [1841] 1883. *Sheilot u-Teshuvot Hatam Sofer — Yoreh Deah.* Vienna: N.p.

Sefer ha-Bahir. [1651] 1951. Edited by Reuven Margaliot. Jerusalem: Mosad ha-Rav Kook.

Sefer ha-Hinukh. [1533] 1978. Edited and translated by Charles Wengrov. Jerusalem: Feldheim.

Sefer Hasidim. [1538] 1924. Edited by Jehuda Wistinetzki and J. Freimann. Frankfurt: Wahrmann Verlag. Edited by Reuven Margaliot. 1960. Jerusalem: Mosad ha-Rav Kook.

Sefer ha-Temunah. [1784] 1892. Lwow: N.p.

Sefer Yetzirah. [1562] 1965. [with commentaries]. Jerusalem: Levin-Epstein.

Shannon, Thomas, ed. 1976. *Bioethics.* New York: Paulist Press.

Shapira, Zevi Hirsch. 1967. *Darkhei Teshuvah.* 7 vols. Jerusalem: N.p.

Shapiro, David S. 1963. "The Doctrine of the Image of God and *Imitatio Dei.*" *Judaism* 12, no. 1: 57–77.

Sherwin, Byron L. 1973. "Bar Mitzvah." *Judaism* 22, no. 1: 53–65.

———. 1974. "Jewish Views on Euthanasia." *The Humanist* 34, no. 4: 19–21.

———. 1979. "Louis Jacobs: Man of Controversy, Scholar of Distinction." *Judaism* 28, no. 1: 95–108.

———. 1982. *Mystical Theology and Social Dissent: The Life and Works of Judah Loew of Prague*. London: Littman Library of Jewish Civilization.

———. 1985. *The Golem Legend: Origins and Implications*. Lanham, Md.: University Press of America.

———. 1989. "The U.S. Catholic Bishops' Pastoral Letter on the Economy and Jewish Tradition." In *Prophetic Visions and Economic Realities*, edited by Charles Strain, 81–93. Grand Rapids, Mich.: William B. Eerdmans Publishing Co.

———. 1990. *In Partnership with God*. Syracuse, N.Y.: Syracuse Univ. Press.

———. 1991a. *Toward a Jewish Theology*. Lewiston, N.Y.: Edwin Mellen Press.

———. 1991b. "The Human Body and the Image of God." In *A Traditional Quest: Essays in Honour of Louis Jacobs*, edited by Dan Cohn-Sherbok, 75–85. Sheffield, England: Sheffield Academic Press.

———. 1992. "My Master." In *No Religion Is an Island: Abraham Joshua Heschel and Interreligious Dialogue*, edited by Harold Kasimow and Byron L. Sherwin, 42–62. Maryknoll, N.Y.: Orbis Books.

———. 1993. "The Life and Legacy of Solomon Schechter." In *The Solomon Goldman Lectures*, edited by Mayer I. Gruber, 153–182. Chicago: Spertus College of Judaica Press.

———. 1995a. "The Golem, Zevi Ashkenazi and Reproductive Biotechnology." *Judaism* 44, no. 3: 314–24.

———. 1995b. "Toward a Just and Compassionate Society: A Jewish View." *Cross Currents* 45, no. 2: 149–63.

———. 1997 (June 24). "Religious Perspectives on Cloning: A Jewish View." Presentation at U.S. Capitol, June 24.

Shindler, Pesah. 1973. "The Holocaust and *Kiddush ha-Shem* in Hasidic Thought." *Tradition* 13/14, no. 4: 88–104.

Shi'ur Qoma. 1983. Translated by Martin S. Cohen. Lanham, Md.: University Press of America.

Shohet, David. 1952. "Mercy Death in Jewish Law." *Conservative Judaism* 8, no. 3: 1–15.

Siegel, Seymour. 1978. "Genetic Engineering." *Proceedings of the Rabbinical Assembly* 40: 164–67.

Siemet, M. 1972–73. "The *Besamim Rosh* of Rabbi Saul Berlin" [in Hebrew]. *Kiryat Sefer* 48: 509–23.

Sifra. [1862] 1947. New York: Ohm.

Sifre on Deuteronomy. [1546] 1939. Edited by Louis Finkelstein. Berlin: Judischer Kulturbund in Deutschland — Abteilung Verlag. Translated by Reuven Hammer under the title *Midrash Sifre on Deuteronomy* (New Haven: Yale Univ. Press, 1986).

Silberg, Moshe. 1973. *Talmudic Law and the Modern State.* Translated by Ben Zion Bokser. New York: Burning Bush Press.

Silver, Lee M. 1997. *Remaking Eden: Cloning and Beyond in a Brave New World.* New York: Avon.

Simon, Ernest. 1948. "Martin Buber and His Way Between Thought and Deed." *Jewish Frontier* 15, no. 2: 25–28.

Sinclair, Daniel B. 1980. "The Legal Basis for the Prohibition on Abortion in Jewish Law." *Israel Law Review* 15, no. 1: 109–30.

———. 1989. *Tradition and the Biological Revolution.* Edinburgh: Edinburgh Univ. Press.

Singer, Isaac Bashevis. 1982. *The Golem.* New York: Farrar, Straus and Giroux.

Sirkes, Joel. *Bayyit Hadash.* In Ben Asher, *Arba'ah Turim.*

Soloveitchik, Joseph B. 1978. "Redemption, Prayer, Talmud Torah." *Tradition* 17, no. 2: 55–72.

———. 1983. *Halakhic Man.* Translated by Lawrence Kaplan. Philadelphia: Jewish Publication Society of America.

Spiegel, Shalom. 1967. *The Last Trial.* Translated by Judah Goldin. Philadelphia: Jewish Publication Society of America.

Stein, Sigfried, and Raphael Loewe. 1979. *Studies in Jewish Religious and Intellectual History.* University, Ala.: Univ. of Alabama Press.

Steinberg, Abraham. 1978. "Mercy Killing" [in Hebrew]. *Assia* 5, no. 3: 5–38.

Strain, Charles, ed. 1989. *Prophetic Visions and Economic Realities.* Grand Rapids, Mich.: William B. Eerdmans.

Talmud. [1520] 1895. [with commentaries]. 20 vols. Vilna: Romm. English translated and edited by Isadore Epstein. *The Talmud.* 18 vols. 1948–52. London: Soncino.

Tamari, Meir. 1987. *With All Your Possessions.* New York: Macmillan.

Telushkin, Nissan. 1961. "Ha-Nimuk ha-Musari she-ha-Mitzvot ha-Teluyot ha-Aretz." *Or ha-Mizrah* 2, no. 6: 12–15.

Tishbi, Isaiah. 1961. *Mishnat ha-Zohar.* Vol. 2. Jerusalem: Mosad Bialik.

Tolstoy, Leo. 1960. *The Death of Ivan Ilych and Other Stories.* New York: New American Library.

Twersky, Isadore. 1963. "Some Aspects of the Jewish Attitude Toward the Welfare State." *Tradition* 5, no. 2: 137–58.

U.S. Commissioner of Patents and Trademarks v Ananda Chakrabarty. 1980. 446 US 303.

Urbach, Ephraim. 1951. "Political and Social Tendencies in Talmudic Concepts of Charity" [in Hebrew]. *Zion* 16, no. 3: 1–27.

———. 1987. *The Sages.* Translated by Israel Abrahams. Cambridge, Mass.: Harvard Univ. Press.

Vital, Hayyim. 1966. *Pri Etz Hayyim.* Tel Aviv: Eshel.

Watson, James. 1971. "Moving Toward the Clonal Man." *Atlantic Monthly,* May, 50–53.

Weiss, Abner. 1969. "Rabbi Loew of Prague: Theory of Human Nature and Morality." Ph.D. diss., Yeshiva Univ.

Weiss, Joseph. 1985. *Studies in East European Jewish Mysticism.* Edited by David Goldstein. New York: Oxford Univ. Press.

Werner, Samuel. 1976. "Euthanasia" [in Hebrew]. *Torah she-Ba'al Peh* 18: 28–45.

Wertheim, Aaron. 1960. *Halakhot ve-Halikhot ba-Hasidut.* Jerusalem: Mosad ha-Rav Kook.

Wiener, Norbert. 1964. *God and Golem, Inc.* Cambridge, Mass.: MIT Press.

Wiesel, Elie. 1978. *Four Hasidic Masters.* Notre Dame, Ind.: Univ. of Notre Dame Press.

———. 1983. *The Golem.* New York: Summit.

Winkler, Gershon. 1980. *The Golem of Prague.* New York: Judaica Press.

Wisniewski, David. 1996. *Golem.* New York: Clarion Books.

Woocher, Jonathan. 1986. *Sacred Survival: The Civil Religion of American Jews.* Bloomington, Ind.: Indiana Univ. Press.

Yalkut ha-Makiri. 1900. Edited by Solomon Buber. Berditchev: Sheftal.

Yalkut Shimoni. [1595] 1944. 2 vols. New York: Pardes.

Zabara, Joseph ben Meir. 1932. *The Book of Delight.* Translated by Moses Hadas. New York: Columbia Univ. Press.

Zadok ha-Kohein of Lublin. 1903. *Resisei Laila.* Lublin: N.p.

Zahalon, Jacob. 1683. *Otzar ha-Hayyim.* Venice: N.p.

Zioni, Menahem. 1882. *Sefer Zioni.* Lwow: Nissim Zis.

Zohar. [1558] 1883. 3 vols. Vilna: Romm.

Index

Aboab, Isaac, 136, 147

Abortion rights, 22n. 5, 39, 85, 124

Abraham (patriarch), 127

Abravanel, Don Isaac, 92, 95

Abulafia, Abraham, 111n. 1

Achron, Joseph, 67

Active euthanasia, 42, 43–45, 49–59, 60

Adam: image of, 62–87 passim; legal status of, 85

Adam Ilaya ("Supernal Man"), 16

Adam Kadmon ("Primordial Man"), 16

Adolescence, recognition of, 89

Adoption, 112–13

Adultery, and artificial insemination, 114n. 4

Aesthetics, 72–73

Afterlife. *See* Life after death

Agadat Bereshit, 152

Agriculture, genetic engineering in, 69–70, 122

Aha, Rabbi: on death, 37; on preventive medicine, 30

Air, breathing clean, 30

Akiva, Rabbi: on greatest principle of the Torah, 11; on "image of God," 1; on sanction to heal, 26

Albertus Magnus, 119

Albo, Joseph: on filial duty, 95; on repentance, 156, 157, 158, 163; on Torah interpretation, 8

Almsgiving. *See* Charity; *Zedakah*

Alsheikh, Moses, 141

Angels, lacking moral choice, 3

Anger, 2

Animals: caring for, 136; Golems as, 84; lacking moral choice, 4; parthenogenesis in, 115n. 5

Apostasy, 51

Arba'ah Turim (Ben Asher): *Hoshen Mishpat* chap. 1, sec. 1, 6; *Yoreh De'ah* para. 336, sec. 1, 27, 28; *Yoreh De'ah* para. 339, 44

Aristotle, 19

Art, appreciation of, 72–73

Artificial embryonization, 85

Artificial insemination, 85, 114, 117

Artificial life: creation of, 64–66, 67–73; legal status of, 77–87. *See also* Golem

Artificial persons, legal status of, 79–80

Asceticism, 33n. 8, 155n. 2

Ashkenazi, Zevi, 77–79, 80, 85, 86, 124

Assisted suicide, prohibition on, 45

Assur ("forbidden"), 40, 117

Attitude, in filial duty, 97

Avon (sin), 154, 162–63

Azkiri, Eliezer, 155

Azulai, Hayyim Joseph David, 25

Ba'al tashhit (wasting resources), 80
Babel, Tower of, 72
Bad habits, effects of, 32–33, 157
Banaya, Rabbi, 63
Bar Hiyya, Abraham: on knowledge of God, 15; on repentance, 164
Bar (and bat) mitzvahs, development of, 89
Barrett, William, 75
Bathroom, using, 14, 32
Bat kol (heavenly voice), 42
Be'er ha-Golah (Loew), 119–20
Ben Asher, Bahya, 155–56
Ben Asher, Jacob, 44. *See also Arba'ah Turim* (Ben Asher)
Ben Azriel (of Vilna), Zevi, 47
Ben Betzalel (of Friedberg), Hayyim, 148
Ben Gershon, Levi (Gersonides), 95, 109
Ben Matityahu, Benjamin Ze'ev, 90
Ben Mishle (Samuel the Prince), 29
Ben Samuel, Jacob, 46
Ben Shefatiyah, Amitai, 85
Ben Yehiel, Asher (Rosh), 52n. 3
Berekiah, Rabbi, 63
Berlin, Saul, 51–52
Besomim Rosh, 52n. 3
Bezalel, 5
Bible
— Hebrew Scriptures: Gen. 1:26, 3, 151; Gen. 1:26–27, 1; Gen. 1:28, 121; Gen. 1:31, 15, 152; Gen. 2:24, 100–101; Gen. 3:9, 151; Gen. 3:19, 37; Gen. 4:7, 154; Gen. 5:1, 1, 63; Gen. 5:1–3, 62; Gen. 9:5, 78; Gen. 9:6, 1, 10, 13, 17; Gen. 11, 72; Gen. 18:27, 151; Gen. 37:3, 81; Gen. 47:29, 136; Exod. 20:1, 92; Exod. 20:12, 89, 91; Exod. 20:12–13, 94; Exod. 21:15, 99; Exod. 21:18–19, 24; Exod. 22:1, 40; Exod. 22:24, 134, 141; Exod. 23:10–11, 133–34; Exod. 31:18, 128; Exod. 34:4, 128; Lev. 18:5, 28; Lev. 19:3, 96, 107; Lev. 19:9–10, 133; Lev. 19:16, 24; Lev. 19:18, 11,

24, 56, 61; Lev. 20:9, 99; Lev. 22:9, 1; Lev. 22:32, 78; Lev. 23:22, 133; Lev. 25:9–15, 134; Lev. 25:35, 146; Lev. 25:35–37, 134; Num. 5:6–7, 162; Num. 7:89, 110; Num. 12:8–11, 27; Num. 18:15, 102; Deut. 4:9, 20, 33, 122; Deut. 5:16, 89; Deut. 6:4, 151; Deut. 6:4–9, 105; Deut. 6:18, 8; Deut. 7:15, 30; Deut. 11:13–21, 105; Deut. 11:19, 105; Deut. 15:8, 143, 144; Deut. 15:11, 131, 144; Deut. 15:14, 133; Deut. 16:9–14, 134; Deut. 22:2, 24; Deut. 24:19, 134; Deut. 26:12, 134; Deut. 27:16, 99; Deut. 30:19, 22, 38, 61; 1 Sam. 2:2, 5; 1 Sam. 31:1–6, 50; 2 Sam. 1:9, 50, 51; 2 Sam. 1:13–17, 50; 2 Sam. 21:8, 78; 1 Kings 8:46, 153; Isa. 2:3, 2; Isa. 5:16, 130; Isa. 6:10, 155; Isa. 22:13, 37; Isa. 43:12, 130; Isa. 48:9, 161; Isa. 57:15, 142; Isa. 59:2, 64, 160; Jer. 20:14–18, 92; Ezek. 16:49, 134; Ezek. 20:44, 161; Jon. 4:3, 92; Jon. 4:8, 92; Hag. 2:8, 140; Mal. 3:7, 160; Ps. 24:1, 140; Ps. 34:15, 164; Ps. 41:1, 138; Ps. 41:2, 142; Ps. 60:14, 130; Ps. 85:12, 9; Ps. 103:14, 151; Ps. 103:15, 26; Ps. 121:5, 129; Ps. 139:16, 63; Ps. 144:4, 37; Prov. 1:8, 105; Prov. 10:2, 137; Prov. 11:4, 137; Prov. 11:27, 147; Prov. 15:20, 99; Job 3:11–12, 93; Job 9:24, 128; Job 19:26, 15; Job 42:6, 151; Eccles. 3:1–2, 37; Eccles. 3:2, 38, 47, 61; Eccles. 7:2, 37; 1 Chron. 29:12, 140; 1 Chron. 29:14, 140; 2 Chron. 6:36, 153; 2 Chron. 16:12–14, 23
— Apocrypha: Tob. 4:12, 105
— New Testament: Luke 4:23, 29; Mark 10:25, 150
Biological parents, 101–2, 112–13
Biological warfare, 70
Bleich, J. David, 122
Boaz, Joshua, 46
Bodily functions, 14–15

Body: cabalistic contemplation of, 15; and death, 35–36; dichotomy with soul, 14n. 1, 18–21; as divine, 15–18; as mirror of image of God, 13–15; obligations concerning, 13–15, 39; provided by parents, 94; washing of, 13
Borges, Jorge Luis, 67
Bowels, evacuation of, 14, 32
Brod, Max, 67
Buber, Martin, 128
Bunam (of Przysucha), Rabbi, 35

Cabala: and Golems, 75; and human body, 15, 16; and human sexuality, 111; and repentance, 161; and Torah, 129
Caidin, Martin, 77
Cain, sins of, 153–54
Capek, Joseph and Karel, 67, 69, 74
Capital punishment, 40, 56
Captives, ransoming of, 148
Carter, Jimmy, 68
Chakrabarty, Ananda, 67–68
Charity: defined, 132–33; for parents by children, 98–99
Childhood, recognition of, 89
Children: legal status of, 89, 123–24, 125; means of filial duty by, 95–100; objects of filial duty by, 101–2, 111–12; and precedence of divine obligations, 107, 111; reasons for filial duty by, 88–95, 111; timing of filial duty by, 100–101
Circumcision, 102
Citizenship, obligation to teach, 102, 103
Clinton, Bill, 118–19n. 8
Cloning, 83n. 1, 85, 115–26. *See also* Golem
Commentary on the Mishnah (Maimonides), 24
Compassion, cultivation of, 2, 7
Conception: defined, 115, 123–24; and fate, 165
Confession, 155, 161–63

Confucius, 90
Contentment,and health, 31
Cordevero, Moses, 18
Corporations, legal status of, 79–80
Creativity, 5, 119–20. *See also* Golem
Criminals, execution of, 40, 56
Cronbach, Abraham, 142
Cryonics, 83n. 1, 114
Cybernetics, 74
Cyborg (Caidin), 77

D'Albert, Eugene, 67
Damim ("blood"; money), 148–49
David, King: and death of King Saul, 50; and filial duty, 101; repentance by, 164
Davidson, Avram, 67
Davis v. Davis, 85–86
Dead people, burial of, 136
Death: acceptance of, 36–38; denial of, 36; by euthanasia, 38–61; forbidden to withhold or impede, 45–46, 47, 48, 60; praying for, 53–55; proper ways of, 33–34, 35–38; by suicide, 21, 25–26, 41
Deathbed confessional, 51, 162
Death penalty, for injuring a parent, 99
de La Mettrie, Julien Offray, 76
Depression, and health, 31
Derekh Hayyim (Loew), 3–4, 12, 15, 16, 17
Descartes, René, 76
Deus Absconditus, 15
Diabetes, treatment of, 45
Diet, maintaining proper, 30–31
Dinesen, Isak, 76
Di Trani, Moses, 158
Di Vidas, Elijah, 155, 160
Divine revelation, of obligations, 91–92
Divinity, manifested, 15–16, 18
DNA research, 70
DNR (Do Not Resuscitate) orders, 47
"Dolly" (cloned sheep), 117

Donor insemination, 114, 120
Dorff, Elliot N., 121
Dostoyevsky, F., 9
Drugs, genetic engineering of, 69,
112n. 2, 122

Edels, Samuel: on physicians, 23; on
wealth, 149
Education. *See* Pedagogy
Egyptian death cults, 38
Eibshitz, Jonathan, 150
Eliezer, Rabbi: on creation of
Adam, 63; on repentance, 37–38,
158–59
Eliezer (of Metz), Rabbi, 106
Elijah (of Chelm), Rabbi, 65, 75,
78
Elijah ha-Cohen (of Smyrna), 137–
38n. 2
Elimelekh (of Lizensk), 17
Eliot, George, 14
Embryos: cloning of, 122–24; legal
status of frozen, 86, 114
Emden, Rabbi Jacob, 56, 84
Emet (truth), 66, 136. *See also* Truth
Emotions: and heart, 152; in moral
choice, 9; regulation of, 31
Emunah Ramah (ibn Daud), 19
Enosh, 66
En Sof, 15
Epitropos, 141
Erudition, 7
Etchison, Dennis, 77
Ethics. *See* Jewish ethics; Secular
ethics
Euthanasia, 38–61; justification of,
40–41; obligations concerning, 40;
permissible, 42, 43, 45–49, 52, 59,
60; prohibited, 43–45, 59, 60;
rights concerning, 39–40; Talmudic
precedent concerning, 40–43; types
of, 42
Exercise, benefits of, 31
Exile, voluntary, 155n. 2
Experimental medical therapies, 57
Ezekiel (prophet), 134

Family structure: and political struc-
ture, 95
Al-Fasi, Isaac, 46, 156–57n. 3
Fasting, penitential, 155
Fate, 2–3, 165
Feinstein, Moshe, 114n. 4
Fetal tissue, use of, 121, 123
Filial duty. *See* Children
Financial support: of children by par-
ents, 103–4; of parents by children,
98–99; priorities in, 147–48; as
purpose of wealth, 149. *See also*
Zedakah
Fires of Night (Etchison), 77
Fletcher, Joseph F., 118–19n. 8
Foolish behavior, 105
Frankenstein (Shelley), 67, 69
Free will, 3–5, 9, 153
Freud, Sigmund, 36
Frischmann, David, 67

Galen, 31
Gamete intrafallopian transfer
(GIFT), 117
Ganzfried, Solomon, 44
Gaylin, Willard, 118–19n. 8
Gehinom (purgatory), 137
Gemilut hasadim. *See* Loving-kindness,
acts of
Gender, of Golems, 73–74
General Secretaries of the National
Council of Churches, 68
Gene therapy, 83n. 1, 112n. 2, 123
Genetic engineering: controls on, 70–
71; development of, 67–73, 83n. 1.
See also Golem
Gene splicing, 70, 112
Gerondi, Jonah, 159, 163
Gershuni, Judah, 85
Gersonides (Levi ben Gershon), 95,
109
Gilgamesh, 38
Gluttony, 30
God: actions of, 2, 7–8, 10; belief in,
xvii–xviii; corporeality of, 16n. 4;
essential attributes of, 2; human

beings created in image of, 1–12 passim; nature of, 2; as physician, 21–24; and sanction to heal, 24–29. *See also Imago Dei* ("image of God")

God and Golem, Inc. (Wiener), 74

Goethe, Johann Wolfgang von, 36, 67

Golem, The (Meyrink, novel), 67, 87

Golem, The (Wegener, film), 67

Golem: creation of, 64–66; dangers inherent in, 65–66, 68–69, 71–73, 74, 75; defined, 63, 85, 124; description of, 62–87 passim; influence of legend of, 66–67; legal status of, 77–87; sexual relations with, 81

"Golem Suite, The" (Achron), 67

Good deeds, importance of, 153

Goses (terminally ill person), 43, 49, 58–59

Grace After Meals, 148, 149

Grandchildren, filial duty to, 102

Grandparents, filial duty to, 102

Gratitude, 14

Group medical practice, 29

Guide of the Perplexed, The (Maimonides), 3, 127, 136, 154

Habit, and repentance, 157

Halakhah (Jewish law), 8, 40

Ha-Levi (of Barcelona), Aaron, 91

Ha-Levi, David ben Samuel, 26

Ha-Levi, Judah, 22

Hanina, Rabbi, 64, 84, 119

Hanina ben Teradion, Rabbi, 41–42, 43, 44, 45, 50

Happiness: and filial duty, 99; and health, 31

Hasid (pious person), development of, 64

Hasidei Ashkenaz, 65, 155n. 2, 162n. 4

Hasidism: and confession, 162n. 4; and health (illness), 20, 21; and human sexuality, 111n. 1

Hasidut (piety), 65. *See also* Piety

Healing: by patients, 29–34; by physicians, 21–29. *See also* Repentance

Health: biomedical model of, 20–21; defined, 19–21; and physicians, 21–29; purpose of, 21; responsibility for, 20–21, 29–30

Heart transplants, 120

Hegel, Georg Wilhelm Friedrich, 69, 72–73

Heit (sin), 154, 162–63

Heller, Aryeh Leib, 9

Heresy, 72

Heroic measures, use of, 47, 60, 122

Herz, Marcus, 22n. 5

Heschel, Abraham Joshua: on death, 38; on redemption, 131; on relationship between physicians and God, 22

Hesed (mercy, divine grace), 136, 160. *See also* Mercy

Hiddushei Agadot (Loew), 23, 73, 151

High Holiday liturgy, 137

Hillel, Rabbi: on death, 37, 159; on ethics, 11; on washing the body, 13

Hillel, the Elder: on *zedakah*, 144

Hippocratic Oath, 22n. 5

Holiness, 2

Holy Letter, The (*Iggeret ha-Kodesh*), 14–15, 111

Honor, defined, 96–97

Horowitz, Isaiah: on confession, 162; on "Golem abuse," 80–81; on repentance, 157, 160

Hovah ("obligation"), 27, 40, 117

Human beings: acting as God acts, 2, 7–8, 10; created in Adam's image, 62–64; created in God's image, 1–12 passim; free will of, 3–5; as God's cocreators, 5–6, 64–66, 71, 118, 119–20; Golems created by, 64–66; as machines, 75–77, 87; posture of, 4; self-definition of, 76; as unique, 4, 83. *See also* Body

Human nature: and filial duty, 90–91, 92; polarities in, 151; reflected in Golems, 74–75; similitude to God's nature, 2

Human sexuality, 111n. 1
Humiliation, 105
Humility, cultivation of, 7
Huna, Rabbi, 37
Hygiene. *See* Health; Preventive medicine
Hygiene of the Soul (Ibn Aknin), 19

Ibn Adret, Solomon (Rashba), 101, 120
Ibn Aknin, Joseph: on health, 31; on healthy soul, 19
Ibn al-Nakawa, Israel: on filial duty, 93, 106–7; on *zedakah*, 139n. 3
Ibn Daud (ben David), Abraham, 19
Ibn Ezra, Abraham, 91
Ibn Falaquera, Shem Tov ben Joseph, 33
Ibn Gabirol, Solomon, 73–74
Ibn Pakuda, Bahya: on filial duty, 93; on repentance, 156–57, 159; on spiritual development, 33n. 8
Ibn Tibbon, Judah, 29
Ibn Verga, Solomon, 28
Ibn Zimra, David, 6
Idolatry, dangers of, 66, 72–73
Illness. *See* Health; Medical ethics
Imagination, 5
Imago Dei ("image of God"), 2, 3–5, 7
Imitatio Dei (virtuous acts that imitate God's actions), 2, 7, 64, 71, 119, 136, 164
Ingersoll, Robert, 76
In-laws, filial duty to, 101–2
Insulin, 45, 112n. 2
Intellect (intelligence): function of, 3, 9; of Golems, 81–83
Intra-Cytoplasmic Sperm Injection (ICSI), 117
Intuition, 9
In vitro fertilization, 85, 114, 117, 120
Involuntary euthanasia, 42, 55
Isaac, Rabbi, 137
Ishmael, Rabbi, 24, 26
Israeli, Isaac, 22–23
Isserles, Moses, 46

Jacob (patriarch), 81, 136
Jacobs, Louis, 14n. 1
Jakobovits, Immanuel, 48
Jealousy, 2
Jeremiah (prophet), 66, 72
Jethro, 101
Jewish ethics: defined, xvii; methodology of, 7, 8, xviii–xix; objective foundation of, 8–10; purpose of, 7–8; purview of, 11–12. *See also* Secular ethics
Jewish identity, and maternal identity, 113, 114n. 4
Jewish Medical Ethics (Jakobovits), 48
Johanan ben Hanina, Rabbi, 62
John Paul II, Pope, 124
Jonah, Rabbi, 145
Jonas, Hans, 118–19n. 8
Jonathan, Rabbi, 37
Jose ben Kisma, Rabbi, 41
Joseph, 81, 136
Joshua ben Levi, Rabbi: and charity, 137; and "image of God," 1
Joy: and filial duty, 99; and health, 31
Judah, Rabbi: and charity, 137; and parental obligations to children, 102, 103; and prayers for death, 53–54
Judah ben Simon, Rabbi, 63
"Judeo-Christian ethics," 132
Justice, cultivation of, 7, 130–31, 133, 135–36
Just society, 134

Kaku, Michio, 115n. 5, 125
Kal va-homer ("the light and the weighty"), 56
Karo, Joseph: on euthanasia, 44; on interpretation of Torah, 8; on parental obligations to children, 104. *See also Shulhan Arukh* (Karo)
Kass, Leon R., 118–19n. 8
Kattina, Rabbi, 110
Keter (divine will), 17
Kiddush ha-Shem, 41

Killing: of criminals, 40, 56; justified, 40–41; obligatory, 41. *See also* Murder; Suicide
Kimhi, David (Radak), 50–51
Kitzur Shulhan Arukh (Ganzfried), 44
Korban (sacrifice), 154

Lainer (of Radzyn), Gershon Hanokh, 81–82, 85
Lampronti, Isaac, 53n. 4
Lederberg, Joshua, 118–19n. 8
Leivick, Halper, 67
Leprosy, 27
Levi Yitzhak (of Berditchev), 129–30
Liberalism, xvii
Lieberman, Saul, 31–32n. 7
Life, purpose of, 35, 37–38
Life after death (afterlife), 35, 36, 90, 159
Life support, withdrawal of, 42, 45, 46–47, 52, 53
Lincoln, Abraham, 142
Lipschutz, Israel, 54
Loans, giving of, 145–46
Loew (of Prague), Rabbi Judah: on creation (creativity), 6, 119–20; on creation of Golem, 64, 65, 68, 69, 70, 73, 75, 82; on evil inclination, 152; on honoring parents, 90; on "image of God," 3–4, 15; on Jewish ethics, 11–12; on knowledge of God, 17; on manifested divinity, 16; on medical practice, 23; on polarities, 151; on wealth, 149; on *zedakah*, 135
Longevity, 89–90
Lost property, return of, 24
Lother, Rudolph, 67
Love: cultivation of, 2, 7; and filial duty, 97–98, 100–101; and repentance, 159–60
Loving-kindness, acts of (*gemilut hasadim*): cultivation of, 7, 135–36; motivation of, 135; toward parents, 91
Lunshitz, Ephraim, 149
Luzzatto, Moses Hayyim, 32–33, 157

Machines, human-like, 73–77
Maimonides, Moses: on body-soul dichotomy, 18, 19–20; on confession, 161–62; on euthanasia, 43–44; on filial duty, 95, 96, 100, 102, 106; and human sexuality, 111n. 1; on "image of God," 3; on medical care, 21, 22n. 5, 24, 25, 29; and parental obligations to children, 104, 105; on pedagogy, 105; on preventive medicine, 30–33; on repentance, 154, 155, 156–57n. 3, 160, 161–62, 163; on *Shi'ur Qoma*, 16n. 4; on *tereifah* ("torn"), 59n. 5; on *zedakah*, 134–35, 136, 139–40, 143, 144, 145, 146, 147
Mamzer (illegitimate), 114n. 4
Man, A Machine (L'homme-machine) (de La Mettrie), 76
Manslaughter. *See* Murder
Marital strife, and filial duty, 100–101, 102
Marriage: and filial duty, 100–101; obligation to, 102, 103; and procreation, 111
Martyrdom, 41–42, 49, 50, 51, 56–57
Marx, Karl, 77
Matt, Moses, 21
Medical Aphorisms (Maimonides), 19–20
Medical ethics, 13–34 passim
Mehilah (renunciation of legal claim or entitlement), 108
Me'il Zedakah, 137, 138, 142, 146
Meir, Rabbi: on death, 43; on *zedakah*, 147
Meiri, Menahem, 9, 119
Mekhilta d'Rabbi Yishmael (MRY), 2, 5, 8, 102
Mena, Rabbi, 144
Mendel (of Kotzk), Rabbi, 64
Menorat ha-Ma'or (Ibn al-Nakawa), 139n. 3
Mercy, 2, 135, 136
Mercy killing. *See* Euthanasia
Meyrink, Gustav, 67, 87

Midrash Rabbah: Deuteronomy Rabbah
chap. 2, sec. 31, 151; *Deuteronomy
Rabbah* chap. 4, sec. 4, 1; *Deuteronomy Rabbah* chap. 6, sec. 2, 96;
Deuteronomy Rabbah chap. 6, sec.
13, 27; *Ecclesiastes Rabbah* chap. 1,
sec. 1, 37; *Exodus Rabbah* chap. 31,
sec. 12, 143; *Exodus Rabbah* chap.
31, sec. 14, 143; *Exodus Rabbah*
chap. 34, sec. 6, 144; *Exodus Rabbah* chap. 47, sec. 2, 128; *Genesis
Rabbah* chap. 8, sec. 11, 151; *Genesis Rabbah* chap. 9, sec. 7, 152;
Genesis Rabbah chap. 14, sec. 3,
151; *Genesis Rabbah* chap. 22, sec.
6, 153; *Leviticus Rabbah* chap. 5,
sec. 8, 164; *Leviticus Rabbah* chap.
10, sec. 5, 154; *Leviticus Rabbah*
chap. 16, sec. 8, 30; *Leviticus Rabbah* chap. 21, sec. 5, 164; *Leviticus
Rabbah* chap. 29, sec. 1, 63; *Leviticus Rabbah* chap. 34, sec. 3, 13;
Leviticus Rabbah chap. 34, sec. 6,
143; *Leviticus Rabbah* chap. 35, sec.
7, 7
Midrash Samuel, 26
Midrash Tanhuma, 7
Midrash Tehillim (Midrash on Psalms),
1, 138
Midrash Temurah, 26
Minyan, Golems excluded from, 77–
79, 80, 124
Miracles, and healing, 25
Mishnah: Kiddushin chap. 4, sec. 14,
23; *Pe'ah* chap. 1, sec. 1, 136; *Pe'ah*
chap. 8, sec. 9, 147; *Sanhedrin* chap.
4, sec. 5, 62
Mishneh Torah (Maimonides): *Hilkhot
De-ot* chap. 1, secs. 2–4, 31; *Hilkhot
De-ot* chap. 1, sec. 6, 2; *Hilkhot De-ot* chap. 2, sec. 1, 19; *Hilkhot De-ot*
chap. 4, sec. 1, 32; *Hilkhot De-ot*
chap. 4, sec. 13, 32; *Hilkhot De-ot*
chap. 4, sec. 14, 31, 32; *Hilkhot De-ot* chap. 4, sec. 15, 30; *Hilkhot De-ot*
chap. 4, sec. 20, 32; *Hilkhot Kiddushin* chap. 13, secs. 12–14, 101;

Hilkhot Mamrim chap. 6, sec. 7,
105, 106; *Hilkhot Mamrim* chap. 6,
sec. 8, 100; *Hilkhot Mamrim* chap.
16, sec. 14, 96; *Hilkhot Matnat
Ani'im* chap. 6, sec. 12, 148; *Hilkhot
Matnat Ani'im* chap. 7, secs. 1–2,
134; *Hilkhot Matnat Ani'im* chap. 7,
sec. 3, 144; *Hilkhot Matnat Ani'im*
chap. 7, sec. 5, 139; *Hilkhot Matnat
Ani'im* chap. 7, sec. 6, 146; *Hilkhot
Matnat Ani'im* chap. 7, sec. 9, 147;
Hilkhot Matnat Ani'im chap. 7, sec.
13, 147; *Hilkhot Matnat Ani'im*
chap. 10, sec. 1, 135; *Hilkhot Matnat Ani'im* chap. 10, sec. 18, 147;
Hilkhot Nedarim chap. 6, sec. 8, 25;
Hilkhot Rozeah chap. 4, sec. 5, 43–
44; *Hilkhot Talmud Torah* chap. 1,
sec. 1, 105; *Hilkhot Teshuvah* chap.
1, sec. 1, 161–62; *Hilkhot Teshuvah*
chap. 1, sec. 3, 155; *Hilkhot Teshuvah* chap. 2, sec. 1, 163; *Hilkhot
Teshuvah* chap. 2, sec. 2, 161;
Hilkhot Teshuvah chap. 5, sec. 3, 4;
Hilkhot Teshuvah chap. 5, sec. 4, 4;
Hilkhot Teshuvah chap. 7, sec. 6,
160; *Hilkhot Teshuvah* chap. 7, sec.
7, 160
Mitah yafah (a good death), 56
Mitochondrial DNA, 116
Mitzvah (religious obligation/commandment), 27, 40
Moral choice (free will), 3–5, 9, 153
Moral rehabilitation, 157–65
Moral volition, 3–4, 32, 153
Mortality. *See* Death
Moses: and filial duty, 101; and redemption, 128–29
Moses Hayyim Ephraim (of Sudlykow), 6
Moses of Coucy, 139n. 3
Mourning: comforting the mourner,
136; of parents by children, 98; for
suicides, 51n. 2
Murder: of cyborgs and Golems, 77,
78, 79, 80, 81, 84, 86, 124; defined,
58; of embryos, 123; as morally

wrong, 10; by physicians, 23, 28, 58; sanctioned incidence of, 40–41. *See also* Euthanasia

Naftali of Ropshitz, 150
Nahmanides, Moses: on filial duty, 94; on interpretation of Torah, 8; on sanction to heal, 24–25; and spousal love, 100–101
Nahman of Bratslav: on "image of God," 5; on medical treatment, 20
National Bioethics Advisory Committee, 118–19n. 8
National Institute of Health, 70
National Science Foundation (NSF), 69
Neshekh (interest), 134
Netivot Olom (Loew), 135
Nezah Yisrael (Loew), 23
Nissim (Ran, Rabbenu Nissim), 54, 156–57n. 3

Occupation, obligation to teach, 102, 103
Orhot Zaddikim, 138–39, 164
Original sin, 153–54n. 1
Oshaia, Rabbi, 64, 84, 119
Overbearing parents, duty to, 99–100, 108
Overeating, 30
Ovum donation, 114, 116, 117
Ozick, Cynthia, 67

Pahad Yitzhak (Lampronti), 53n. 4
Palaggi, Hayyim, 54–55, 57, 137–38n. 2
Palestinian Talmud: Berakhot chap. 1, sec. 2, 7; *Kiddushin* chap. 1, sec. 7, 97; *Kiddushin* chap. 4, sec. 12, 14n. 1; *Pe'ah* chap. 1, sec. 1, 96; *Pe'ah* chap. 8, sec. 8, 144; *Rosh ha-Shanah* chap. 4, sec. 8, 165; *Shekalim* chap. 2, sec. 16, 145; *Shekalim* chap. 5,

sec. 4, 145; *Terumot* chap. 8, sec. 4, 149; *Yebamot* chap. 4, sec. 12, 1
Palm Tree of Deborah, The (Tomer Deborah) (Cordevero), 18
Parenting, 88–109 passim; and cloning, 115–26; definition of parents, 101–2, 111–12; obligation of children to parents, 88–102, 111; obligation of parents to children, 88–89, 102–9; and reproductive biotechnology, 112–15
Parthenogenesis, 85, 115
Passive euthanasia, 42, 45–49, 52, 60
Patents, on artificial life-forms, 67–68, 84
Pedagogy: of parents, 104–9; of physicians, 29
Peretz, Y. L., 67
Pesha (sin), 154, 162–63
Pesikta d'Rav Kahana (PRK), 8, 130
Pesikta Rabbati (PR), 141, 160
Philanthropy. *See* Charity
Physical gratification, 14n. 1
Physicians: destined for hell, 23, 28; gentile, 49n. 1; murder by, 23, 28, 58; in partnership with God, 21–24; payment of, 28; relationship to patients, 22; sanction to heal, 24–29
"Physician's Prayers," medieval, 21–22
Pikadon ("deposit"), doctrine of, 141
Pikuah nefesh (obligation to save a life), 27, 122
Pirke d'Rabbi Eliezer, 137
Plato: on body-soul dichotomy, 19, 35, 110; on filial duty, 90, 95
Polarities, 151–52
Poverty, Jewish conception of, 141–43
President's Commission for the Study of Ethical Problems in Medicine and Biomedical and Behavioral Research, 68–71
Preventive medicine, 29–34
Pride, of physicians, 23
Procreation, 111, 121–22

Prosperity, 90
Puberty, 89

Quality of life, 44, 49
"Quickening," 123

Ramsey, Paul, 118–19n. 8
Rape, permissible death to avoid, 50
Rashi (Solomon Yitzhaki): on acts of loving-kindness, 136; on cherubs in the Temple, 110; on filial duty, 97, 108; on interest, 134; on parental obligations to children, 103, 108; on pathenogenesis, 115n. 5; on physicians, 23; on *tereifah* ("torn"), 59n. 5; on *zedakah*, 135, 146
Rava, 64, 65, 73, 77, 119
Reason, 9, 152
Redemption, 128–31, 137
Remorse, 158, 161
Repentance: cultivation of, 7, 151–65 passim; and death, 37–38; and moral rehabilitation, 157–65; obstacles to, 156–57; purpose of, 153
Reproductive biotechnology: legal status of children conceived by, 84–85, 86–87; legal status of embryos, sperm, and eggs, 86, 114; and new conception of parenting, 112–15. *See also* Cloning
Rescuing. *See* Captives, ransoming of; Saving a life, obligation to
Reshit Hokhmah (di Vidas), 155
Reshut (permission), 24, 27, 40, 117
Resolve, to repent, 158, 161
Resuscitation, of terminal patients, 47, 60
Reverence, defined, 96–97
Righteousness, 2, 65, 131, 133
Rights, in Anglo-American legal discourse, 39
Robots, 73–77
Rokeah, Eleazar, 73
Rosenfeld, Azriel, 83n. 1, 115n. 5, 117n. 6

Rosensweig, Franz, 36
Rothberg, Abraham, 67
R.U.R. (Capek and Capek), 67, 69, 74

Saadya Gaon, 149
Sabbath observance, reasons for setting aside, 27–28, 45
Salus, Hugo, 67
Samuel, 37
Samuel of Uceda, 159
Satan, creation of, 66
Saul, King: death of, 50–51; and filial duty, 101
Saving a life, obligation to, 24, 27, 122
Scholem, Gershom: on divine corporeality, 16n. 4; on Golems, 75; on Torah, 129
Schooling. *See* Pedagogy
Schreiber, Moses, 51n. 2
Schwartz, Rabbi Yosef, 117n. 6
Secular ethics, xvii–xviii, 8, 9
Sefer ha-Bahir, 81
Sefer ha-Hinukh, 91
Sefer Hareidim, 97, 101–2
Sefer Hasidim: on euthanasia, 43, 45, 46–48; on filial duty, 100; on medical care, 21, 29; on poverty, 142; on *zedakah*, 141
Sefer Ma'alot ha-Middot (ben Yekutiel), 136, 140
Sefer Mitzvot Gadol (Moses of Coucy), 139n. 3
Sefer Yetzirah (*The Book of Creation*), 64, 66, 77, 81
Sefirot, 15–17, 130
Self-defense, killing in, 40
Self-definition, 76
Self-determination, 4
"Self-excuse," 158
Self-flagellation, 155n. 2
Self-injury, 21, 45, 57
Self-knowledge, 17
Selflessness, 137
Self-mortification, 155n. 2
Self-worship, 72

Sexual sins, avoiding, 51
Shapira, Zevi Hirsch, 81
Shekhinah, 110, 127, 129
Shelley, Mary, 67
Shema: recitation of, 38; teaching of, 105
Shiur komah ("measurement of the height"), 17
Shi'ur Qoma, 16n. 4
Shmor et nafshotekha ("guarding one's self"), 122
Shnei Luhot ha-Brit (Horowitz), 157
Shohet, David, 59
Shulhan Arukh (Karo): *Orah Hayyim* para. 230, sec. 4, 26; *Orah Hayyim* para. 329, secs. 1–3, 28; *Yoreh De'ah* para. 155, sec. 57, 49n. 1; *Yoreh De'ah* para. 240, sec. 9, 98; *Yoreh De'ah* para. 240, sec. 13, 108; *Yoreh De'ah* para. 240, sec. 18, 106; *Yoreh De'ah* para. 240, secs. 22–23, 102; *Yoreh De'ah* para. 241, sec. 4, 106; *Yoreh De'ah* para. 242, sec. 1, 108; *Yoreh De'ah* para. 245, sec. 4, 104; *Yoreh De'ah* para. 249, secs. 1–2, 139; *Yoreh De'ah* para. 336, sec. 1, 28; *Yoreh De'ah* para. 339, sec. 1, 44, 46
Siblings, filial duty to, 102
Sick people, visiting of, 136
Sidrei Taharot (Lanier), 81
Siegel, Seymour, 70
Sifre on Deuteronomy, 130, 145
Sin: defined, 154–57; and moral rehabilitation, 157–65; and moral volition, 153–54
Singer, Isaac Bashevis, 67
Sira, son of Jeremiah, 66
Sitra ahara (demonic "other side"), 16n. 3
"Six-Million-Dollar Man, The" (TV series), 77
Slaves, genetically engineered, 71
Sleep, and health, 30
Social welfare, Jewish, 131–32. *See also Zedakah* (social welfare)
Soloveichik, Rabbi Joseph B., 5

"Sorcerer's Apprentice, The" (Goethe), 67, 69
Sorcery, 119
Soul: death as liberation of, 35; dichotomy with body, 14n. 1, 18–21, 110; as distinction between humans and Golems, 83; provided by God, 94
Sports, and exercise, 31–32n. 7
Spousal love, 100–101
Steinberg, Abraham, 53n. 4
Stepparenting, and filial duty, 102
Strangers, hospitality to, 136
Suicide: mourning for, 51n. 2; obligatory, 41; permissible, 50–52; prohibited, 21, 25–26, 45
Surrogate mothers, 117
Swimming, obligation to teach, 102, 103
Synagogue Council of America, 68

Talmud: *Arakhin* 6b, 56; *Avodah Zara* 18a, 33, 41–42, 44, 50; *Avodah Zara* 27b, 49n. 1; *Avot d'Rabbi Natan* chap. 3, 9a, 139; *Avot d'Rabbi Natan* chap. 16, 64, 11; *Avot d'Rabbi Natan* chap. 28, 43a, 14n. 1; *Avot d'Rabbi Natan* chap. 30, 33b, 13; *Avot d'Rabbi Natan* chap. 41, 66a, 146; *Avot d'Rabbi Natan*, Version B, chap. 26, 27a, 11; *Bava Batra* 9b, 137; *Bava Batra* 116a, 143; *Bava Kamma* 81b, 24; *Bava Kamma* 85a, 24, 28; *Beitzah* 32b, 49; *Berakhot* 5a, 38; *Berakhot* 10a, 5; *Berakhot* 16b, 148; *Berakhot* 17a, 37, 155; *Berakhot* 34b, 165; *Berakhot* 55a, 5, 32; *Berakhot* 60b, 14, 32; *Berakhot* 61b, 150; *Erubin* 41b, 143; *Gittin* 7a, 139; *Gittin* 9b, 28; *Gittin* 23b, 123; *Gittin* 57b, 50; *Hagiga* 16a, 151; *Ketubot* 49–50, 104; *Ketubot* 67a, 150; *Ketubot* 67b, 144, 147; *Ketubot* 103, 102; *Ketubot* 104a, 53; *Kiddushin* 29a, 102, 103; *Kiddushin* 30b, 94, 97, 101, 103; *Kiddushin* 31a, 96;

Talmud (cont.)
Kiddushin 31b, 96–97, 98; Kiddushin 32a, 105; Kiddushin 82a, 23; Megillah 16b, 108; Mo'ed Katan 16b, 46; Nedarim 64b, 137; Neddah 64b, 143; Niddah 16b, 165; Niddah 31a, 94, 111; Pesahim 75a, 61; Pirke Avot chap. 1, sec. 14, 37, 159; Pirke Avot chap. 2, sec. 5, 7; Pirke Avot chap. 3, sec. 1, 151; Pirke Avot chap. 3, sec. 14, 1, 4; Sanhedrin 19a, 78; Sanhedrin 37a, 151; Sanhedrin 38a, 151; Sanhedrin 38b, 62; Sanhedrin 39a, 134; Sanhedrin 46b, 13; Sanhedrin 65b, 64; Sanhedrin 67b, 119; Sanhedrin 72a-b, 40; Sanhedrin 74a, 41; Semahot chap. 1, sec. 1, 43; Shabbat 10a, 5, 24, 111, 120, 151; Shabbat 31a, 11; Shabbat 63a, 146; Shabbat 127a, 105; Shabbat 133b, 2; Shabbat 153a, 38, 158–59; Soferim chap. 15, sec. 10, 23; Sota 14a, 2; Sota 49a, 100; Sukkot 46b, 105; Sukkot 49b, 134, 135; Sukkot 52a, 152; Sukkot 52b, 153; Ta'anit 21b, 28; Yebamot 62b, 102, 105; Yoma 36b, 162; Yoma 54a, 110; Yoma 82a, 41; Yoma 83a, 28; Yoma 84–85, 45; Yoma 85b, 28; Yoma 86, 155. See also Palestinian Talmud
Tam, Jacob, 50
Tanhuma, Rabbi, 63
Tarfon, Rabbi, 96
Temple, cherubs in, 110–11
Ten Commandments, 88–89, 93–94, 95–96, 128
Tendler, Moshe, 125
Tereifah ("torn"), 58–59
Terrorism, 70
Teshuvah ("return"; repentance), 154, 155n. 2, 164. See also Repentance
Test-tube babies. See In vitro fertilization; Reproductive biotechnology
Thomas Aquinas, Saint, 119
Tiferet Yisrael (Loew), 4, 6
Tikkun ("correction"; repair), 6

Toilet, using, 14, 32
Tolstoy, Leo, 36
Torah: content of, 11; creation (completion) of, 6, 8; obligation to study and teach, 102, 103, 105, 108, 153; vocalization of, 6–7; writing of, 128–29
Torat Moshe (Alsheikh), 141
Tosafot: Bava Kamma 85a, 27; Gittin 57b, 50
Tower of Babel, 72
Treatise on Asthma (Maimonides), 30, 31
Truth, 2, 9, 66
Tzayyar ("artist"), 5
Tzur ("rock"), 5

Urinary tract, health of, 32
"U.S. Catholic Bishops' Pastoral Letter on the Economy," 131
U.S. Catholic Conference, 68

Victims, protection of, 41
Virtue, defined, 19
Voluntary euthanasia, 42

Waldenberg, Eliezer, 114n. 4
Wars, killing during, 40
Watson, James, 118–19n. 8
Wealth: moral dangers of, 148–50; ownership of, 140–41
Wegener, Paul, 67
Wiener, Norbert, 74
Wiesel, Elie, 67
Wisniewski, David, 67
Witchcraft, 119
Worry, and health, 31

Yalkut Shimoni, 13
Yetzer ha-ra (inclination to do evil), 152–53
Yetzer ha-tov (inclination to do good), 152

Yishuv medinah (good citizenship),
102, 103
Yose ben Halafta, Rabbi, 52

Zabara, Joseph ben Meir, 31
Zadok ha-Kohein (of Lublin): on
Golem, 84; on polarities, 152
Zahalon, Jacob: on medical care, 25–
26, 29; on physician's healing
power, 22
Zedakah (social welfare): anonymity
of, 145; biblical roots of, 133–35;
determining need for, 146–47; with
finite resources, 147–48; Jewish,
131–32; limitations on, 139; and
moral dangers of wealth, 148–50;

motivation of donors of, 136–40;
theological assumptions about,
140–43; types of, 135–36; and welfare recipients, 143–47
Zedakah le-Hayyim, 137–38n. 2
Zedek (righteousness), 133. *See also*
Righteousness
Zera, Rabbi, 64, 77–78, 79, 80, 81,
84
Zerufei ha-otiot, 75
Zohar: on creation, 16; on filial duty,
94, 97–98; on original sin, 153–
54n. 1; on polarities, 152; on poverty, 142; on repentance, 161,
165
Zygote intrafallopian transfer
(ZIFT), 117